Library of the Chathams
Chatham, New Jersey
Presented by
The Friends of
The Library
This book purchased
with funds raised at
the annual Book Sale

APPALACHIAN LEGACY

JAMES P. ZILIAK
Editor

APPALACHIAN LEGACY

Economic Opportunity after the War on Poverty

BROOKINGS INSTITUTION PRESS
Washington, D.C.

ABOUT BROOKINGS

The Brookings Institution is a private nonprofit organization devoted to research, education, and publication on important issues of domestic and foreign policy. Its principal purpose is to bring the highest quality independent research and analysis to bear on current and emerging policy problems. Interpretations or conclusions in Brookings publications should be understood to be solely those of the authors.

1775 Massachusetts Avenue, N.W., Washington, D.C. 20036
www.brookings.edu

Library of Congress Cataloging-in-Publication data
Appalachian legacy : economic opportunity after the war on poverty / James P. Ziliak, editor.
p. cm.
Includes bibliographical references and index.
ISBN 978-0-8157-2214-4 (hbk. : alk. paper)
1. Poverty—Appalachian Region. 2. Appalachian Region—Economic policy.
3. Appalachian Region—Economic conditions. I. Ziliak, James Patrick.
HC107.A127A64 2012
339.4'60974—dc23 2011051163

9 8 7 6 5 4 3 2 1

Printed on acid-free paper

Typeset in Adobe Garamond

Composition by Circle Graphics
Columbia, Maryland

Printed by R. R. Donnelley
Harrisonburg, Virginia

Contents

Acknowledgments

I AM GRATEFUL FOR financial support from the University of Kentucky Center for Poverty Research, underwritten by a grant from Office of the Assistant Secretary of Planning and Evaluation in the U.S. Department of Health and Human Services. I thank Gary Burtless, Hilary Hoynes, Chris Kelaher, Mark Schweitzer, and an anonymous reviewer for insightful comments on earlier versions of the chapters. The views expressed herein are solely those of the authors and do not necessarily reflect the views of any sponsoring agency.

JAMES P. ZILIAK

1

Introduction: Progress and Prospects for Appalachia

Appalachia is a region apart—both geographically and statistically.
President's Appalachian Regional Commission, 1964

Much of the Southern Appalachians is as underdeveloped, when compared with the affluence of the rest of the nation, as the newly independent countries of Africa.
Julius Duscha, 1960[1]

IN APRIL 1964 PRESIDENT Lyndon Johnson traveled to Martin County, Kentucky, in the heart of Appalachia to launch the nation's War on Poverty. Within a year—with passage of the Appalachian Regional Development Act of 1965 (ARDA)—Appalachia was designated as a special economic zone. The act created a federal and state partnership known as the Appalachian Regional Commission (ARC), whose mission is to expand the economic opportunities of the area's residents by increasing job opportunities, human capital, and transportation. The ARC-designated region is depicted by its 1967 boundaries and associated subregions in figure 1-1. The ARC region covers the Appalachian Mountains from southern New York to northern Mississippi and spans parts of twelve states and all of West Virginia. As of 2010, 420 counties were included in

1. Julius Duscha, "A Long Trail of Misery Winds the Proud Hills," *Washington Post,* August 7, 1960.

Figure 1-1. *Regions of Appalachia as of 1967*

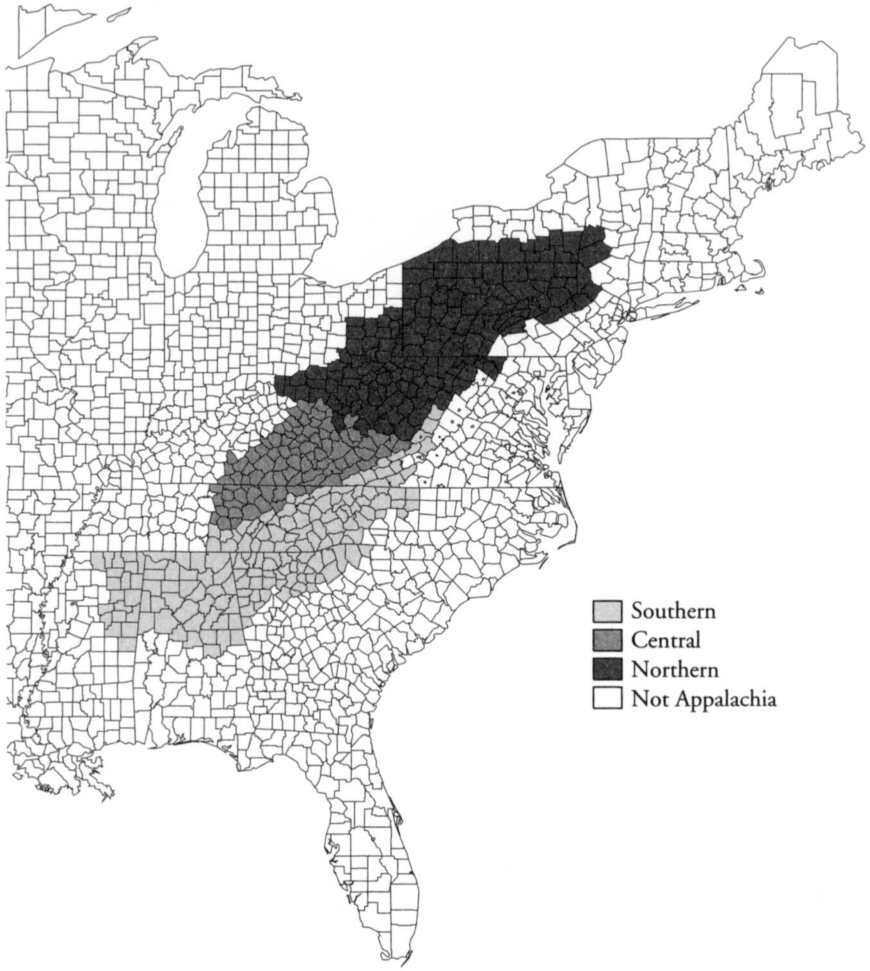

Southern
Central
Northern
Not Appalachia

Appalachia (23 more than in 1967), and over $23 billion had been spent on the region through the auspices of ARDA; roughly half of the funds were from ARC and the remainder were from other federal, state, and local programs.[2]

Five decades later, is there evidence of a convergence between Appalachia and the rest of the nation? As a place-based policy was ARDA effective at ameliorating hardship in the region? Or is Appalachia caught in a poverty trap? Do the

2. ARC (2009).

urban areas of the region offer growth opportunities for the highly skilled? If not, what policies could attract such workers and firms and at whose expense? The answers to these and related questions are important not only for a better understanding of the enduring legacy of the War on Poverty in Appalachia but also for antipoverty policy in general as the United States confronts a rising tide of poverty and inequality.

The authors in this volume look back over the past several decades to examine whether, where, and how progress has been made in terms of earnings, income, poverty, education, and health in Appalachia compared to the nation overall. They not only inform us of past successes and failures of policy and the broader social science research underpinning the analyses, but they also point us toward gaps in research knowledge as well as toward policy options going forward. The authors suggest that a new commitment to investment in human and physical capital through expanded prekindergarten programs, public health campaigns, and regionally focused infrastructure improvements in higher education and tourism-oriented industries is likely to offer the greatest long-term payoff for Appalachia and for similarly depressed regions of the nation.

A Region Apart

During the early 1960s poverty, and in particular Appalachian poverty, entered the American consciousness with the classic works of Michael Harrington's *The Other America* and Harry Caudill's *Night Comes to the Cumberlands.* Indeed, the case for action gained steam during the 1960 West Virginia presidential primary when the future president, John F. Kennedy, witnessed firsthand the stark deprivation facing the region. At the time more than half of West Virginians lived in poverty, many suffered from malnutrition, and basic amenities such as indoor plumbing were the exception in the rural areas. In 1960 county poverty rates were on average 10 percentage points higher in Appalachia than in the rest of the country (figure 1-2). In the Central Appalachian counties in Kentucky, Tennessee, Virginia, and West Virginia poverty rates approached 60 percent, or nearly double the rate outside Appalachia.

At the same time real per capita income in Central Appalachian counties lagged not only the nation as a whole but even its neighbors in the Northern Appalachian region by $2,800 per person (figure 1-3). Part of the reason for deep poverty and low incomes in Central Appalachia owed to the fact that high school completion rates, which stood at about 17 percent in 1960, were about 20 percentage points lower than the remainder of the country. The level of hardship led Kennedy in 1963 to establish the President's Appalachian Regional Commission

Figure 1-2. *County Poverty Rates in Appalachia and Major Subregions, 1960*

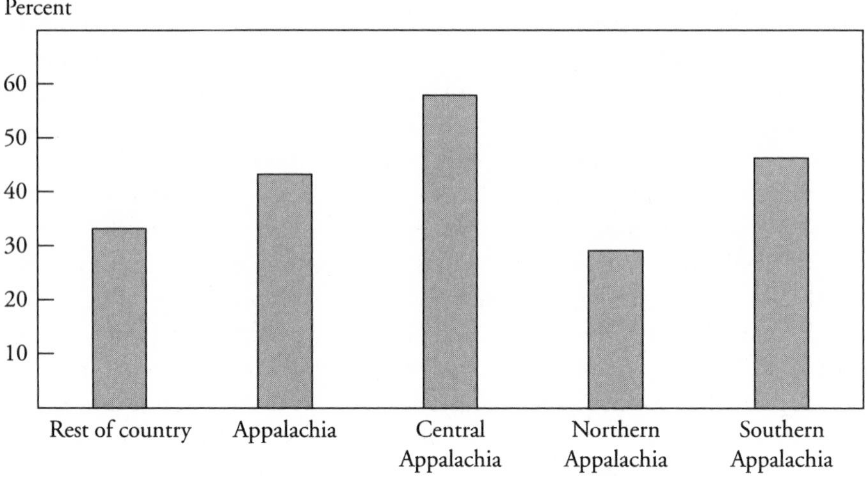

Source: Author's calculations of 1960 Census data.

Figure 1-3. *County Real per Capita Income and High School Completion Rates for Appalachia and Major Subregions, 1960*

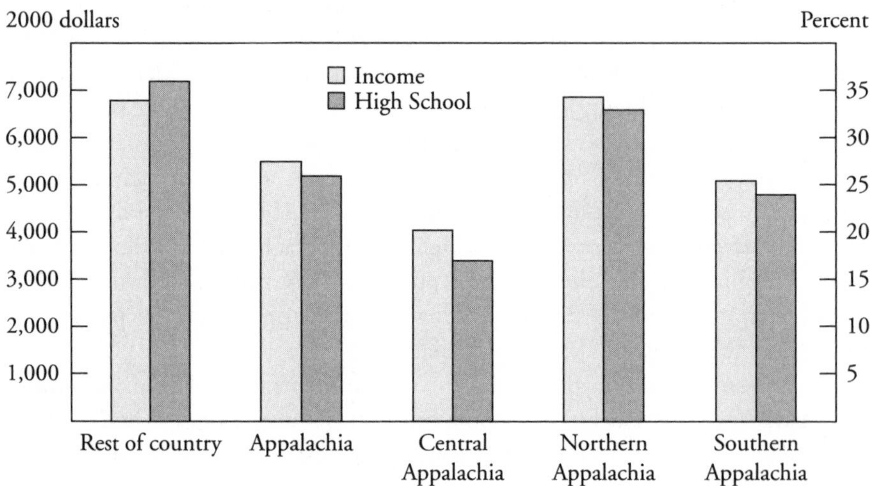

Source: Author's calculations of 1960 Census data.

(PARC) to develop a comprehensive economic development program for the region. The PARC, chaired by Franklin D. Roosevelt Jr., submitted its report to President Johnson in 1964. The report states, with no hint of exaggeration, that Appalachia was "a region apart."[3]

Congress agreed with PARC's basic assessment of Appalachia in the passing of ARDA as Public Law 89-4 on March 9, 1965. The act opens with the following language:

> The Congress hereby finds and declares that the Appalachian region of the United States, while abundant in natural resources and rich in potential, lags behind the rest of the Nation in its economic growth and that its people have not shared properly in the Nation's prosperity. The region's uneven past development, with its historic reliance on a few basic industries and a marginal agriculture, has failed to provide the economic base that is a vital prerequisite for vigorous, self-sustaining growth.[4]

In addition to creating ARC, the act established several new transportation and human development programs, such as the Appalachian Development Highway System and regional health clinics and vocational education centers. The initial congressional appropriation to ARC was about $1.1 billion, with about three-fourths of it dedicated to highway construction. Although the initial investment in human development programs seemed low given the high levels of poverty in the region, Congress and the Johnson administration were simultaneously expanding the broader social safety net with the introduction of food stamps, Medicaid, Medicare, Head Start, and other targeted programs for low-income families, and thus from their perspective the additional funds made available in ARDA were to complement the wider investment in human capital.

Progress was made in the ensuing four decades to reduce the abject poverty found in much of Appalachia in the 1960s. By 2000 poverty rates had fallen in all of the United States, including Appalachia (figure 1-4), while real per capita incomes and high school attainment increased across the board (figure 1-5). Moreover there is some indication of convergence, as the Appalachian poverty rate in 2000 was about 20 percent higher than the rest of the country, down from 30 percent higher in 1960. Most notably, poverty rates in Central Appalachia plummeted from 58 percent in 1960 to 23 percent in 2000. Additionally, the high school attainment gap narrowed, especially between the rest

3. PARC (1964).
4. Bradshaw (1992), p. 41.

Figure 1-4. *County Poverty Rates in Appalachia and Major Subregions, 2000*

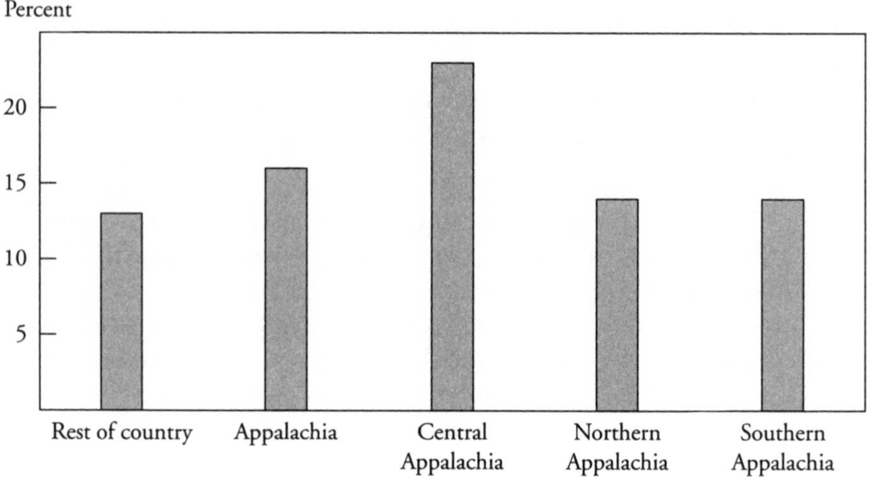

Source: Author's calculations of 2000 Census data.

Figure 1-5. *Country Real per Capita Income and High School Completion Rates for Appalachia and Major Subregions, 2000*

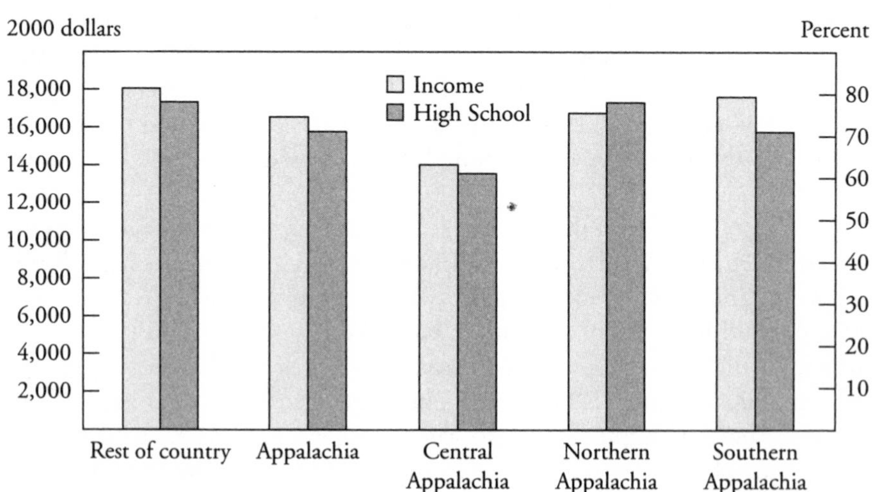

Source: Author's calculations of 2000 Census data.

of the nation and Northern and Southern Appalachia. There is little doubt that the progressive changes were palpable.

However, the region continues to lag behind the rest of the nation on many measures of economic development and health, and parts of Central Appalachia share lingering characteristics of a poverty trap. While levels of poverty fell dramatically in the Central region, the rate is still roughly double the rate of the rest of the nation. Real per capita incomes in the Central region are now $4,000 below those outside Appalachia, or $1,200 more than in 1960, and the gap in high school completion rates narrowed only slightly. Thus the shared regionwide convergence envisioned by the President's Appalachian Commission appears to have bypassed the Central region. And perhaps because of the searing portraits of grinding poverty in the books by Caudill and Harrington, to this day Appalachia, or at least the Central region, is often viewed as "the other America."

A number of excellent accounts of Appalachia and of ARC provide a rich historical and sociological background on the region and thus will not be reexamined here.[5] In contradistinction, there is a paucity of research by economists and demographers on Appalachia, and this is the point of departure for this book. Guided by rigorous theoretical underpinnings, the authors provide extensive evidence on earnings and inequality, human capital, health disparities, economic development programs, and poverty—and the way the Appalachian region has fared in relation to the country overall since the 1960s.

Progress against Poverty

Should policymakers subsidize firms, industries, or even regions (such as Appalachia)? Unlike most other OECD nations, policymakers in the United States have had an uneasy relationship with so-called place-based economic policy. Economists generally agree that industrial policy is often not welfare improving for local citizens. Instead, they argue in favor of investing in people, not in places or firms. And yet we regularly see governments engage in place-based investments, such as a city or state providing tax subsidies to a firm for locating an industrial plant in its jurisdiction.

One of the earliest, and subsequently longest running, efforts at regional economic development came about from passage of ARDA. However, there have been few attempts to formally test whether or not the program improved the lives of Appalachians. Thus the book begins with an evaluation of the effect of ARDA

5. See for example Caudill (1963); Bradshaw (1992); Duncan (1999); Billings and Blee (2000); Eller (2008).

on economic progress in Appalachia. In chapter 2 James Ziliak assembles county-level data from the 1960 and 2000 decennial censuses on poverty, per capita income, education, labor force growth, and other variables. His analysis improves upon prior efforts to evaluate ARDA by including data five years before passage of the act, thus placing the Appalachian and comparison counties on a prereform baseline (instead of postreform, as in earlier studies).[6]

Ziliak finds that ARDA reduced Appalachian poverty between 1960 and 2000 by 7.6 percentage points relative to the rest of the country and by 4 percentage points relative to border counties, with half to two-thirds of the effect realized within the first five years of the act's passage. These antipoverty gains were most pronounced in Central Appalachia, where poverty rates fell by 5–16 percentage points, depending on the comparison group. Additionally, he presents strong evidence of convergence in per capita income growth rates, resulting in 14 percent faster growth overall and about 25 percent faster growth in Central and Southern Appalachia compared to the rest of the country. The results suggest that ARDA did succeed in reducing hardship and boosting income growth. However, other forces caused the region—especially Central and Northern Appalachia, to diverge from the country in terms of income level.

It is well documented that inequality of earnings has increased since the 1970s, with the most pronounced increase in the 1980s.[7] In this literature, understanding the role of skill levels, and the market returns to those skills, has been at the core of the research effort. This literature links the growth in inequality to expanding wage premiums paid to college graduates, rising returns to unobserved skills, and the skill composition of the workforce, among others. Recent work suggests a polarization of the earnings structure in the United States: the rich are gaining and the middle class is falling further behind.[8] The inequality research to date, however, is comparatively silent on earnings inequality within and between geographic regions, including whether the polarization of the earnings distribution within and between regions holds equally or whether it differs between urban and rural areas. Knowledge of differences in inequality within and between regions is important for understanding widening inequality in general and for considering regional policy responses in particular.

In chapter 3, Dan Black and Seth Sanders use a special tabulation of the 1960–2000 internal long form of the decennial census to construct county-level earnings profiles of men at multiple points of the distribution. They find that in

6. See for example Isserman and Rephann (1995); Glaeser and Gottlieb (2008).
7. Bound and Johnson (1992); Katz and Autor (1999); Lemieux (2006).
8. See for example Autor, Katz, and Kearney (2006).

1960 prime-age working men in Appalachia earned 80 percent as much as their peers in the rest of the country. Some forty years later that ratio has barely moved. But breaking down the era into two twenty-year time periods tells a different story. In 1980 men in Appalachia earned 85 percent of those outside the region, an increase attributable to the boom in the coal industry in the 1960s and 1970s. In the subsequent two decades inflation-adjusted income among men in Appalachia continued to grow, but without the engine of a booming coal sector, it lagged growth in the rest of the country and so sank to 81 percent in 2000. This same pattern holds in Central Appalachia but not in Northern and Southern Appalachia: wages were stable in the North between 1960 and 1980 and then fell thereafter, while in the South they increased progressively across the four decades.

Even more provocative, Black and Sanders find that there are large differences between rural and urban areas in earnings distribution and that this is the principal reason that Appalachia's earnings distribution differs from the rest of the country. The bottom half of the earnings distribution increased in rural counties between 1960 and 1980 both in absolute terms and relative to the bottom half in urban areas. But between 1980 and 2000 urban areas exhibited far more polarization of earnings than rural areas. Echoing the findings in chapter 2, Black and Sanders argue that a key factor underlying these trends in earnings is slower growth in educational attainment, especially at the baccalaureate and professional levels, suggesting that a key to long-term improvement in the economic status of Appalachian men is to invest more in the types of advanced education needed to compete in the global economy.

In addition to macroeconomic forces placing upward pressure on poverty and inequality, secular changes in the structure of the American family are another possible causal mechanism. It is widely known that children growing up in a single-parent family (usually the mother) are at much great risk of poverty than children growing up with both parents present (nationally, poverty rates among single-parent, female-headed families are three times higher their two-parent counterparts). But in 1960 only 5 percent of children were born to single women, while in 2004, that share was 36 percent.[9]

In chapter 4, Daniel Lichter and Lisa Cimbaluk document that recent changes in family structure, especially the rise in female-headed families, have placed upward demographic pressure on poverty rates nationally and that Appalachian families and children have not been immune to the economic consequences of declining marriage rates, high rates of nonmarital fertility, and rising numbers of female-headed families, especially in rural areas. They find

9. Cancian and Reed (2009).

that the implications of these family changes for family poverty are larger in Appalachia than in non-Appalachia areas, independent of regional differences in employment opportunities, industrial structure, demographic variables, and other factors. Moreover, family effects, notably those associated with changing female roles, are estimated to be larger than those for conventional economic and human capital variables. Their simulations suggest that from 1990 to 2009 changes in family poverty would have been roughly 15–20 percent lower than the observed poverty rate if Appalachian families had not changed since 1990. This suggests that, in addition to policies that encourage economic growth, policies that encourage healthy marriages may help reduce poverty.

Future Challenges for Appalachia

Research increasingly indicates that poor health in childhood may be important in transmitting health disparities across the income distribution later in life and that these links are especially pronounced among individuals from lower socioeconomic backgrounds. Indeed, this process likely starts from poor maternal health while the child is in utero. The fetal origins hypothesis implies that conditions in utero affect not only birth weight but features such as basic metabolism, which in turn affect future health. This may be particularly problematic for families in Appalachia, who tend to be poorer and in worse health than other Americans.

In chapter 5, Janet Currie and Mariesa Herrmann provide an exhaustive review of the social science research that links childhood socioeconomic status with adult outcomes. They supplement their review with a detailed analysis of health trends both between Appalachia and the nation overall and within Appalachia. They find that Appalachians, especially Central Appalachians, are in poor health relative to other Americans and that health disparities start before birth from maternal behaviors. For example, the incidence of low birth weight is 95 per 1,000 in Central Appalachia compared to 83 per 1,000 outside the region. Moreover, although African Americans are generally in poorer health relative to white Americans, disparities between Appalachia and the rest of the country are much greater for whites in the region than blacks. In rural Appalachia 25 percent of women smoked during pregnancy in 2005, compared to about 12 percent in the country as a whole, and smoking is a leading cause of low birth weight. Maternal obesity may also be a factor. Obese women are at higher risk for many complications of pregnancy and delivery, and their infants are more likely to be higher than normal birth weight, which has been linked to higher body weight in later life and metabolic disorders such as diabetes. Although Currie and

Herrmann do not have data on obesity rates in Appalachia, obesity-related correlates such as chronic hypertension do tend to be higher in Appalachia. Because many poor health outcomes trace their roots to childhood deprivation, it will be difficult to eradicate adult health disparities without significant efforts to improve child health. This suggests an increasing role for public health campaigns to combat maternal smoking and obesity.

The past two decades have witnessed a flurry of new research on the role of cities in economic development.[10] The research confirms that in cities ideas travel faster, transportation is more efficient, education is enhanced, and workforce specialization allows for higher per capita incomes. In general, these economies of scale are greater the larger the city. Smaller cities and rural areas tend to have less diverse economies, often based on a single industry, which in turn makes them more vulnerable to boom and bust cycles when that industry suffers.

In chapter 6 Matthew Kahn surveys the economic research on the association between economic development and urban areas and the attendant implications for the types of place-based policies that might be effective in promoting economic growth in Appalachia. Kahn observes that the fundamental development challenge that Appalachia faces is that its cities are comparatively small and located far from the high-amenity coasts. Moreover, relative to the rest of the nation, its educational attainment is low and its local economies have not specialized in the high-technology sector. Based on the findings of Black and Sanders in chapter 3, this in turn implies that returns to skill are lower in Appalachia. These drawbacks are reflected in migration data Kahn presents, which show that skilled workers are voting with their feet: those who grew up in the region are leaving and those living elsewhere do not move there. This is more evident among those with higher educational attainment; the college educated are even more likely to leave and less likely to move in than those with only high school degrees or less.

While there is debate within the economics community about whether local efforts to stimulate an economy benefit those who live there or simply encourage in-migration, Kahn argues that the evidence suggests that in Appalachia the benefits might accrue to residents. Research on the phenomenon of coal price swings finds that Appalachians leave the area during depressed times but people who live outside don't come in during boom times.[11] However, there is evidence that during coal booms out-migration falls and some prime-working-age men who had left the region return. This leads Kahn to advocate a homegrown strategy for

10. Glaeser (1998).

11. Black, McKinnish, and Sanders (2005).

Appalachia—of educating its young people and encouraging a significant number to stay in the region through economic opportunity, social networks, and family. Valuable lessons for encouraging the growth of Appalachia's medium-sized cities that emphasize improving household quality of life can be learned from cities, such as Pittsburgh, that have reinvented themselves as high-skill, consumer cities.

That there has been economic progress in Appalachia in an absolute sense since the 1960s is unequivocal. The results in chapters 2 through 6 make clear that real earnings and incomes are higher, extreme poverty is abated, health outcomes overall are better, workers are more skilled, and infrastructure has been modernized. And yet in a relative sense there are some unsettling developments. This is especially true in Central Appalachia, where real earnings and per capita income levels have diverged from the rest of the nation, and health disparities such as low birth weight, smoking during pregnancy, and chronic hypertension have widened. Although poverty has fallen, it remains persistently high in this region.

In chapter 7 Steven Durlauf explores whether or not there are the footprints of a poverty trap in Appalachia. He begins by describing exactly what is and what is not a poverty trap: a poverty trap can be suspected when poverty is persistent, is not self-correcting, and is perpetuated by the institutions and culture of the region. There is an important distinction between the first two characteristics and the third. The first two refer specifically to the income process: how much income people make and the duration of those income levels. These two characteristics often reflect the supply of and demand for human capital and the interaction of these two sides of the labor market. The third characteristic, though, refers to the supernumerary reasons that account for an income deficit. Examples of the latter include the diversity of work opportunities (or lack thereof, in the case of coal towns), the concentration of control over physical and financial capital, the level of participation in the political process, and amenities such as arts and recreation. Although regions per se are not the usual scale at which poverty traps are studied, there are several aspects of the socioeconomic environment in Central Appalachia that are consistent with a poverty trap.

Understanding the causal channels generating a trap is the first step for designing a possible policy response. For example, if a shortage of skilled labor is the problem, then a policy response might be to enhance opportunities for formal schooling and training or to foster the in-migration of skilled labor. But if the trap largely emanates from institutional barriers, then political reforms affecting the distribution of resources and political participation may be warranted. Durlauf notes that empirical work is scarce on this fundamental issue and calls for new research on the roots of persistent poverty in Appalachia.

Missing Markets and Other Appalachian Challenges

The chapters in this volume suggest that the residents of Appalachia, and in particular those of Central Appalachia, suffer from deficits in human capital and health capital. The region faces a shortage of highly educated workers and high-tech employers, leading some researchers to speculate that there is a "missing market" of skill in the region.[12] In a somewhat ironic turn of events, this deficit is particularly pronounced in the urban areas of the region. The irony stems from the fact that many policymakers and advocates in the early 1960s pushed for a massive infusion of resources into the rural areas, but out of fear of pork-barrel spending the ARDA legislation directed that "investments shall be concentrated in areas where there is a significant potential for future growth and where the returns will be the greatest."[13] In practice this meant the urban areas of the region.

Moreover, on nearly every barometer of good health, Appalachians (particularly white Appalachians) come up short. One might be led to believe that once again the deficits arise from a missing market, in this case health markets. Expectant women in Central Appalachia are twice as likely to have to travel to a hospital out of the county to give birth than a pregnant woman in the rest of the nation (and one-third more likely than in rural America in general), which suggests poor access to care. However, there is little difference in prenatal care in the first trimester or in delivery by C-section, which counters the access problem. Again, though, expectant women in Appalachia have significantly lower education, once again pointing to a human capital shortage. One health market that does appear to be in chronic short supply is dental care, which is largely served by volunteer efforts such as the Remote Area Medical Volunteer Corps, though this group serves only of fraction of the need.

So what is to be done? On the research front the list of potential projects is extensive. For example, it would be fruitful to move beyond descriptive trends of health outcomes and behaviors to a more formal analysis of possible underlying determinants of health capital. There is broad scope for both experimental and nonexperimental health evaluations. To wit, field experiments pervade the research agenda among economists in the developing country context, and yet this effort has completely bypassed opportunities in depressed areas here in

12. Bollinger, Ziliak, and Troske (2011).

13. Bradshaw (1992).

America, such as Appalachia. In a related vein, the analysis of ARDA's effectiveness could be broadened to assess which types of grants for specific human development investments paid off for Appalachia. The results of this work could then guide such policy interventions as early childhood investments, along the lines of the Perry Preschool Project and with an evaluation component. Moreover, fundamental research into the existence of and mechanisms behind poverty traps in the region is crucial. One recent effort to link income growth in the latter part of the twentieth century to data on institutional structure, culture, and human capital from the late nineteenth century seems promising.[14]

The broad policy prescriptions seem clear. Substantial investment in education from prekindergarten through higher education, coupled with incentives to retain the recipients of the investments, are needed for Appalachia to have any chance of catching up to the rest of the nation, as was so strongly desired by the President's Appalachian Regional Commission nearly fifty years ago. Likewise, substantial investment in health is essential, especially maternal health, in order to reduce disparities between future generations of Appalachian children and the rest of the country. Public health campaigns highlighting the dangers of smoking while pregnant are one option; direct taxation is another, especially given that cigarette excise taxes in the Appalachian states are the lowest in the nation.

Who should pay for these policy investments? Is a federal recommitment to ARC needed to oversee policy implementation? Or, as Matthew Kahn suggests, should local governments in Appalachia adopt a homegrown strategy? These are challenging questions, the answers to which are often contingent upon difficult equity and efficiency trade-offs. General economic policies that promote growth in the major border cities of Charlotte, Atlanta, Pittsburgh, Cleveland, and Washington are likely to reap important benefits for Northern and Southern Appalachia. However, given its comparative isolation, Central Appalachia may require direct federal intervention to encourage economic growth and alleviate persistent hardship. The evidence makes clear that inaction should not be considered an option, given the enduring challenges facing the region. It is hoped that the research discussed in this volume will serve as a guide to future research and will lead to policies that will improve the lives of the residents of Appalachia.

14. Islam, Minier, and Ziliak (2010).

References

ARC (Appalachian Regional Commission). 2009. *Performance and Accountability Report* (www.arc.gov/publications/FY2009PerformanceandAccountabilityReport.asp).

Autor, David, Lawrence Katz, and Melissa Kearney. 2006. "The Polarization of the U.S. Labor Market." *American Economic Review Papers and Proceedings* 96, no. 2: 189–94.

Billings, Dwight, and Kathleen Blee. 2000. *The Road to Poverty: The Making of Wealth and Hardship in Appalachia.* Cambridge University Press.

Black, Dan, Terra McKinnish, and Seth Sanders. 2005. "The Economic Impact of the Coal Boom and Bust." *Economic Journal* 115, no. 503: 449–76.

Bollinger, Christopher, James Ziliak, and Kenneth Troske. 2011. "Down from the Mountain: Skill Upgrading and Wages in Appalachia." *Journal of Labor Economics* 29, no. 4: 819–57.

Bound, John, and George Johnson. 1992. "Changes in the Structure of Wages in the 1980s: An Evaluation of Alternative Explanations." *American Economic Review* 82, no. 3: 371–92.

Bradshaw, Michael. 1992. *The Appalachian Regional Commission: Twenty-Five Years of Government Policy.* University Press of Kentucky.

Cancian, Maria, and Deborah Reed. 2009. "Family Structure, Childbearing, and Parental Employment: Implications for the Level and Trend in Poverty." In *Changing Poverty, Changing Policies,* edited by Maria Cancian and Sheldon H. Danziger, pp. 92–121. New York: Russell Sage.

Caudill, Harry. 1963. *Night Comes to the Cumberlands: A Biography of a Depressed Area.* New York: Little, Brown.

Duncan, Cynthia. 1999. *Worlds Apart: Why Poverty Persists in Rural America.* Yale University Press.

Eller, Ronald. 2008. *Uneven Ground: Appalachia since 1945.* University of Kentucky Press.

Glaeser, Edward L. 1998. "Are Cities Dying?" *Journal of Economic Perspectives* 12, no. 2: 139–60.

Glaeser, Edward, and Joshua Gottlieb. 2008. "The Economics of Place Making Policies." *BPEA,* no. 1: 155–253.

Harrington, Michael. 1962. *The Other America.* New York: Scribner.

Islam, Tonmoy, Jenny Minier, and James Ziliak. 2010. "On Persistent Poverty in a Rich Country." Center for Poverty Research, University of Kentucky.

Isserman, Andrew, and Terance Rephann. 1995. "The Economic Effects of the Appalachian Regional Commission." *Journal of the American Planning Association* 61, no. 3: 345–65.

Katz, Lawrence, and David Autor. 1999. "Changes in the Wage Structure and Earnings Inequality." In *Handbook of Labor Economics,* edited by Orley Ashenfelter and David Card, vol. 3A, pp. 1463–555. Amsterdam: Elsevier–North Holland.

Lemieux, Thomas. 2006. "Increasing Residual Wage Inequality: Composition Effects, Noisy Data, or Rising Demand for Skill?" *American Economic Review* 96, no. 3: 461–98.

PARC (President's Appalachian Regional Commission). 1964. *Appalachia: A Report by the President's Appalachian Regional Commission.* Washington: Government Printing Office.

PART I

Progress against Poverty

JAMES P. ZILIAK

2

The Appalachian Regional Development Act and Economic Change

More than forty-five years ago—on March 9, 1965—President Lyndon Johnson signed the Appalachian Regional Development Act (ARDA), solidifying Appalachia's place as a galvanizing force in the nation's War on Poverty. The ARDA created a unique federal and state partnership known as the Appalachian Regional Commission (ARC), whose mission was to expand the economic opportunities of the Appalachians by increasing job opportunities, human capital, and transportation. Through fiscal year 2009 about $23.5 billion had been spent on ARDA programs, around $12.7 billion coming from federal funds and $10.8 billion from state and local funds.[1] Of the total, roughly half was spent on highways and the other half on human services. This has been the longest serving place-based regional development program in the United States (after the Tennessee Valley Authority, which was established by President Roosevelt during the Great Depression). To this day ARDA remains the largest program in terms of geographic scope. In this chapter I evaluate the effect of ARDA on economic progress in Appalachia since 1960.

The case for federal intervention in local and regional economic development along the lines of ARDA has generally been met with skepticism by economists.[2] Proponents of place-based policy typically make an appeal either on redistributive grounds or on the need to redress a negative externality (or to

1. ARC (2009).
2. Schultze (1983); Glaeser and Gottlieb (2008); Matthew Kahn, chapter 6, this volume.

subsidize a positive externality such as agglomeration economies). The case against such intervention follows from the belief that helping poor places is not the same thing as helping poor people—business subsidies may just induce new firms to bring new migrants to the area and not hire locals, leading to upward pressure on local house prices and rents. Although such price pressure benefits current owners, it harms current renters, who are more likely to be poor. And these place-based interventions, while possibly making the area more attractive, reduce the incentive for the poor to migrate away to areas with greater economic opportunities. Charles Schultze goes straight to the heart of the matter when he argues that "there are many important tasks that only governments can do. . . . But the one thing that most democratic political systems—and especially the American one—cannot do well at all is make critical choices among particular firms, municipalities, or regions, determining cold-bloodedly which shall prosper and which shall not."[3] And yet this is exactly what the ARDA set out to accomplish—to direct resources to Appalachia in hopes of lifting its economic status.

There have been scores of papers and books written on the history of ARDA, but perhaps surprising is that there have been few attempts to test empirically the effect of the act on economic outcomes in the region.[4] Ralph Widner, who was the first director of the Appalachian Regional Commission, on the twenty-fifth anniversary of the passage of ARDA, provided a basic overview of economic progress by comparing mean outcomes in Appalachia to the rest of the country from 1970 to the mid-1980s.[5] He found that incomes and employment improved but that education lagged and that the promise of development flowing from improved transportation access was only partially met.

Andrew Isserman and Terance Rephann conducted a more formal analysis by comparing the economic growth, between 1969 and 1991, of Appalachian counties to their "twins" outside of Appalachia.[6] The matched twins were to serve as the counterfactual for the Appalachian county. Using variables characterizing population and economic status in 1959, along with a distance metric to combine these variables into a single index, each Appalachian county was matched with a county (or group of counties in the case of ties) located at least sixty miles outside

3. Schultze (1983).

4. See for example Widner (1990); Bradshaw (1992); Glen (1995); Eller (2008), and the references therein.

5. Widner (1990).

6. Isserman and Rephann (1995).

the region.[7] So for example Wayne County, West Virginia, which is part of the Huntington metropolitan statistical area (MSA), was matched with Hamilton County, Indiana, a part of the Indianapolis MSA. Isserman and Rephann find that earnings grew 48 percent faster in Appalachia than in the control counties, per capita incomes grew 17 percent faster, and population grew 5 percent faster. They infer that these income growth differences imply an additional $8.4 billion in income for Appalachia in 1991, a huge return on the $13 billion spent as of that year.

Edward Glaeser and Joshua Gottlieb adopt a more standard multivariate regression model to evaluate the effect of ARC on per capita income growth and population growth.[8] Instead of matching to counties around the nation, their sample is all counties in states that contain parts of Appalachia, excluding those counties within ninety kilometers of the coast. The sample is intended to compare counties in Appalachia to "similar" neighboring counties in the region. The authors find that population growth between 1970 and 1980 was 3.4 log points faster but that there was no difference between 1970 and 2000. They find no evidence that income grew faster between 1970 and 1980, and indeed it actually fell by 2000. In light of the conflicting estimates, the authors sum up with the rather pessimistic view: "The ARC may or may not be cost effective, but there is little chance that its effectiveness will ever be evident in the data."[9]

In this chapter I provide improved estimates of the effect of ARDA on poverty and real per capita incomes in Appalachia. First, my evaluation spans the 1960 to 2000 decennial censuses, which begin five years before passage of the act and thus places the Appalachian and comparison counties on a pretreatment baseline—instead of post-treatment as in the previous evaluations. Second, my regression framework controls for county changes in demographics and the labor force, whereas the prior papers did not control for confounding factors, even though there were substantial differences in human capital, urban density, and labor force growth in 1960 as well as over the past four decades. Third, I provide a more refined characterization of the treatment and comparison groups and of the robustness of ARDA to these alternative assignments. Like the previous studies, I observe only whether counties were included within the coverage area

7. The distance metric they used is the Mahalanobis distance, or quadratic distance. It differs from its Euclidean counterpart in that Mahalanobis distance weights the squared deviation of a random variable about its mean by the covariance matrix of the random variables. It also differs from the more commonly used propensity score of Rosenbaum and Rubin (1983), which uses regression methods to create the index, or propensity score, to match across treatment and comparison groups.

8. Glaeser and Gottlieb (2008).

9. Ibid., p. 200.

of the act and not specific policy interventions; thus the parameter identified in the difference-in-differences model is known in the treatment effects literature as the *intent to treat on the treated.*[10] However, some counties within the ARDA jurisdiction were never eligible for financial grants, and some border counties may have benefited indirectly from the ARDA programs, and thus I separate grant-eligible from grant-ineligible counties from border counties to identify the parameter more closely aligned to average treatment effect on the treated: that is, those counties directly affected by ARDA. Finally, I also allow heterogeneity of treatment effects by disaggregating Appalachia into the major regions of Northern, Central, and Southern.

The results suggest that, between 1960 and 2000, ARDA reduced Appalachian poverty by 7.6 percentage points relative to the rest of the United States and 4 percentage points relative to border counties, with half to two-thirds of the effect realized within the first five years of the act's passage. These antipoverty gains were most pronounced in Central Appalachia, where poverty rates fell by 5 to 16 percentage points, depending on the comparison group. Comparing grant-eligible to grant-ineligible counties suggests a modest additional boost to human development programs. Although there is some evidence that levels of real per capita income diverged after passage of ARDA, there was strong evidence of convergence in growth rates, resulting in 14 percent faster growth overall and about 25 percent faster growth in Central and Southern Appalachia compared to the rest of the country, whether restricted to rural regions or not. Together, the results suggest that ARDA was a positive intervention in Appalachia in terms of lifting the incomes for the lower half of the income distribution.

Poverty and the Appalachian Regional Development Act

The 1960 presidential campaign set the stage for ARDA when then senator John F. Kennedy toured West Virginia. Figure 2-1 depicts county poverty rates in 1960 when nearly every other person in a typical West Virginia county was living in poverty. Extreme poverty was not unique to West Virginia—rates in excess of 50 percent were the norm from West Virginia to Texas—but it was eminently clear that poverty in this part of the country was distinct from poverty in most of the Northeast, Midwest, and West.[11] Prompted by the urging of several proactive governors in the region, in 1963 President Kennedy formed the President's

10. Heckman, LaLonde, and Smith (1999); Blundell and Costa-Dias (2009).

11. See Harrington (1962); Caudill (1963).

Figure 2-1. *County Poverty Rates in 1960*

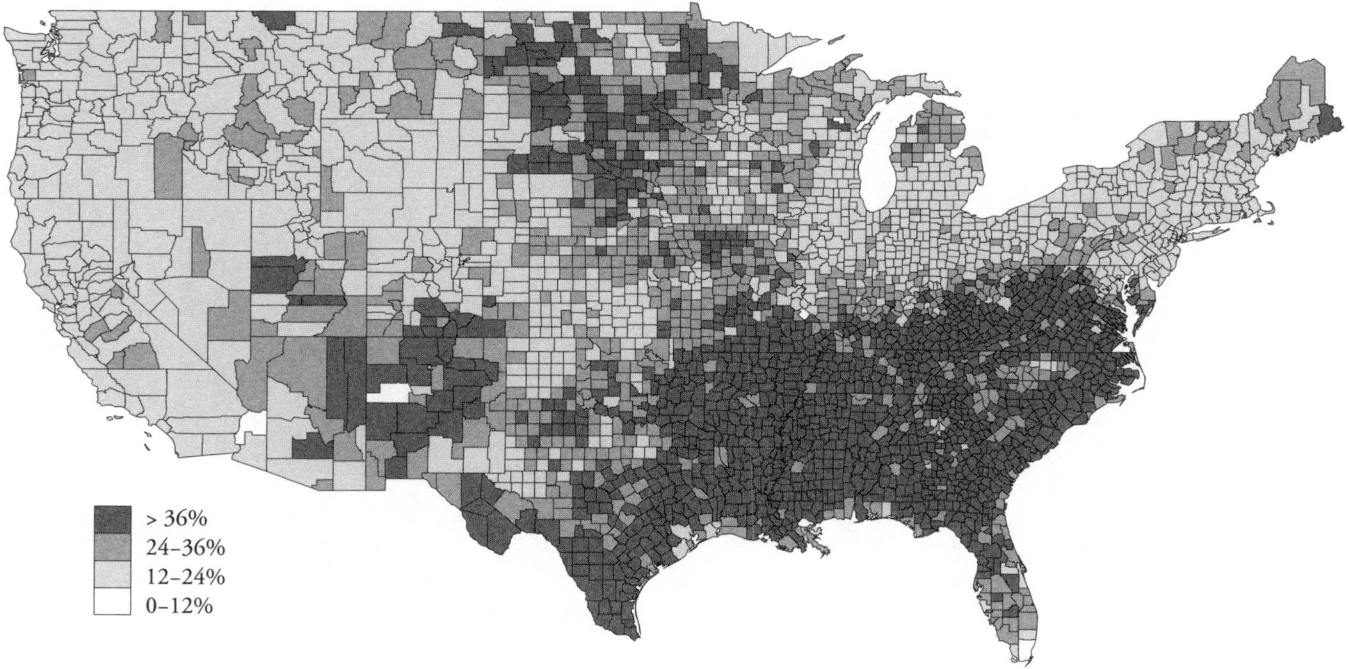

Appalachian Regional Commission (PARC) "to prepare a comprehensive action program for the economic development of the Appalachian Region."[12] The work of the commission was continued by President Johnson after the assassination of President Kennedy, and in 1964 PARC issued its final report, recommending an ambitious program of investment in transportation, water and natural resources, and human capital via education, training, health, and nutrition programs.

PARC opened its report by noting that "Appalachia is a region apart—both geographically and statistically. . . . The average Appalachian, whether he lives in a metropolis, in town, on the farm, or in a mountain cabin, has not matched his counterpart in the rest of the United States as a participant in the Nation's economic growth."[13] To make such a statement required a definition of precisely what comprised Appalachia. This definition was complicated by both economic and political considerations. The 1960 poverty rates in figure 2-1 suggest that the region in need of assistance was the sixteen states in the South, but this would preclude inclusion of Pennsylvania, whose governor served on the PARC. Moreover, to secure passage of the ARDA legislation it was necessary to first add counties in Ohio, and then later counties in New York and South Carolina, to those in the original nine states recommended by PARC.[14]

The 1967 amendments to ARDA added yet a thirteenth state (Mississippi). By 1967 the ARDA region spanned parts of twelve states and all of West Virginia, 397 counties in total, or 12.6 percent of all U.S. counties, as depicted in figure 1-1. The PARC report made clear that certain parts of the region were worse off economically, and in particular Central Appalachia, encompassing eastern Kentucky, central Tennessee, southern West Virginia, and western Virginia. Thus for reporting purposes the Appalachian Regional Commission separated Northern Appalachia, Central Appalachia, and Southern Appalachia, a division that has been historically significant.

The ambition of ARDA was also spelled out in the PARC report in its goal of bringing Appalachia up to the rest of the United States on several measures. From an evaluation perspective this suggests that PARC viewed the "treatment" group as counties included in ARDA and the "comparison" group as the rest of the country. However, a cursory look at county poverty rates in 2000 depicted in figure 2-2 suggests much lower levels *and* greater homogeneity of poverty rates across the nation relative to 1960. Thus with the possible exception of parts of Central Appalachia, a key benchmark of ARDA had been attained in the

12. PARC (1964), p. ii.
13. Ibid., p. xv.
14. Bradshaw (1992).

Figure 2-2. *County Poverty Rates in 2000*

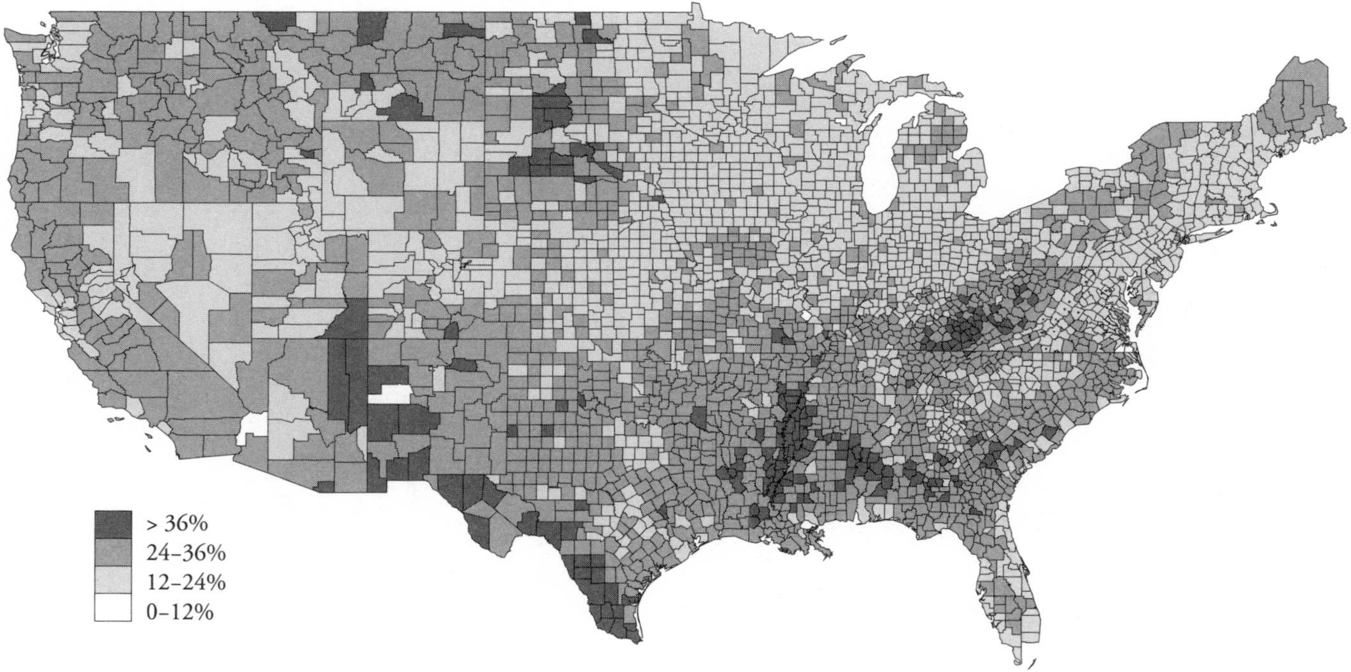

thirty-five years since passage. Whether or not ARDA had a causal role in effecting that change is the focus of this chapter.

Leading up to the creation of PARC, the Area Redevelopment Act of 1961 (ARA) made limited funds available to upward of one-third of needy counties across the nation. However, about 20 percent of counties within the newly drawn Appalachian region either were never eligible for ARA grants or were initially eligible but were removed from eligibility by 1965 primarily because they were deemed "too rich" for federal intervention.[15] Some of these counties were not included in the PARC's original conception of Appalachia (such as New York and South Carolina), but most others were included. This suggests that in evaluating the effects of ARDA on the region it is important to differentiate economic change in those counties that were grant eligible from those that were grant ineligible. That is, while PARC viewed the rest of country as the comparison group for Appalachia, a more appropriate comparison group might in fact be those counties within the region not eligible for ARA grants. But this is probably too conservative because it suggests that only ARA grant-eligible counties were the focus of policymakers. Indeed in its report, PARC states:

> In some of these urban complexes, income and living standards far exceed the regional norm and in some cases surpass the national average. . . . But these cities, standing with one foot in Appalachia and one foot in industrial America, prosperous as they are, fall far short of the performance of urban areas in the rest of the country. . . . At the onset of its work the Commission was confronted by a major problem of strategy: whether to concentrate its efforts on the hard core of Appalachian distress—the largely rural interior country of marginal farms, coal, and timber—or devote its attention to the entire region. . . . Solutions must be devised to assist both.[16]

The quotation suggests that the actual intent was to treat the entire region, and indeed, it is important to note that grant-ineligible counties received highway funds from other federal, state, and local sources, even though they were not eligible for human development grants.[17] Exploiting these programmatic differences should isolate the intent to treat effects of ARDA more precisely and, indeed, yield a parameter more closely aligned to the average treatment effect on the treated.

At the time the PARC report was submitted, President Johnson expressed concern that other poor regions of the country might also claim need for redevelop-

15. See ibid.
16. Ibid., pp. xv and xviii.
17. I thank Ronald Eller for clarifying this distinction.

ment funds, thus leading to federal budgetary pressures.[18] This concern was prescient, for later in 1965 the president signed the Public Works and Economic Development Act (PWEDA), which established multicounty economic development districts through the auspices of a new Economic Development Administration (EDA).[19] This suggests that identifying any causal impact of ARDA might be confounded with PWEDA, especially if PWEDA funds were directed to areas near Appalachia. As a consequence, border counties to Appalachia serve as an additional comparison group for grant-eligible ARDA counties. Moreover, at the same time that ARDA and PWEDA were being enacted, the broad Great Society programs (such as Aid to Families with Dependent Children, the Food Stamp Program, Head Start, Medicaid, and Medicare) were also being created. Although these programs were nationwide, they were often rolled out at different times for different regions. For example, the Food Stamp Program was introduced sooner in Central and Northern Appalachia than in the South and the West as a whole, while Head Start was introduced first in the 300 poorest counties in the country.[20] This suggests that an additional advantage of these alternative comparison groups is to control for the regional spillover effects of concurrent legislative changes.

Appalachia and Economic Change, 1960–2000

I begin with a general overview of economic change in Appalachia in the four decades from 1960 to 2000. The outcomes I focus on are a subset of those that PARC used as background justification for intervention in the region. Because PARC believed that the goal was to raise the well-being of Appalachia in comparison to the rest of the country, I initially compare Appalachian counties in 1967 to the rest of the country. However, because Appalachia is largely rural, a more appropriate comparison group to identify the intent to treat might in fact be other parts of rural America. Likewise, as indicated in the prior section, to examine the possible role of policy spillovers, I also consider two variants of

18. Indeed, Charles Schultze was the director of the budget for President Johnson and was not sympathetic to the creation of ARC (Schultze 1983; personal correspondence).

19. The EDA continues to this day, and a major growth policy of President Obama is the creation or expansion of regional innovation clusters that "are geographic concentrations of firms and industries that do business with each other and have common needs for talent, technology, and infrastructure" (www.eda.gov/AboutEDA/RIC).

20. See Ludwig and Miller (2007); Hoynes and Schanzenbach (2009). With the exception of AFDC none of the Great Society programs have a mechanical effect on the county poverty rates or per capita income used in the evaluation, because in-kind transfers are not included in the census definition of income, in general, and for poverty measurement specifically. However, it is possible that the programs have behavioral effects via altered labor supply, thus affecting poverty and per capita income.

border counties as comparison groups—those counties immediately adjacent to Appalachia and those counties surrounding the adjacent counties, which in most cases are the first two or three counties beyond the Appalachian border. Thus there are four comparison groups—the rest of the country, rural regions of the country, adjacent border counties, and surrounding border counties.[21]

The county-level data used in the analysis come from the 1960–2000 decennial censuses. Information on 1960 income, population, civilian labor force, number of high school degree holders, number of blacks, and number of urban residents was obtained from the 1962 *County and City Data Book.*[22] The United States did not produce its first estimates of poverty until the 1960s, but in the special tabulation the Economic Research Service of the U.S. Department of Agriculture produced estimates for the 1960 census.[23] The data for the 2000 census were obtained from "USA Counties" basic information database.[24]

The variables of interest include real per capita income earned by county residents and its log, the poverty rate defined as the ratio of the number of persons living below the family-size-specific poverty threshold to the total population of the county, the proportion of people residing in the county who are over the age of twenty-five and have at least a high school degree, the labor force growth rate defined as the percentage change in the civilian labor force residing in the county from one decade to the next, the proportion of people residing in an urban area, and the proportion of residents who are black.[25] The income data in 1960 were converted to real 2000 dollars using the personal consumption expenditure deflator from the Bureau of Economic Analysis (BEA). It is important to note that the income data in the census is money income, which differs from personal income reported in the BEA's Regional Economic Information System, which includes in-kind transfers.

Table 2-1 presents 1960 mean outcomes for Appalachia and the four comparison groups, along with the differences between Appalachia and the four groups. In real terms Appalachian per capita income is significantly below that of

21. The latter is akin to the comparison group adopted by Glaeser and Gottlieb (2008).

22. See also www.icpsr.umich.edu/icpsrweb/ICPSR/studies/2896/system.

23. We thank Robert Gibbs of ERS for providing these data.

24. See http://censtats.census.gov/usa/usa.shtml.

25. To construct labor force growth in 1960 we obtained the corresponding labor force data from 1950 to calculate the 1950–60 growth. The definition of what constitutes an urban area has changed over time. For the years 1960–90, any area that was one of the census-designated places with more than 2,500 people, or was incorporated in an urban area, was considered to be urban. In 2000 the definition of an urban area was a core census block group or census block that had at least 1,000 people per square mile and surrounding census blocks that had at least 500 people per square mile (www.census.gov/geo/www/ua/ua_2k.html).

Table 2-1. *Outcomes on Seven Variables, Appalachia and Four Comparison Groups, 1960*[a]

Units as indicated

Variable	*Appalachia*	*Rest of country*	*Difference*	*Rural America*	*Difference*	*Adjacent counties*	*Difference*	*Surrounding counties*	*Difference*
Real per capita income ($)	5,507	6,799	−1,292	6,195	−688	6,484	−977	6,570	−1,063
	(84.85)	(38.65)	[93.24]	(40.39)	[95.5]	(182.2)	[181.7]	(150.3)	[160.5]
Log real per capita income	8.564	8.779	−0.215	8.691	−0.126	8.720	−0.156	8.719	−0.154
	(0.016)	(0.006)	(0.017)	(0.007)	[0.016]	(0.031)	[0.033]	(0.024)	[0.028]
Poverty rate (%)	0.425	0.325	0.100	0.366	0.059	0.355	0.070	0.363	0.063
	(0.008)	(0.003)	[0.009]	(0.004)	[0.009]	(0.016)	[0.017]	(0.012)	[0.014]
High school completion (%)	0.257	0.360	−0.102	0.339	−0.082	0.308	−0.050	0.310	−0.053
	(0.005)	(0.002)	[0.005]	(0.002)	[0.006]	(0.008)	[0.009]	(0.007)	[0.008]
Labor force growth (%)	−0.014	0.058	−0.072	−0.035	0.021	0.082	−0.096	0.095	−0.109
	(0.009)	(0.006)	[0.011]	(0.005)	[0.011]	(0.016)	[0.018]	(0.015)	[0.016]
Population that is urban (%)	0.228	0.336	−0.107	0.225	0.003	0.369	−0.141	0.364	−0.136
	(0.011)	(0.006)	[0.013]	(0.005)	[0.013]	(0.022)	[0.023]	(0.017)	[0.020]
Population that is black (%)	0.062	0.103	−0.042	0.104	−0.042	0.166	−0.104	0.192	−0.131
	(0.005)	(0.003)	[0.006]	(0.004)	[0.009]	(0.017)	[0.013]	(0.013)	[0.012]

Source: Author's calculations.

a. Means are presented in the first line of each variable, standard deviations are in parentheses, and standard errors for difference in means are in square brackets. Rural America refers to those counties outside of Appalachia with a 1974 rural-urban value of more than 5. Adjacent counties are those immediately bordering Appalachia; surrounding counties include adjacent counties plus counties immediately bordering them.

the counties outside Appalachia. Moreover, county poverty rates in Appalachia are about 10 percentage points higher than they are outside the region, and labor force growth is over 7 percentage points lower. Counties in Appalachia are much less likely to have citizens who graduated from high school by age twenty-five, are much less likely to be urban, and are less likely to have black residents. At the dawn of the 1960s residents of these counties were indeed a people apart.

The remaining columns of table 2-1 present the same set of calculations for Appalachia against the other three comparison groups. The most widely applied definition of *rural* is based on the Economic Research Service's rural-urban continuum code.[26] This code takes a value between 1 and 9, with larger numbers reflecting more rural locations. The earliest categorization by ERS of rurality was conducted in 1974, and while there were likely some implicit changes in designation between 1960 and 1974, the 1974 data are clearly preferred to the more recent 2003 codes. I define rural America as any county outside of Appalachia with a rural-urban value of 6 or higher. About 70 percent of Appalachian counties fell into this category in 1960, and thus counties with rural-urban values greater than 5 serve as a useful comparison.

Table 2-1 shows that the differences in income, poverty, and education between Appalachia and rural America in 1960 are narrower relative to those with the rest of the country, and in fact labor force growth was even more sluggish in rural parts of the country in the 1950s compared to Appalachia. Table 2-1 also presents comparisons with the two border county designations: Appalachia was less similar to its immediate neighbors than rural United States overall, except for high school completion. The other difference with border counties is that they are more urban than the rest of the United States and have higher shares of black residents.

Table 2-2 presents a similar set of calculations for each of the three regions of Appalachia in comparison to the rest of the country. In the baseline year of 1960 the deficit between Appalachia and the rest of the nation was greatest in Central Appalachia, followed by Southern Appalachia. Real per capita income was $2,752 lower in Central Appalachia, county poverty rates were an astonishing 26 percentage points higher in Central Appalachia relative to the rest of the country, and labor force growth was 20 percentage points lower owing to the negative 15 percent labor force growth between 1950 and 1960. On the other hand, across many major economic indicators Northern Appalachian counties in 1960 were either no different or actually better off than those outside

26. This is sometimes referred to as the Beale code, after Calvin Beale, who, while at ERS, was instrumental in the development of the index. See www.ers.usda.gov/Briefing/Rurality/ruralurbcon/.

Table 2-2. *Outcomes on Seven Variables, Appalachia, by Region, 1960*[a]

Units as indicated

	1960			*Difference from rest of country*		
Variable	*Central Appalachia*	*Northern Appalachia*	*Southern Appalachia*	*Central Appalachia*	*Northern Appalachia*	*Southern Appalachia*
Per capita income ($)	4,047	6,876	5,095	−2,752	77.74	−1,703
	(127.2)	(120.0)	(94.13)	[217.5]	[126.1]	[155.3]
Log per capita income	8.266	8.812	8.507	−0.513	0.033	−0.272
	(0.030)	(0.019)	(0.019)	[0.034]	[0.026]	[0.024]
Poverty rate (%)	0.584	0.288	0.461	0.259	−0.038	0.136
	(0.013)	(0.010)	(0.008)	[0.018]	[0.014]	[0.013]
High school completion (%)	0.167	0.335	0.238	−0.193	−0.025	−0.121
	(0.007)	(0.006)	(0.005)	[0.012]	[0.009]	[0.008]
Labor force growth (%)	−0.150	−0.003	0.044	−0.208	−0.061	−0.013
	(0.017)	(0.012)	(0.013)	[0.036]	[0.028]	[0.026]
Population that is urban (%)	0.115	0.313	0.214	−0.220	−0.022	−0.122
	(0.018)	(0.020)	(0.016)	[0.031]	[0.025]	[0.023]
Population that is black (%)	0.027	0.016	0.118	−0.077	−0.088	0.015
	(0.004)	(0.002)	(0.010)	[0.018]	[0.014]	[0.013]

Source: Author's calculations.

a. Means are presented in the first line of each variable, standard deviations are in parentheses, and standard errors for difference in means are in square brackets.

Appalachia. For example, poverty rates were lower in Northern Appalachia and incomes were no different.

Tables 2-3 and 2-4 present a parallel set of calculations for census year 2000. In absolute value terms, and relative to the rest of the country, the real difference in per capita income actually widened over the forty years for Appalachia overall, and for both Central and Northern Appalachia, but it narrowed for Southern Appalachia. At the same time, the absolute differences in poverty rates, high school completion, and labor force growth compared to the rest of the country fell in all regions of Appalachia (except for poverty in Northern Appalachia). In short, there is prima facie evidence that the complex story of convergence and divergence in the earnings of men across Appalachia (see chapter 3, this volume) appears to carry over to a host of other economic outcomes.

ARDA and Economic Well-Being in Appalachia

In this section I use a multivariate regression model to more precisely estimate the effect of ARDA on economic well-being in Appalachia. I focus attention on three outcomes: poverty rates, real per capita incomes, and log real per capita incomes. Poverty rates provide a summary of the economic status of individuals in the lower tail of the income distribution. Even though these are a major focus of PARC, they have not been used in the previous evaluations of ARDA.[27]

The baseline regression model I estimate for county i ($i = 1, \ldots, N$, in time period t, $t = 1960$ or 2000) is given as

$$y_{it} = \alpha + \beta App_i + \delta_{2000} + \gamma\left(App_i * \delta_{2000}\right) + x_{i1960}\varphi + u_{it},$$

where y_{it} is the outcome (poverty rate, real per capita income, or log per capita income); App_i takes a value of 1 if the county is located in ARDA-designated Appalachia as of 1967 and 0 otherwise; δ_{2000} is an indicator variable that equals 1 in the year 2000 and 0 in 1960; $App_i * \delta_{2000}$ is an interaction term that equals 0 for all counties in 1960 and 1 for Appalachian counties in 2000; and x_{i1960} is a vector of observable factors measured in 1960 at the county level that have been shown to affect poverty rates at the regional level (such as high school completion rates, labor force growth, urbanicity, and race).[28]

The parameter of interest in the equation is γ, the coefficient on the interaction term that yields the intent to treat. With the model assumptions above, least squares estimation of the equation gives the regression-adjusted difference-in-

27. See Isserman and Rephann (1995); Glaeser and Gottlieb (2008).

28. Gundersen and Ziliak (2004).

Table 2-3. *Outcomes on Seven Variables, Appalachia and Four Comparison Groups, 2000*[a]

Units as indicated

Variable	*Appalachia*	*Rest of country*	*Difference*	*Rural America*	*Difference*	*Adjacent counties*	*Difference*	*Surrounding counties*	*Difference*
Real per capita income ($)	16,555	18,053	−1,498	16,788	−233	19,040	−2,484	19,657	−3,102
	(141.6)	(79.28)	[162.3]	(71.41)	[167.2]	(332.8)	[312.8]	(308.9)	[304.7]
Log real per capita income	9.700	9.778	−0.078	9.713	−0.013	9.836	−0.135	9.857	−0.157
	(0.008)	(0.004)	[0.011]	(0.004)	[0.010]	(0.017)	[0.018]	(0.015)	[0.016]
Poverty rate (%)	0.158	0.134	0.024	0.143	0.015	0.127	0.030	0.127	0.031
	(0.003)	(0.001)	[0.003]	(0.001)	[0.004]	(0.006)	[0.006]	(0.004)	[0.005]
High school completion (%)	0.713	0.782	−0.069	0.767	−0.055	0.759	−0.047	0.761	−0.048
	(0.004)	(0.002)	[0.005]	(0.002)	[0.005]	(0.007)	[0.008]	(0.005)	[0.007]
Labor force growth (%)	0.123	0.138	−0.015	0.128	−0.006	0.132	−0.009	0.139	−0.016
	(0.007)	(0.003)	[0.008]	(0.004)	[0.009]	(0.013)	[0.014]	(0.010)	[0.012]
Population that is urban (%)	0.303	0.414	−0.111	0.277	0.026	0.465	−0.162	0.471	−0.168
	(0.013)	(0.006)	[0.014]	(0.006)	[0.013]	(0.024)	[0.026]	(0.019)	[0.022]
Population that is black (%)	0.054	0.093	−0.039	0.089	−0.033	0.146	−0.093	0.172	−0.118
	(0.005)	(0.003)	[0.006]	(0.004)	[0.008]	(0.016)	[0.012]	(0.012)	[0.011]

Source: Author's calculations.

a. Means are presented in the first line of each variable, standard deviations are in parentheses, and standard errors for difference in means are in square brackets. Rural America refers to those counties outside of Appalachia with a 1974 rural-urban value of more than 5. Adjacent counties are those immediately bordering Appalachia; surrounding counties include adjacent counties plus counties immediately bordering them.

Table 2-4. *Outcomes on Seven Variables, Appalachia, by Region, 2000*[a]

Units as indicated

	2000			*Difference from rest of country*		
Variable	*Central Appalachia*	*Northern Appalachia*	*Southern Appalachia*	*Central Appalachia*	*Northern Appalachia*	*Southern Appalachia*
Per capita income ($)	14,040	16,773	17,638	–4,013	–1,281	–415.2
	(243.6)	(169.1)	(222.2)	[445.9]	[186.8]	[319.6]
Log per capita income	9.537	9.720	9.765	–0.241	–0.058	–0.013
	(0.017)	(0.010)	(0.012)	[0.023]	[0.018]	[0.016]
Poverty rate (%)	0.229	0.140	0.136	0.096	0.006	0.003
	(0.008)	(0.004)	(0.003)	[0.007]	[0.005]	[0.005]
High school completion (%)	0.614	0.779	0.707	–0.168	–0.003	–0.075
	(0.007)	(0.005)	(0.005)	[0.009]	[0.007]	[0.007]
Labor force growth (%)	0.092	0.084	0.171	–0.046	–0.054	0.033
	(0.012)	(0.008)	(0.013)	[0.018]	[0.014]	[0.013]
Population that is urban (%)	0.188	0.370	0.305	–0.225	–0.044	–0.109
	(0.021)	(0.020)	(0.020)	[0.034]	[0.027]	[0.024]
Population that is black (%)	0.017	0.019	0.101	–0.076	–0.074	0.008
	(0.002)	(0.002)	(0.010)	[0.016]	[0.013]	[0.011]

Source: Author's calculations.

a. Means are presented in the first line of each variable, standard deviations are in parentheses.

difference estimate of the effect of ARDA on y_{it}. Indeed, with two years of data, 1960 and 2000, and dropping the control variables x_{i1960}, the equation yields the unadjusted difference-in-difference estimates that can be computed comparing tables 2-1 and 2-3 with 2-2 and 2-4. However, the simple difference-in-difference estimates ignore that there were significant pretreatment differences in the confounding factors like education and labor force growth in table 2-1 and thus may not reflect causal effects of the role that ARDA had in accounting for convergence in poverty, on the one hand, or divergence in per capita incomes, on the other. Controlling for initial observed heterogeneity will provide more accurate estimates of ARDA than the simple difference-in-difference estimates.

The baseline model in the equation identifies the effect of ARDA by comparing Appalachian counties to the balance of counties in the United States. As noted earlier, this is a useful exercise because the PARC believed that the goal of ARDA was to lift the region up to the rest of the country, and as such γ in the equation represents the intent to treat. However, because the ARDA county designation is somewhat arbitrary (inclusion in the original counties was determined by the governor of each state and subject to Senate approval), and because of the possibility of spillover of programs into neighboring counties, I also estimate the model using the three alternative comparison groups of rural America, adjacent border counties, and surrounding border counties.

Table 2-5 reports the results of the four comparison groups described above where the dependent variable is the county poverty rate in the census years 1960 and 2000. For ease of presentation I provide only estimates of the intent-to-treat parameter, though in all cases the initial-period demographic controls are quantitatively and statistically significant and have the expected signs. That is, higher high school completion, faster labor force growth, higher urban shares, and lower shares of black residents are each associated with lower poverty rates. The high R-square of 0.75 or greater indicates that the model does a good job explaining the variation in county poverty rates.

The first row and column tabulates the baseline specification in the equation, suggesting that after passage of ARDA poverty rates in Appalachia fell 7.6 percentage points relative to the rest of the United States in the ensuing thirty-five years. On an initial baseline poverty rate of 42.5 percent, this is an impressive 18 percent reduction. If we restrict attention to the narrower comparison group of rural America, the table suggests that ARDA reduced poverty in Appalachia by 4.5 points relative to rural America, which is about 60 percent of the total effect against the rest of the country. Moreover, in the next two columns, where we compare Appalachia to the two border county designations, we also find smaller antipoverty gains—4 percent and 3.2 percent, respectively.

Table 2-5. *Effects of ARDA on Poverty Rates, Regression Adjusted, 1960–2000*[a]
Percent

Region	*Rest of country*	*Rural America*	*Adjacent counties*	*Surrounding counties*
Appalachia	– 0.076	–0.045	–0.040	–0.032
	(0.007)	(0.007)	(0.012)	(0.010)
Central Appalachia	–0.163	–0.132	–0.053	–0.059
	(0.014)	(0.013)	(0.019)	(0.016)
Northern Appalachia	0.044	0.075	–0.076	–0.081
	(0.011)	(0.010)	(0.014)	(0.011)
Southern Appalachia	–0.133	–0.101	–0.003	0.012
	(0.010)	(0.010)	(0.004)	(0.012)
Appalachia, ARA eligible	–0.084	–0.052	–0.047	–0.039
	(0.008)	(0.007)	(0.012)	(0.011)
Central, ARA eligible	–0.166	–0.135	–0.056	–0.062
	(0.014)	(0.013)	(0.019)	(0.016)
Northern, ARA eligible	0.036	0.068	–0.084	–0.089
	(0.011)	(0.011)	(0.014)	(0.011)
Southern, ARA eligible	–0.158	–0.126	–0.028	–0.013
	(0.012)	(0.010)	(0.015)	(0.013)

Source: Author's calculations.

a. Standard errors are in parentheses. All models control for 1960 county-level shares of high school graduates, shares of blacks, shares of persons living in urban areas, and labor force growth. Rural America refers to those counties outside of Appalachia with a 1974 rural-urban value of more than 5. Adjacent counties are those immediately bordering Appalachia; surrounding counties include adjacent counties plus counties immediately bordering them.

The next three rows of table 2-5 separate App_i into Central, Northern, and Southern Appalachia in order to admit heterogeneity of treatment effects within Appalachia. Each row represents a separate regression model, and while the comparison groups in each of the first two columns are identical, in the latter two comparisons I only use the border counties in the respective regions (that is, for Central Appalachia I use border counties in Kentucky and Tennessee; for Northern Appalachia I use border counties in Ohio, New York, Pennsylvania, Maryland, New Jersey, and Delaware; and for Southern Appalachia I use border counties in Tennessee, Mississippi, Alabama, Georgia, North Carolina, South Carolina, and Virginia). In these three rows we find astounding heterogeneity in the effect of ARDA on poverty both across regions as well as within regions but across comparison groups. Compared to the rest of the country, poverty in Central Appalachia fell 16.3 percentage points and 13.3 percentage points in Southern

Appalachia, or 28 percent on the respective 1960 baseline rates of 58.4 and 46.1 percent. On the other hand, poverty in Northern Appalachia actually diverged from the rest of the country by 4.4 percentage points. Central Appalachia consistently outperformed rural America, as well as its own border counties, in terms of poverty reduction. Southern Appalachia likewise outperformed rural parts of the country in general but did no better than border counties, perhaps because the border regions include fast-growing metropolitan areas such as Atlanta and Charlotte. Northern Appalachia, on the other hand, diverged in terms of poverty against rural America but made substantive gains against border counties, highlighting the particular challenges facing counties in Rust Belt states.

The Area Redevelopment Act of 1961 excluded many counties in Appalachia from funding eligibility, and ARDA expanded upon that set of counties so that by 1965 there were seventy-two ARDA-ineligible counties.[29] This suggests that the intent to treat did not necessarily apply to all Appalachian counties but rather to only grant-eligible counties. Thus in the last four rows of table 2-5 I consider an alternative definition of App_i where it equals 1 if the county was ARA eligible and 0 for the comparison group, excluding ARA-ineligible counties. This is perhaps the most conservative approach to identifying the effect of ARDA, as it assumes that the only true treatment effect occurs in counties that are eligible for human development grants. In fact, an alternative approach is to view the highway development funds and human development funds as multiple treatments, and thus comparing the models with ARA grant-eligible-only counties with the full set in the baseline will yield the extra impact from human development programs. Overall the human development programs boosted the antipoverty effectiveness of ARDA by about 0.8 percentage points (8.4 versus 7.6), or about 11 percent on the baseline effect of 7.6 points. Southern Appalachia particularly benefited from these programs, with an additional poverty reduction of 19 percent (from 13.3 to 15.8). Even still, the results suggest that the major incremental gains against poverty in the region were from improvements in transportation and infrastructure.

All of the estimates in table 2-5 are identical to the difference-in-difference estimates one obtains without demographic controls in tables 2-1 through 2-4. For example, we can construct the unadjusted effect of ARDA on poverty relative to the rest of the country by noting that 0.024 in table 2-3 less 0.100 in table 2-1 yields –0.076, which is exactly the same as reported in table 2-5. The only difference is that the estimates in table 2-5 are more precise. This is a remarkable outcome. In the standard random assignment treatment control experiment, controlling for demographics should have no effect on the treatment parameter if

29. Bradshaw (1992).

random assignment is carried out correctly. Controlling for demographics could improve the efficiency of the estimated treatment effect if those demographics help explain variation in the outcome variable, but they will not affect the parameter itself. This is exactly what we find here, suggesting that pretreatment differences in high school completion rates, black share, urban share, and labor force growth had no effect on the estimated treatment provided by ARDA other than the variance of the estimate. Or in other words, assignment into Appalachia was random with respect to initial demographics. If we modify the specification and instead allow the demographics to change over time, then the effect of ARDA on poverty rates falls by about one-third (to 5.1 percentage points), which suggests that ARDA likely improved some of the demographic outcomes observed in 2000 over and above the direct effect on poverty.

Tables 2-6 and 2-7 present a parallel set of estimates, but instead of poverty rates the dependent variables are the level of real income per capita (table 2-6) and natural log of real income per capita (table 2-7). The main difference in interpretation across these models is that in the difference-in-difference specification of log income per capita approximates a percent change. Thus in table 2-6 we identify the effect of ARDA on income levels, while in table 2-7 we identify the effect of ARDA on income growth.

The tables reveal a complex story of the effect of ARDA on the level and growth of real incomes. Relative to the rest of the country, Appalachia showed no progress as a result of ARDA on income levels, but income growth converged by 14 percent. This growth convergence is consistent with the much lower income at baseline. Compared to rural America, though, Appalachia converged in both levels and growth. At the same time, it diverged in levels compared to border counties and did no better in terms of growth. This analysis helps reconcile the diverging conclusions of Andrew Isserman and Terance Rephann (1995) and Edward Glaeser and Joshua Gottlieb (2008). The comparison group used in the former was based on a matching algorithm, which in practice likely approximates my use of rural America, while Glaeser and Gottlieb used a comparison group akin to the surrounding border counties. When compared to its neighbors, Appalachia did not fare so well in terms of income convergence, but it showed substantive gains against a more general rural counterpart. Income levels in Central Appalachia diverged, but growth rates converged, whereas both levels and growth diverged in Northern Appalachia (or stayed the same in terms of growth compared to border counties). Southern Appalachia actually converged in income levels and growth in relation to the rest of the country and rural America but showed no relative improvement in light of ARDA relative to border counties.

Table 2-6. *Effects of ARDA on Real per Capita Income, Regression Adjusted, 1960–2000*[a]
U.S. dollars

Region	*Rest of country*	*Rural America*	*Adjacent counties*	*Surrounding counties*
Appalachia	−206	455	−1,507	−2,039
	(193)	(161)	(254)	(239)
Central Appalachia	−1,261	−600	−2,275	−2,847
	(405)	(326)	(354)	(352)
Northern Appalachia	−1,358	−697	−2,164	−3,215
	(315)	(255)	(325)	(380)
Southern Appalachia	1,288	1,950	−602	−766
	(291)	(237)	(399)	(367)
Appalachia, ARA eligible	−479	187	−1,781	−2,312
	(212)	(174)	(255)	(251)
Central, ARA eligible	−1,331	−670	−2,344	−2,917
	(413)	(322)	(354)	(355)
Northern, ARA eligible	−1,313	−651	−2,118	−3,170
	(322)	(268)	(339)	(398)
Southern, ARA eligible	1,057	1,719	−833	−997
	(352)	(285)	(436)	(442)

Source: Author's calculations.

a. Standard errors are in parentheses. All models control for 1960 county-level shares of high school graduates, shares of blacks, shares of persons living in urban areas, and labor force growth. Rural America refers to those counties outside of Appalachia with a 1974 rural-urban value of more than 5. Adjacent counties are those immediately bordering Appalachia; surrounding counties include adjacent counties plus counties immediately bordering them.

The baseline models of the effect of ARDA on Appalachia shown in tables 2-5, 2-6, and 2-7 are reestimated in table 2-8 but only for 1960–70. These models capture the immediate effects of ARDA five years after passage and thus abstract from any intervening social and economic developments in the decades after 1970 that are not controlled for in table 2-5 and yet may confound the estimate of the program. Each row pertains to a dependent variable from each of the earlier tables. Thus, the baseline estimate of a 5 percentage point reduction in the first column and row of table 2-8 indicates that in comparing this to column 1 of table 2-5 nearly two-thirds of the antipoverty effectiveness of ARDA relative to the rest of the country occurred in the first five years of the program. This is perhaps not surprising given that the major influx of resources into the region occurred in the initial years of the program. This increases to three-fourths of the

Table 2-7. *Effects of ARDA on Log Real per Capita Income, Regression Adjusted, 1960–2000*[a]

Region	*Rest of country*	*Rural America*	*Adjacent counties*	*Surrounding counties*
Appalachia	0.137	0.114	0.021	−0.003
	(0.014)	(0.014)	(0.024)	(0.019)
Central Appalachia	0.272	0.249	0.042	0.046
	(0.029)	(0.028)	(0.043)	(0.034)
Northern Appalachia	−0.091	−0.114	0.027	0.020
	(0.023)	(0.022)	(0.026)	(0.023)
Southern Appalachia	0.259	0.236	−0.012	−0.037
	(0.021)	(0.020)	(0.030)	(0.026)
Appalachia, ARA eligible	0.145	0.122	0.029	0.005
	(0.016)	(0.015)	(0.024)	(0.020)
Central, ARA eligible	0.276	0.253	0.047	0.051
	(0.030)	(0.029)	(0.043)	(0.034)
Northern, ARA eligible	−0.078	−0.101	0.050	0.033
	(0.024)	(0.023)	(0.027)	(0.023)
Southern, ARA eligible	0.300	0.277	0.029	0.004
	(0.025)	(0.024)	(0.033)	(0.030)

Source: Author's calculations.

a. Standard errors are in parentheses. All models control for 1960 county-level shares of high school graduates, shares of blacks, shares of persons living in urban areas, and labor force growth. Rural America refers to those counties outside of Appalachia with a 1974 rural-urban value of more than 5. Adjacent counties are those immediately bordering Appalachia; surrounding counties include adjacent counties plus counties immediately bordering them.

total impact in comparison to rural America but to only about one-half the total gain relative to the border counties. On the other hand, only about 20–40 percent of the effect of income levels and income growth was realized by 1970. This suggests that Appalachian counties benefited with continued investments after 1970.

Conclusion

The passage of the Appalachian Regional Development Act was a major legislative achievement given the historic federal-state partnership that it envisioned and the formalization of local development districts, the efficacy of which was often met with considerable skepticism by economists and politicians wary of too much government intervention into economic life. It faced many critics at its origin and at subsequent congressional reauthorizations and has had its share of

Table 2-8. *Short-Run Effects of ARDA, Regression Adjusted, 1960–70*[a]
Units as indicated

Variable	*Rest of country*	*Rural America*	*Adjacent counties*	*Surrounding counties*
Poverty rates (%)	−0.050	−0.035	−0.019	−0.019
	(0.006)	(0.006)	(0.010)	(0.009)
Real per capita income ($)	−59	7	−395	−410
	(87)	(79)	(107)	(92)
Log real per capita income	0.061	0.042	0.003	0.001
	(0.012)	(0.012)	(0.019)	(0.015)

Source: Author's calculations.

a. Standard errors are in parentheses. All models control for 1960 county-level shares of high school graduates, shares of blacks, shares of persons living in urban areas, and labor force growth. Rural America refers to those counties outside of Appalachia with a 1974 rural-urban value of more than 5. Adjacent counties are those immediately bordering Appalachia; surrounding counties include adjacent counties plus counties immediately bordering them.

operational and funding challenges over the years.[30] Yet despite this criticism the evidence presented here suggests that ARDA, or more specifically the *intent* of the act, has delivered at least partially on two key goals, that of alleviating extreme poverty and that of improving income growth in Appalachian counties.

As elucidated in chapter 6, this volume (by Matthew Kahn), the economic case for federal investment in local areas and regions is often difficult to make—one must justify the investment on equity grounds that it will reduce inequality, or on efficiency grounds that it will reduce negative externalities or enhance positive externalities such as agglomeration economies. The case made by PARC (1964) focuses on both—extreme poverty was a blight that at once violated Americans' sense of fairness and inhibited the nation's economic growth. The results here suggest that the ARDA investment did succeed in reducing hardship and brought Appalachian incomes closer to the national average.

However, even with ARDA, other forces at work caused the region to diverge from the country in terms of incomes per capita among Central and Northern Appalachians. The findings of several writers point to skill deficits as a leading factor in income divergence.[31] Over twenty years ago, at the twenty-fifth anniversary of ARDA, Ralph Widner reached a similar conclusion: "Yet in the years immediately ahead, the quality of labor will be the most powerful determinant of

30. Ibid.; Eller (2008).

31. Bollinger, Ziliak, and Troske (2011); also see chapters 3 and 6, this volume.

local economic development and, in this respect, Appalachia shares a major problem with America's inner cities and other distressed parts of nonmetropolitan America: its education gap."[32] The positive treatment effect attributed to infrastructure and human development programs in this chapter suggests that continued investments in this area are needed—and probably more intensively than in the past. In the hope of guiding future investments in the people in this and other disadvantaged regions of the country, additional empirical work on ARDA is called for to ascertain which specific programs were successful.

References

ARC (Appalachian Regional Commission). 2009. *Performance and Accountability Report* (www.arc.gov/publications/FY2009PerformanceandAccountabilityReport.asp).

Blank, Rebecca, and David Card. 1993. "Poverty, Income Distribution, and Growth: Are They Still Connected?" *BPEA,* no. 2: 285–339.

Blundell, Richard, and Monica Costa-Dias. 2009. "Alternative Approaches to Evaluation in Empirical Microeconomics." *Journal of Human Resources* 44, no. 3: 565–640.

Bollinger, Christopher, James Ziliak, and Kenneth Troske. 2011. "Down from the Mountain: Skill Upgrading and Wages in Appalachia." *Journal of Labor Economics* 29, no. 4: 819–57.

Bradshaw, Michael. 1992. *The Appalachian Regional Commission: Twenty-Five Years of Government Policy.* University Press of Kentucky.

Caudill, Harry. 1963. *Night Comes to the Cumberlands: A Biography of a Depressed Area.* New York: Little, Brown.

Eller, Ronald. 2008. *Uneven Ground: Appalachia since 1945.* University Press of Kentucky.

Glaeser, Edward, and Joshua Gottlieb. 2008. "The Economics of Place Making Policies." *BPEA,* no. 1: 155–253.

Glen, John. 1995. "The War on Poverty in Appalachia: Oral History from the 'Top down' and the 'Bottom up.' " *Oral History Review* 22, no. 1: 67–93.

Gundersen, Craig, and James P. Ziliak. 2004. "Poverty and Macroeconomic Performance across Space, Race, and Family Structure." *Demography* 41, no. 1: 61–86.

Harrington, Michael. 1962. *The Other America.* New York: Scribner.

Heckman, James, Robert LaLonde, and Jeffrey Smith. 1999. "The Economics and Econometrics of Active Labor Market Programs." In *Handbook of Labor Economics,* edited by Orley Ashenfelter and David Card, vol. 3A, pp. 1865–2097. Amsterdam: Elsevier–North Holland.

Hoynes, Hilary, and Diane Whitmore Schanzenbach. 2009. "Consumption Reponses to In-Kind Transfers: Evidence from the Introduction of the Food Stamp Program." *American Economic Journal: Applied Economics* 1, no. 4: 109–39.

Isserman, Andrew, and Terance Rephann. 1995. "The Economic Effects of the Appalachian Regional Commission." *Journal of the American Planning Association* 61, no. 3: 345–65.

32. Widner (1990), p. 310.

Ludwig, Jens, and Douglas L. Miller. 2007. "Does Head Start Improve Children's Life Chances? Evidence from a Regression Discontinuity Approach." *Quarterly Journal of Economics* 122, no. 1: 159–208.

PARC (President's Appalachian Regional Commission). 1964. *Appalachia: A Report by the President's Appalachian Regional Commission.* Washington: Government Printing Office.

Rosenbaum, Robert, and Donald Rubin. 1983. "The Central Role of the Propensity Score in Observational Studies for Causal Effects." *Biometrika* 70, no. 1: 41–55.

Schultze, Charles. 1983. "Industrial Policy: A Dissent." *Brookings Review* (Fall): 3–12.

Widner, Ralph. 1990. "Appalachian Development after 25 Years: An Assessment." *Economic Development Quarterly* 4, no. 4: 291–312.

DAN A. BLACK
SETH G. SANDERS

3

Inequality and Human Capital in Appalachia, 1960–2000

When President Lyndon B. Johnson signed the Appalachian Regional Development Act in 1965 (which created the Appalachian Regional Commission), analysts could indeed classify Appalachia as economically distressed—particularly when compared to the rest of the United States. Per capita income in the region was $1,267 in 1960, 77 percent of the national average. Nearly one-third (31 percent) of Appalachians lived below the federal poverty line, compared to just over one-fifth (22 percent) of all Americans.[1] Labor force and employment levels in Appalachia also compared unfavorably with those in the rest of the United States.

The results of the 2000 decennial census, however, show that Appalachia, in some dimensions, more closely resembles the rest of the United States economically than it did in 1964. For example:

—Per capita income in 1999 was $18,200, 84 percent of the national average of $21,600 (figures in 2000 dollars). In fourteen Appalachian counties, per capita income exceeded the national average.

—At 13.6 percent, Appalachia's poverty rate in the 2000 census was less than half its level forty years earlier. Moreover, the rate was just 1.3 percentage points higher than in the rest of the United States.

—Appalachia's labor force participation rate in 2000 was 67 percent for men and 53 percent for women—only slightly less than the rates outside the

1. Wood and Bischak (2000), table 3. Appalachia's income figure is in 1960 dollars.

region (71 percent and 58 percent, respectively). And the 2000 census shows that 5.8 percent of Appalachia's civilian labor force was unemployed, almost identical with the 5.7 percent rate in the rest of the country.

—The typical Appalachian county had a median household income ($32,500), which was 89 percent of the median for the typical U.S. county.[2]

Many of the cited statistics on economic well-being are measured at the family or household level. This means that shifts in household composition, in female labor supply and earnings, and in male labor supply and earnings all might have contributed to this convergence. Models of human capital suggest that an individual's level of human capital should be related to earnings capacity. To focus on issues of human capital we first need to shift the analysis from the family or household level to the individual level.

We focus on the earnings of men ages twenty-five through sixty-four in 1960 through 2000. First we ask, What have been the *average* earnings of these working-age men in Appalachia relative to the same cohort in the rest of the United States? Of course changes in average earnings potentially obfuscate important changes in earnings at different points in the earnings distribution. For example, even if there was no change in the average earnings of these men living in Appalachia relative to those in the rest of the United States, the interpretation of this statement is quite different if earnings inequality grew within Appalachia, leaving the poorest Appalachians relatively worse off. The Appalachian Regional Development Act and the War on Poverty were not born out of a concern about *average* earnings; the chief concern was the earnings (and earnings potential) of the bottom part of the income distribution. For this reason we examine the earnings of working-age men in Appalachia relative to those in the rest of the United States at different points in the earnings distribution.

Besides understanding whether the poor in Appalachia have gotten richer since 1960, there is another reason to examine the relative change in the earnings distribution. Several studies document that, starting in the late 1970s and going through the middle 1990s, earnings at the bottom of the distribution fell while earnings at the top of the distribution rose. Most of this evidence is about earnings trends in the United States as a whole, but some analysis shows that this bifurcation of the earnings distribution holds by census region. What we know much less about is whether within regions bifurcation of the earnings distribution holds in all areas equally or whether it holds more in urban areas than in rural areas. Knowing this could be important. The most prevalent explanation for this earnings bifurcation, skill-biased technological change (SBTC), suggests that a

2. Black and Sanders (2004), table 5.

shift in production technology that favors skilled over unskilled workers increased the relative demand for skilled workers and their earnings. As we show, in rural areas education is lower at all quantiles of the earnings distribution; a considerable number of men at the top of the earnings distribution, in fact, have relatively low levels of education historically; and at the bottom of the distribution, education levels in rural areas in general, and in Appalachia specifically, are astonishingly low. This suggests that if SBTC is important, all else equal, the top end of the earnings distribution should rise faster in urban areas than in rural areas, and the bottom end of the distribution should fall faster in rural areas than in urban areas. Of course shifting levels of education at various quantiles also affect the relative earnings distribution.

Although the three regions of Appalachia show very different trends, average male earnings in Appalachia as a whole remained at a constant of about 80 percent of the national average for the forty years. And although there has been no improvement in *average* male earnings, there was an impressive rise in the bottom of the earnings distribution between 1960 and 1980. Interestingly, the convergence of Appalachia in the bottom of the earnings distribution toward earnings of the remainder of the United States appears to be driven almost entirely by a convergence of earnings in rural areas toward those in urban areas. In fact between 1960 and 1980 a rising fraction of men in urban areas were in the bottom of the distribution, while a falling fraction of men in rural areas were in the bottom of the distribution. Between 1960 and 1980 the upper end of the earnings distribution was increasing similarly within and outside of Appalachia.

Average earnings remained constant over the entire period of 1960–2000, while relative earnings in the bottom of the earnings distribution increased between 1960 and 1980, which means that either the upper end of the earnings distribution was rising faster outside of Appalachia or the bottom end of the distribution was falling faster inside of Appalachia after 1980—or both. On balance, we find evidence that the most important factor is that Appalachia has a smaller fraction of people in urban areas and that between 1980 and 2000 there was a rapid rise in the upper end of the earnings distribution in cities. Our general conclusion from this analysis is that the changes over time in earnings distribution are pronounced between rural and urban areas; what drives differences between earnings inside and outside Appalachia is simply that a somewhat higher fraction of Appalachian men live in rural areas.[3]

We then turn to the degree to which changes in the relative level of human capital and the relative return to human capital can explain these changes in

3. This is consistent with the findings of Bollinger, Ziliak, and Troske (2011).

relative earnings at different points in the earnings distribution. We find that the rise in education plays an important role in explaining the rise in earnings at the bottom of the earnings distribution between 1960 and 1980; at the top of the earnings distribution it plays much less of a role. Between 1980 and 2000, however, both the level and return to education are important explanations for the relative rise in the upper tail of the earnings distribution outside of Appalachia and, more specifically, in cities.

The Rise of Wage Inequality

There are now dozens of studies on changes in wage and income inequality in the United States since 1970.[4] They identify a set of facts about income inequality on which there is considerable agreement:

—Wage dispersion increased substantially for both men and women from the end of the 1970s to the mid-1990s. The weekly earnings of the 90th percentile worker relative to the 10th percentile worker increased by over 25 percent for both men and women from 1979 to 1995.

—Wage differentials by education, occupation, and age (experience) have increased. The relative earnings of college graduates and those with advanced degrees increased dramatically in the 1980s.

—Wage dispersion expanded within demographic and skill groups. The wages of individuals of the same age, education, and sex (and even those working in the same occupation and industry) were much more unequal in the mid-1990s than two decades earlier.

—Because these wage structure changes occurred in a period of rather slow mean real wage growth, the real earnings of less educated and lower paid workers (especially young, less educated males) appear to be lower in the 1990s than those of analogous workers two decades earlier. The employment rates of less skilled workers also appear to have fallen relative to those of more skilled workers.[5]

There is a great deal of debate on the causes of these changes in the wage and income distribution. Labor economists emphasize two explanations, the most prominent being that skill-biased technological change, often thought to be associated with the adoption of computer and automation technology, caused an increase in the demand for more skilled workers.[6] A second explanation used by

4. This literature is summarized in Katz and Autor (1999).

5. Juhn (1992); Murphy and Topel (1997).

6. Berman, Bound, and Griliches (1994); Autor, Katz, and Kruger (1998).

labor economists focuses on the supply of skill to the market. For example, one study argues that inflows of less-skilled immigrants increased the supply of less-skilled workers, particularly workers with less than a high school education.[7] This study estimates that 30–50 percent of the fall in wages of high school dropouts is due to immigration. Others, though, emphasize the relative changes in the supply of college graduates as a potential explanation for both the rise in the returns to education and increased wage inequality.[8] In contrast, trade economists emphasize falling barriers to international trade and its effect on U.S. manufacturing employment, long a bastion of high-paid jobs for low-skilled workers. Adrian Wood made a dramatic calculation, adjusting skill intensities to account for low-skilled goods that had been totally transferred to developing countries.[9] He estimates that 100 percent of the rise in the skilled/unskilled wage ratio could be attributed to increased North-South trade. Finally, there are studies that emphasize the role of institutional factors, such as changing rates of unionization or falling minimum wages.[10]

In this chapter we examine earnings inequality that is a function of both a changing wage structure and changes in the number of hours worked. There is also now a large literature on changes in labor supply of working-age men over the last thirty years.[11] Part of the labor market dropout literature emphasizes the same factors as the wage inequality literature and suggests that falling wages for some groups have led to falling labor supply. This is especially true for low-skilled labor, especially young, black urban workers.[12] But labor market dropout of working-age men also seems to have increased since the 1970s. Some scholars suggest that a rise in the after-tax Social Security disability income replacement rate has strengthened the incentives for workers to seek benefits and leave the labor market.[13] For workers over the age of forty-five, there is also evidence of increased rates of early retirement.

Robert Topel (1994) offers some evidence on variation in income inequality by census region. He estimates wage inequality between the 84th and 16th percentile of the wage distribution and finds that the West, North Central, and Atlantic regions had higher growth in wage inequality between 1972 and 1990

7. Borjas, Freeman, and Katz (1992).

8. Katz and Murphy (1992); Card and Lemieux (2001).

9. Wood (1994).

10. DiNardo, Fortin, and Lemieux (1996); Freeman (1996); Lee (1999).

11. Juhn and Potter (2006) give a through review of this literature.

12. Edelman, Holzer, and Offner (2006).

13. Black, Daniel, and Sanders (2002); Autor and Duggan (2006).

than other regions. The change in wage inequality between the 50th and 16th percentile plays a large role in the high growth in inequality in these regions. Topel's central conclusion is that what explains regional differences in the growth in inequality lies on the supply side. In the West he finds evidence of immigration affecting the wages of low-skilled men; he also finds evidence that increased female labor force participation decreases men's wages. He specifically rejects that demand factors such as deindustrialization in the Atlantic and North Central regions play a role in differences in the regional growth in inequality.

The work that is most closely related to ours is that of Christopher Wheeler (2001). He develops a model in which capital and worker skill are complementary in production, a model that formalizes the idea that urban agglomeration generates more efficient but segregated matches between workers and firms. As a result, market size not only is positively correlated with average productivity, it also generates greater between-skill-group wage inequality and higher returns to market skills. He tests the wage inequality prediction using a cross section from the 1980 public use microdata sample (PUMS) of the census that identifies 286 metropolitan areas. While Wheeler does not look directly at measures of wage inequality, he does present evidence that city size significantly increases wages and does so more for more educated workers. This is consistent with his sorting model, in which larger markets generate more stratified matches, allocating high-skilled workers to more productive firms. This leaves low-skilled workers in less-productive firms and raises wages of skilled workers relative to unskilled workers.

To our knowledge, there is no work that directly addresses the *growth* in income inequality in urban versus rural areas. When this issue has been addressed it has been examined only in a single cross section. And typically because of the limited geographic detail in public use data files, rural areas are not analyzed at all. Our contribution is to describe the evolution of earnings inequality across time and between rural and urban areas, with a particular focus on Appalachia.

Appalachia and the Distribution of Earnings

We use the definition of Appalachia employed by the Appalachian Regional Commission (ARC). In addition to examining the entire region, we analyze convergence levels and patterns in Appalachia's three subregions: Northern Appalachia (from southern New York State through most of West Virginia); Central Appalachia (southern West Virginia, eastern Kentucky, and parts of

Appalachian Virginia and Tennessee); and Southern Appalachia (from southwestern Virginia southward).[14]

The data in this chapter come from two sources. The first is a summary file on the earnings distribution for working-age men for each county in the United States (derived from the long forms of the decennial censuses from 1960 through 2000). We begin with the 1960 census because the data in that survey capture the conditions that ultimately led President Johnson to sign the bill forming the ARC. Since 1970 the Census Bureau has tabulated county-level statistics on various measures of housing and consumption and made these publicly available in electronic form. Two reasons, however, prevent us from using these files for this particular analysis: the files do not measure the same statistics consistently over time or they measure the wrong population subgroup; and no such public statistics are available for the 1960 data.

As a result, we use a special tabulation prepared for ARC from the Census Bureau's internal long-form data files from 1960 to 2000. The tabulation reports for each county the mean earnings as well as the 10th, 25th, 50th, 75th, and 90th percentiles of the earnings distribution for working-age men (and for working-age women). Earnings are defined as wage and salary earnings and earnings from farm and business enterprises. The tabulation reports this for all men and women who are working full time and full year. It also reports the fraction of men and women working full time, full year, and the fraction not in the labor force at any time in the year before the census ("zero earners"). This tabulation was done on 25 percent of all U.S. households in 1960, 20 percent of households in 1970, and 16.7 percent of households in the remaining three census years. The tabulation is cleared for public release through the Census Bureau's Disclosure Review Committee.

Unfortunately, without accessing the confidential long-form data directly, no microdata are available that identify a person's county of residence. The summary data pose a problem for describing the evolution of quantiles of the earnings distribution and for examining the role of education in explaining it. The first issue we deal with statistically as outlined below. The second issue we address in an imperfect form. Applying public use microdata from the 1960–2000 decennial census, we show that the aggregate patterns for rural Appalachia are remarkably close to the aggregate patterns for men living in the rural part of two states, Kentucky and West Virginia. All 55 counties of West Virginia are part of Appalachia, but only 51 of the 120 counties in Kentucky lie within Appalachia. These two

14. For a more detailed description of the Appalachian region, see Pollard (2003), p. 2.

states comprise over one-fourth of the counties of Appalachia. While 69 counties in Kentucky lie outside of Appalachia, the rural counties among them appear to be remarkably similar to the Appalachian counties of Kentucky.

Estimation of Earnings Distributions from Summary Data

With microdata, calculating the quantiles of the earnings distribution for any subregion of the country is straightforward. The challenge we face is that the microdata at our disposal do not have enough geographic detail to identify directly the residents of Appalachia. The best we can do is use the summary data described above, but this poses a challenge.[15]

Appalachia is a collection of counties. If we know the mean earnings for working-age men and their number in each county, then we can ascertain the mean earnings of a collection of counties by calculating a weighted sum of each county's mean earnings. The weights are simply the fraction of men who reside in any specific county. Unfortunately, this weighted approach does not apply to other moments of a distribution. For example, the median earnings in Appalachia are not equal to a weighted average of the median earnings of each county in Appalachia.

Appendix A develops a new approach to calculating the level of earnings at any point in the earnings distribution for Appalachia or its subregions. The method approximates the earnings distribution of each county in each year; with this approximation, we can calculate the number of men in each county who are below any level of income, such as the number of working-age men earning $24,500 a year or less in each rural county of Appalachia in 1980. When we add this number across the counties that make up rural Appalachia, we have the total number of men in rural Appalachia earning $24,500 or less in 1980; dividing this by the total number of men in rural Appalachia in 1980 gives us the fraction of men in rural Appalachia earning $24,500 a year or less; this specific number turns out to be 33.9 percent. We can then calculate this in a different year for rural

15. An alternative is to adopt the inverse probability weighting method of Bollinger, Ziliak, and Troske (2011). They note that the lowest geographic identifier in the public use data is the Public Use Microdata Area (PUMA), which contains 100,000 persons. The PUMA can contain multiple counties, especially in rural areas such as Appalachia, and thus Bollinger, Ziliak, and Troske construct weights that are based on the probability that a person living in a given PUMA resides in Appalachia. For PUMAs wholly contained in Appalachia the weight takes a value of 1, and for those wholly outside a value of 0. For those PUMAs with some counties in Appalachia and some outside, the probability varies between 0 and 1.

Appalachia, which allows us to discuss how the fraction of men earning $24,500 annually changed over time. For example in 1960, 46.3 percent of men in rural Appalachia earned less than $24,500. We can also compare a region like rural Appalachia to other areas in the United States. For example, in 1980, 25 percent of urban residents outside Appalachia earned $24,500 or less annually.

We also report our results a second way. Instead of focusing on the fraction of working-age men in a region who are below a specific level of earnings, we ask what is the level of income that marks a specific point in the earnings distribution? Returning to our example of men in rural Appalachia in 1980, knowing that 33.9 percent of them earned $24,500 a year or less lets us know that, if we want to know the median level of income (that is, the income below which 50 percent of men fall), it must be higher than $24,500 a year (because 33.9 percent of men earned less than this level). Similarly if we are interested in the 25th percentile of earnings, it must be lower than $24,500. Appendix A also shows how we solve for the level of earnings of a subregion that defines specific percentiles of the earnings distribution.

Microdata and Estimating Education Distributions and the Return to Education

Appendix B develops a method of using census microdata to estimate how education affects earnings at different points in the earnings distribution. Take as an example the way the 25th percentile of earnings of working-age men with bachelor's degrees (BA) compares to the 25th percentile of such men with a high school diploma (HD). Because education has been rising over time, on average men with a BA are younger than men with an HD. Because of this, it would not be shocking to find that among men with a BA, the 25th percentile of earnings might be lower than among people with an HD. It seems odd that more education might lower earnings, and in fact it is; this counterintuitive result would stem from the lowest paid people with BAs being substantially younger that those with HDs, reflecting the formers' relatively recent start in the labor market. To isolate the effect of a BA we would want to compare those with a BA and those with an HD who were the same age.

Appendix B discusses how to construct a set of weights so that when the data are weighted the age and sex distribution of people with BAs and people with HDs will be the same. This eliminates any difference in earnings generated by age and sex differences and allows an interpretation of the earnings differences being associated with the level of education. The weights also take into account nonresponse in the census to questions of age, sex, education, earnings, and hours of work.

Given the weighting scheme in equation B-5, we can simply run weighted ordinary least squares on the equation

$$y_{k,i} = \alpha + \Delta BA_i + \varepsilon_i, \tag{3-1}$$

and the estimated Δ will isolate the effect of a BA on earnings at any point in the earnings distribution. The intuition for why this procedure provides an estimate of Δ is that the reweighting scheme given in equation B-5 makes the distribution of covariates in the sample of high school graduates identical to the distribution of covariates in the sample of BA holders. In the matching context, this is often referred to as "inverse probability weighting."[16]

Average Earnings and Employment: One Step Forward, One Step Back

At first glance, the last forty years of the twentieth century show little convergence between the average incomes of working-age men in Appalachia and that of their counterparts in the rest of the country. Appalachian men earned, on average, 81 percent of the incomes of working-age men outside the region in 2000 ($37,600 to $46,600, in 2006 dollars), compared to 80 percent in 1960 ($28,500 to $35,500).

But this masks two stories: evidence of convergence between 1960 and 1980 and evidence of divergence afterward (figure 3-1). In 1980 men's mean income in Appalachia was $35,300 (in 2006 dollars), which is 85 percent of the $41,400 men outside the region earned that year. This convergence coincides with the boom in the coal industry during the 1960s and 1970s—a boom from which Appalachia (particularly Central Appalachia) benefited significantly. Similarly, the post-1980 divergence in men's income coincided with the shift away from Appalachian coal and similar products. (Income for Appalachian men, even when adjusted for inflation, continued to rise in the 1980s and 1990s; the income of men outside the region rose even faster.)

Among the subregions, Central Appalachia (which was especially reliant on the coal industry) followed the above pattern. Between 1960 and 1980 the average income of Central Appalachian working-age men rose from 57 percent to 72 percent of that of non-Appalachian working-age men. By 2000, however, Central Appalachian men were earning 58 percent of men outside the

16. See Hirano, Imbens, and Ridder (2003) and DiNardo, Fortin, and Lemieux (1996) for extended discussions of inverse probability weighting with continuous variables. See Black and others (2006, 2008) for applications to discrete data.

Figure 3-1. *Mean Income of Appalachian Men as Percentage of Income of Non-Appalachian Men, Aged 25–64, 1960–2000*

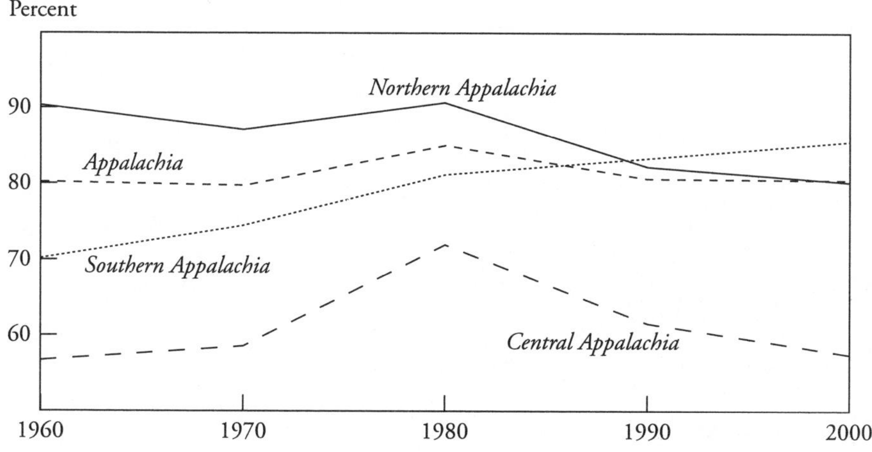

Source: Authors' analysis of the 1960 through 2000 decennial censuses.

Appalachian region—almost their proportion in 1960. In fact, the average income for central Appalachian men (when accounting for inflation) actually *fell* 9 percent between 1980 and 2000.

By contrast, both Northern and Southern Appalachia took different courses. Men's incomes in Northern Appalachia, which on average were 90 percent of those of men outside of Appalachia in 1960, stayed at about that level through 1980, then fell to about 80 percent by 2000. Meanwhile, incomes of men in Southern Appalachia converged toward those of men in the non-Appalachian United States throughout the forty years between 1960 and 2000: 70 percent in 1960, 81 percent in 1980, and 86 percent in 2000.

Employment patterns (figure 3-2) yield similar evidence of economic convergence between residents of Appalachia and those in the rest of the country. Take, for example, year-round employment—considered a key barometer of how a population's skills match with a community's economic opportunities. In 1960 just 64 percent of working-age men in Appalachia were employed during the entire year, compared to 75 percent for working-age men in the rest of the United States. Just ten years later, the share of Appalachian men with full-year employment had risen to 76 percent, much closer to the 80 percent share outside of Appalachia. During the 1970s and 1980s, year-round employment among men slipped at similar paces for both regions, although it rebounded slightly during

Figure 3-2. *Appalachian and Non-Appalachian Men Employed Full Time, 1960–2000*

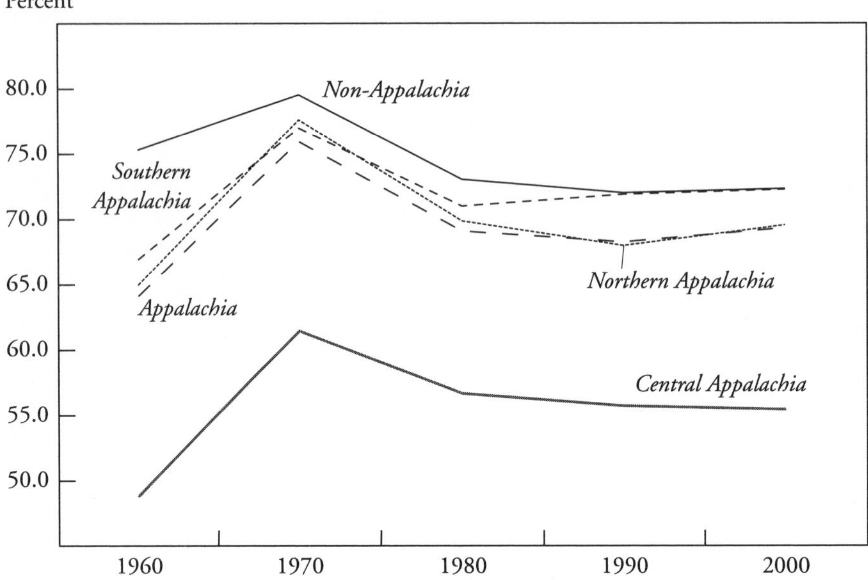

Source: Authors' analysis of the 1960 through 2000 decennial censuses.

the 1990s. In 2000, 70 percent of Appalachian men and 72 percent of men outside the region had full-time employment.

Each subregion exhibits the same pattern. Between 1960 and 1970, the full-year employment rate for working-age men rose from 65 percent to 78 percent in Northern Appalachia, from 49 percent to 61 percent in Central Appalachia, and from 67 percent to 77 percent in Southern Appalachia. By 2000—after slight declines in the 1970s and 1980s followed by small rebounds in the 1990s—these shares stood at 70 percent for Northern Appalachian men, 56 percent for Central Appalachian men, and 73 percent for Southern Appalachian men. Southern Appalachian men actually were slightly more likely to be employed year-round than men outside Appalachia.

There have been rapid changes in the fraction of working-age men not in the labor force. This labor market dropout is noted in several studies, but the regional pattern has not been well documented. In 1960 outside of Appalachia 5.3 percent of working-age men were out of the labor force; within Appalachia 8.3 percent were out of the labor force; and in Central Appalachia 14.7 percent were out of the labor force. In 1960 Appalachia's rate of nonemployment was 56 percent higher than outside Appalachia, and Central Appalachia's rate was 176 percent higher than outside Appalachia. By 2000 the fraction of men not in the labor force rose dramatically in all regions; in 2000, 11.9 percent of men outside of Appalachia and 15.5 percent of men in Appalachia were out of the labor force; for Central Appalachia this figure exceeded 28 percent. Because of the rapid rise in nonemployment outside of Appalachia, the Appalachian rate of nonemployment regressed toward the mean of the United States.

Distribution of Earnings and the Importance of Urban Areas

Figure 3-1 displays the changes in the relative *average* earnings of working-age men in Appalachia versus outside of Appalachia and in the subregions of Appalachia. Except for a notable increase in earnings in Central Appalachia between 1970 and 1980 and an offsetting decline between 1980 and 1990, there was remarkable stability in Appalachia's relative earnings—at 80 percent of the rest of the country.

Table 3-1 shows this analysis at different points in the earnings distribution. There are several findings to note. First, while mean earnings in Appalachia did not improve between 1960 and 1970, there was substantial improvement in relative earnings at the bottom of the income distribution. As a whole Appalachian earnings at the 25th percentile improved from 64 percent to 77 percent of the rest of the country. This was driven largely by a rise in earnings in Southern Appalachia and a small improvement in Central Appalachia.

Second, the rapid rise in average earnings in Central Appalachia between 1970 and 1980 driven by the coal boom hardly affected the earnings in the lower part of the earnings distribution at all but it did raise the median, the 75th percentile, and the 90th percentile of earnings a great deal. The most likely explanation is that coal mining wages are relatively high and hours of work dictate annual earnings to a large degree. In 1970 underemployed miners were likely to be above the 25th percentile of earnings; the boom in 1980 then increased their earnings, causing a rise in the higher earnings quantiles.

Third, the relative earnings of Appalachians in the 90th percentile declined a small amount between 1960 and 2000; as a percentage of earnings at the 90th percentile outside of Appalachia, the 90th percentile of earnings in Appalachia was 87.0 percent in 1960, 85 percent in 1980, and 83.3 percent in 2000. The rapid rise in the upper tail of the earnings distribution implies real declines in the absolute level of earnings in Appalachia versus other areas. The most impressive rise within Appalachia at the top of the earnings distribution was in Southern Appalachia.

Table 3-1. *Earnings of Men, Aged 25–64, Appalachia and Non-Appalachia, Selected Years, 1960–2000*

Units as indicated

	Earnings (2006 $)			*Earnings (2006 $)*			*Relative earnings Appalachia/non-Appalachia (%)*		
Year	*Non-Appalachia*	*Appalachia*	*Appalachia/non-Appalachia (%)*	*Northern Appalachia*	*Central Appalachia*	*Southern Appalachia*	*Northern Appalachia*	*Central Appalachia*	*Southern Appalachia*
10th percentile									
1960	5,400	1,300	24.1	3,000	0	1,300	55.6	0.0	24.1
1970	8,500	2,300	27.1	5,700	0	2,700	67.1	0.0	31.8
1980	700	0	0.0	0	0	0	0.0	0.0	0.0
1990	0	0	0.0	0	0	0	...	...	...
2000	0	0	0.0	0	0	0	...	...	...
25th percentile									
1960	19,000	12,300	64.7	17,800	4,000	9,500	93.7	21.1	50.0
1970	26,500	20,300	76.6	25,600	7,000	17,700	96.6	26.4	66.8
1980	19,200	15,600	81.3	18,300	5,500	14,500	95.3	28.6	75.5
1990	17,600	13,200	75.0	13,900	2,300	15,200	79.0	13.1	86.4
2000	16,900	12,700	75.1	13,600	0	15,000	80.5	0.0	88.8

Median									
1960	32,800	26,600	81.1	30,600	15,300	21,600	93.3	46.6	65.9
1970	42,300	35,000	82.7	38,600	24,200	31,000	91.3	57.2	73.3
1980	36,900	32,200	87.3	35,000	24,900	29,300	94.9	67.5	79.4
1990	36,400	30,800	84.6	32,000	21,700	31,100	87.9	59.6	85.4
2000	35,900	30,900	86.1	31,500	21,700	32,000	87.7	60.4	89.1
75th percentile									
1960	45,500	38,600	84.8	41,500	30,900	34,200	91.2	67.9	75.2
1970	58,500	48,600	83.1	51,200	40,700	45,600	87.5	69.6	77.9
1980	54,300	48,100	88.6	50,100	44,000	45,100	92.3	81.0	83.1
1990	57,400	48,600	84.7	49,400	41,200	49,000	86.1	71.8	85.4
2000	58,400	49,200	84.2	49,400	40,900	50,700	84.6	70.0	86.8
90th percentile									
1960	61,800	51,900	84.0	54,800	44,000	47,900	88.7	71.2	77.5
1970	80,400	64,700	80.5	67,000	55,100	62,900	83.3	68.5	78.2
1980	74,200	64,300	86.7	65,600	61,200	62,600	88.4	82.5	84.4
1990	82,500	68,600	83.2	68,500	60,400	70,600	83.0	73.2	85.6
2000	88,400	72,000	81.4	70,700	63,200	75,600	80.0	71.5	85.5

Figure 3-3. *Earnings of Appalachian Relative to Non-Appalachian Men, Aged 25–64*

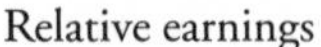

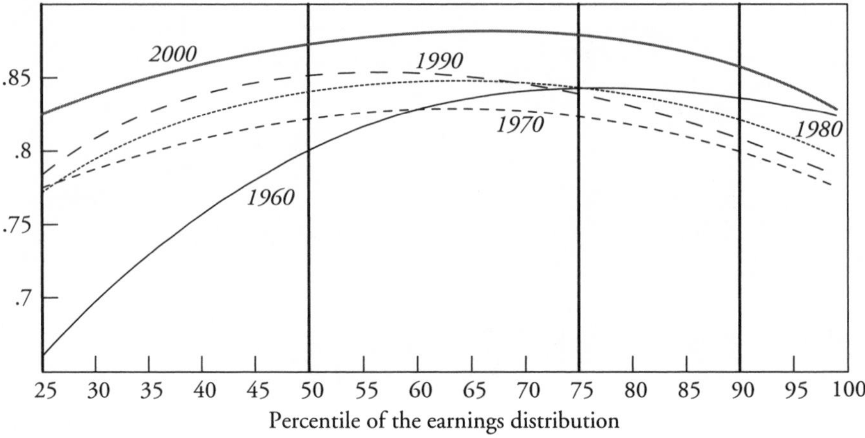

Source: Authors' analysis of the 1960 through 2000 decennial censuses.

Figure 3-3 graphs the relative earnings in Appalachia and in the rest of the country at all points in the earnings distribution, from the 25th percentile to the 98th percentile. Moving along any of the plotted lines shows how the relative earnings change across quantiles within a year. The distance between any two lines shows how the relative earnings changed at that quantile across any two years. In general, each line is an inverted U shape, showing that the highest relative earnings for Appalachians are in the middle of the earnings distribution. The more interesting issue is the relative change in earnings across years at various points in the earnings distribution. The first interesting pattern is a substantial rise in the bottom of the earnings distribution between 1960 and 1970, before the coal boom and despite government programs aimed at aiding poor families that may have limited labor force participation. While the earnings below the 55th percentile improved between 1960 and 1970, relative earnings above the 55th percentile declined. Then between 1970 and 1980 the coal boom had the pronounced effect of raising earnings everywhere in the distribution but by increasing amounts at higher quantiles.

As discussed above, there is a large literature on the increase in earnings at the top of the earnings distribution and the decrease at the bottom in the post-1980 period (see table 3-1). Outside of Appalachia, earnings at the 25th percentile fell from $22,200 in 1980 to $18,900 in 2000, a decline of 15 percent; at the same time earnings in the 90th percentile rose from $85,900 in 1980 to $106,000 in 2000, an increase of 25 percent. In Appalachia, the bottom end of the distribution (25th percentile) declined more (from $16,900 in 1980 to $13,200 in 2000, or 22 percent), while the top end (90th percentile) of the earnings distribution rose from $73,700 to $88,300 (or 20 percent).

One difference between Appalachia and the remainder of the country is the fraction of the population that is rural. Of the 410 counties in Appalachia, all but 37 had less than 100,000 residents in 1960; two-thirds of all Appalachian residents lived in counties with fewer than 100,000 residents, compared to 41 percent in the rest of the country. Outside of Appalachia there are some very large cities. While the largest city in Appalachia in 1960 was Pittsburgh (population 604,332 and population rank 16), New York had almost 8 million residents, Chicago 3.5 million residents, and Los Angeles 2.5 million residents.

To investigate the role of urban density in changes in the earnings distribution we focus on rural Appalachia, rural counties outside of Appalachia, and urban counties outside of Appalachia (figure 3-4). We define an urban county as a county with more than 100,000 residents in 1960.[17] The earnings of rural residents of Appalachia appear to be nearly a constant fraction of the earnings of residents of other rural areas of the country, varying between 75 percent and 90 percent over the earnings distribution. The coal boom between 1960 and 1980 clearly raised the earnings of the lower end of the earnings distribution relative to other rural areas in the country, but this reversed by 2000.

The big story is the relative earnings in rural areas versus urban areas (figure 3-5). In 1960 low-earning urban residents earned substantially more than low-earning rural residents; the 25th percentile of earnings of urban residents was 80 percent higher than rural residents in 1960. The relative earnings of rural and urban residents converge as they move up the earnings distribution; in 1960, at the 90th percentile, urban residents earned 20 percent more than rural residents. By 1980 the relative earnings of rural residents increased substantially at the bottom end of the distribution. Much of this was driven by increasing labor market dropout rates in cities as well as relatively lower earnings among workers. In 1980, regardless of the

17. To give some context, the four counties with closest to 100,000 residents in 1960 were Tazwell County, Ill. (city of Perkins); York County, Maine (towns of York, Lebanon, and Kennebunkport); Rockingham County, N.H. (towns of Derry, Salem, Londonderry, and Portsmouth); and Kenosha, Wis. (city of Kenosha).

Figure 3-4. *Earnings of Rural Appalachian and Urban Non-Appalachian Men Relative to Rural Non-Appalachian Men, Aged 25–64*

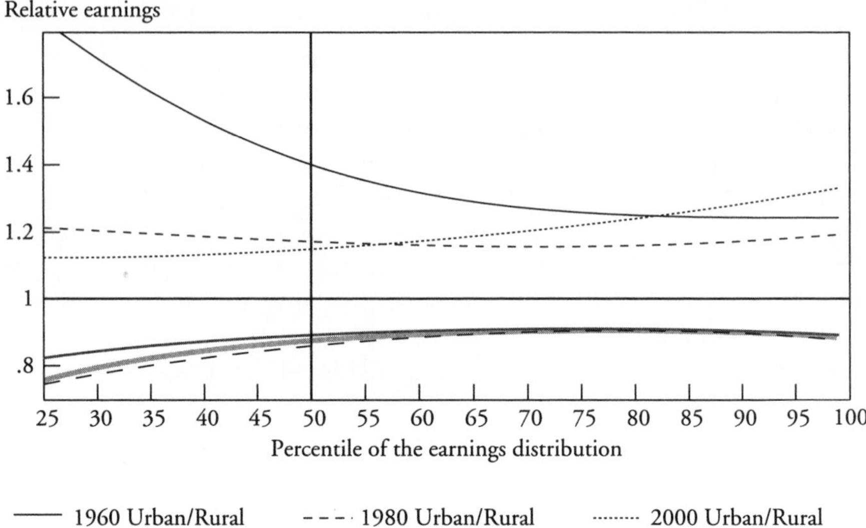

Source: Authors' analysis of the 1960 through 2000 decennial censuses.

point in the earnings distribution, urban residents earned about 20 percent more than rural residents. Between 1980 and 2000 a clear pattern developed: the relative earnings of rural residents at the bottom of the earnings distribution continued to rise while the relative earnings of rural residents at the top of the earnings distribution fell. Put another way, there was more bifurcation of the earnings distribution in urban areas than in rural areas.

The 90th percentile of the earnings distribution rose much faster in urban than rural areas from 1980 to 2000 (figure 3-6). County-level rises in the 90th percentile were pronounced on both coasts. The rise shows on the East Coast, which is the region bounded on the north by the greater Boston area, runs down through New York, Philadelphia, Washington, and Charlotte, and ends in greater Atlanta. On the West Coast the entire area between San Diego and San Francisco experienced a large rise in the 90th percentile of the earnings distribution. Other large cities, including Phoenix, Portland, Seattle, Denver, Dallas, Milwaukee, Chicago, and Detroit, had a rapid rise in the 90th percentile of the earnings distribution. In many rural areas, the 90th percentile of the earnings

Figure 3-5. *Growth in Earnings Distribution, 25th Percentile, 1980–2000*

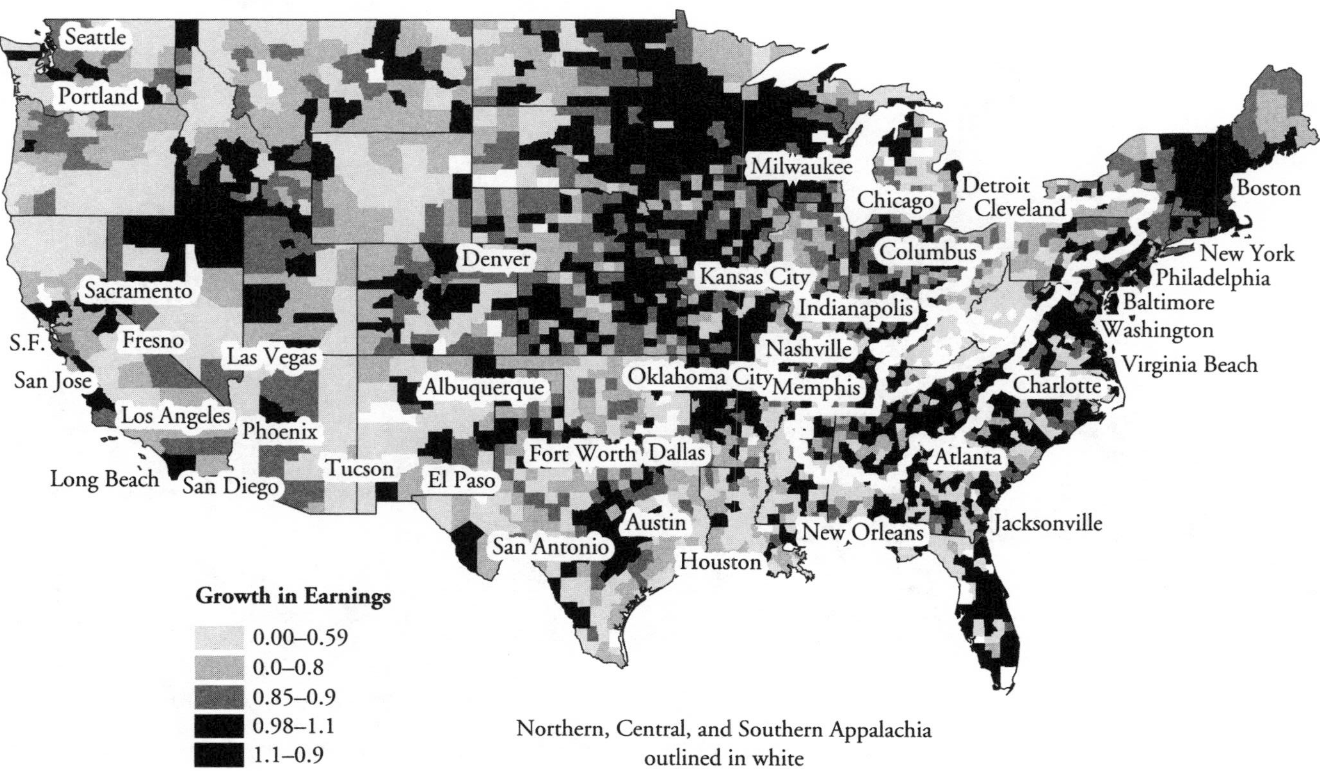

Figure 3-6. *Growth in Earnings Distribution, 90th Percentile, 1980–2000*

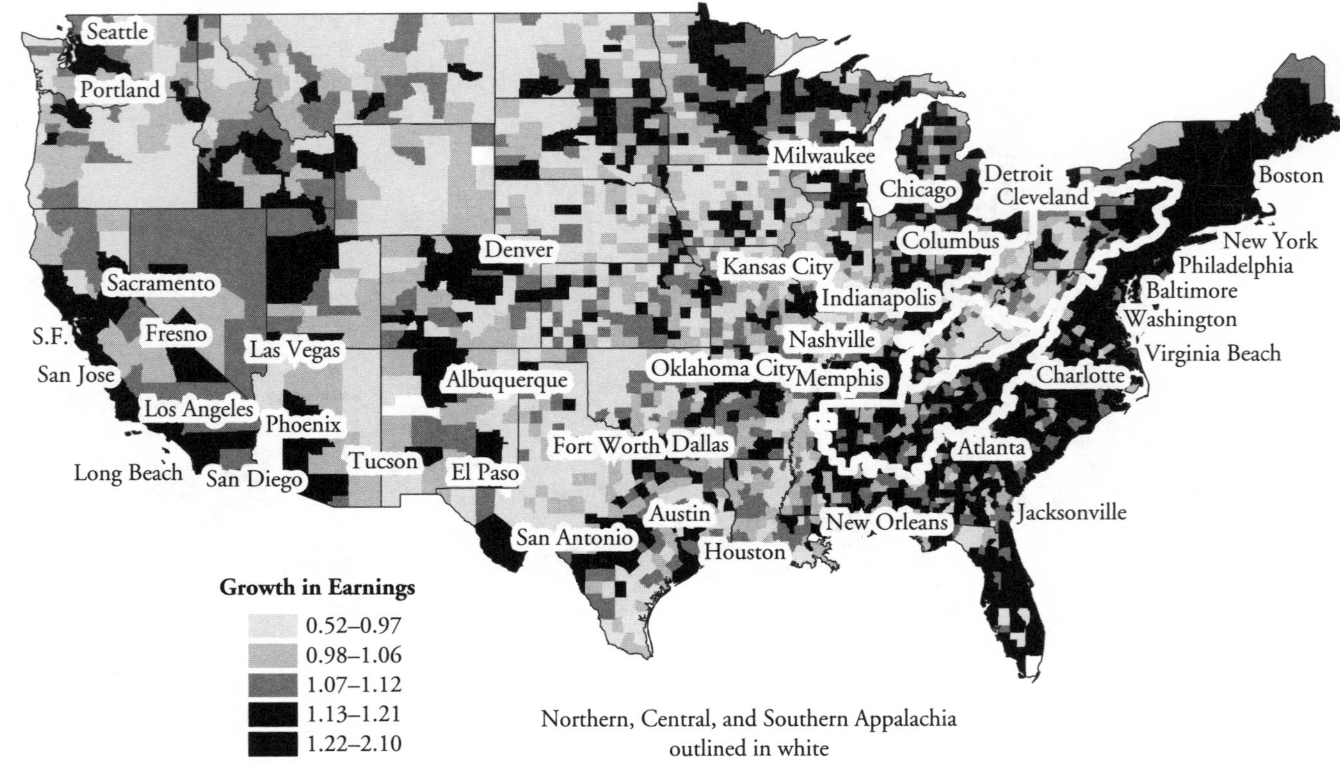

distribution actually fell between 1980 and 2000, including most of the middle of the United States as well as Northern and Central Appalachia. The areas of Appalachia that did experience a rise in the 90th percentile of the earnings distribution are the counties surrounding Charlotte and Atlanta.

In general, the bottom of the earnings distribution fell more in urban than in rural areas, but the pattern is somewhat complicated. Although certain cities led the decline in earnings—for example, Detroit, Cleveland, Chicago, and Milwaukee—other growing cities had large increases in the 25th percentile of earnings. Many rural areas of the Midwest had the largest increases in the 25th percentile. The case of Appalachia is also complicated. Central Appalachia had declines in the 25th percentile, as did Northern Appalachia; Southern Appalachia, especially the counties surrounding Atlanta and Charlotte, were among the places with the fastest growth in the bottom end of the earnings distribution. Overall, the 25th percentile of earnings for rural Appalachia changed in a way that was remarkably similar to rural areas in the country as a whole.

The bifurcation of the earnings distribution since 1980 has received a great deal of attention. The results above suggest that this bifurcation was more pronounced in cities than in rural areas. But the statistics could occur for a second reason. Because the upper quantiles of the earnings distribution were higher in cities in 1980, if earnings rose with their level, then the upper tail of the earnings distribution would rise more in urban areas than in rural areas. Because the 90th percentile of earnings is lower in rural areas, it is likely that the skills of men in the 90th percentile are also lower in rural areas; and if skill-biased technological change is important, we would expect skilled men to benefit more.

We examine the level of education at various quantiles of the earnings distribution below, but before we look at skill directly we examine the following question: How has the fraction of men above (and below) a cutoff level of income changed in urban and rural areas? That is, How has the cumulative distribution function of earnings changed over time for urban and rural areas Table 3-2 addresses this question. It shows that for men in urban areas in 1980 the 25th percentile of earnings was $24,500 and the 90th percentile was $91,500. The fraction of men earning above $91,500 increased significantly more in urban areas than in rural areas. Between 1980 and 2000 outside of Appalachia there was a 35.7 percent increase in men earning above $91,500 in rural areas; in urban areas this increase was 68.1 percent. The fraction of men earning below $24,500 rose faster in urban areas than in rural areas. The fraction of the rural population earning less than $24,500 increased by only 4.3 percent between 1980 and 2000; in urban areas this increase was 13.8 percent.

Table 3-2. *Earnings and Residence of Men, Aged 25–64, Selected Years, 1960–2000*
Units as indicated

Area	*Earning less than $24,500 (%)*	*Earning more than $91,500 (%)*
Urban non-Appalachia		
1960	0.220	0.069
1980	0.250	0.100
2000	0.285	0.168
% change 1960–80	13.6	44.6
% change 1980–2000	13.8	68.1
Rural non-Appalachia		
1960	0.400	0.047
1980	0.298	0.073
2000	0.311	0.098
% change 1960–1980	–25.5	55.5
% change 1980–2000	4.3	35.7
Urban Appalachia		
1960	0.290	0.044
1980	0.274	0.075
2000	0.304	0.115
% change 1960–1980	–5.4	69.4
% change 1980–2000	10.8	54.4
Rural Appalachia		
1960	0.463	0.037
1980	0.339	0.062
2000	0.354	0.081
% change 1960–1980	–26.9	66.7
% change 1980–2000	4.5	31.5

Figure 3-7 compares the cumulative distribution functions of rural areas inside and outside of Appalachia for 1980–2000. The figure shows that rural areas inside and outside of Appalachia had remarkably similar earnings distributions and changes in distribution. Even though the distribution function for rural areas outside of Appalachia stochastically dominates that for Appalachia for 1980 and 2000, it displays remarkably similar changes in distribution. Table 3-2 shows that Appalachian rural areas and rural areas outside of Appalachia had remarkably similar increases in the fraction of men earning less than $24,500 (4.3 percent and 4.5 percent). Similarly the fraction of men earning more than $91,500

Figure 3-7. *CDFs of Appalachia and Non-Appalachia Earnings, 1960 and 1980, Rural Men Aged 25–64*[a]

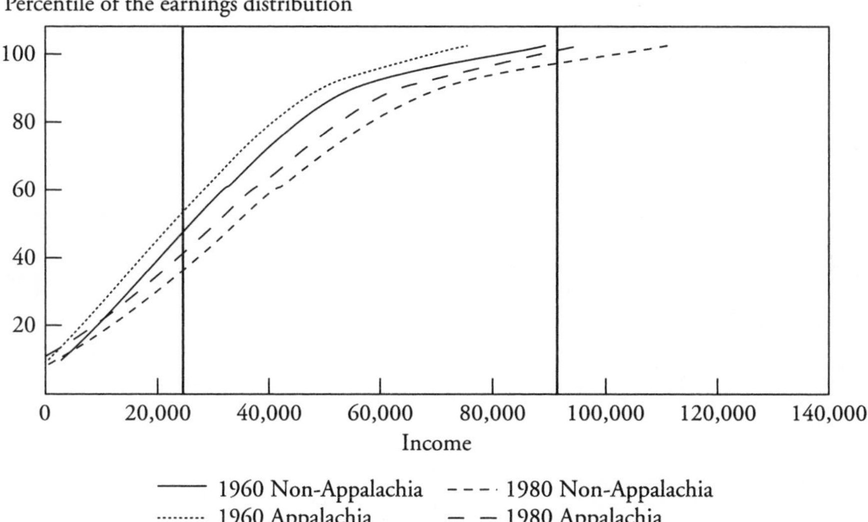

Source: Authors' analysis of the 1960 and 2000 decennial censuses.

a. Vertical lines are 25th and 90th percentile for urban men in 1980.

increased 31.5 percent in rural Appalachia and 35.7 percent in rural areas outside of Appalachia.

Table 3-2 also allows us to examine changes between 1960 and 1980 in the distribution of earnings for rural and urban areas outside of Appalachia. While it appears that both areas experienced a substantial rise in the fraction of men at the top of the earnings distribution, urban and rural areas had very different patterns at the bottom of the earnings distribution. While urban areas show an *increasing* number of men at the bottom of the earnings distribution, rural areas show a *decreasing* number. The table shows that, while the fraction of men earning less than $24,500 increased in cities (by 13.6 percent) it decreased from in rural areas (by 25.5 percent). Finally, just as was true between 1980 and 2000, figure 3-8 shows that rural Appalachia and rural areas outside of Appalachia had extremely similar patterns of changes in the bottom part of the earnings distribution; while between 1980 and 2000 both showed a similar increase in this fraction, between 1960 and 1980 both showed decreases in the fraction of men in the bottom part of the earnings distribution of about the same size.

Figure 3-8. *CDFs of Appalachia and Non-Appalachia Earnings, 1980 and 2000, Rural Men Aged 25–64*[a]

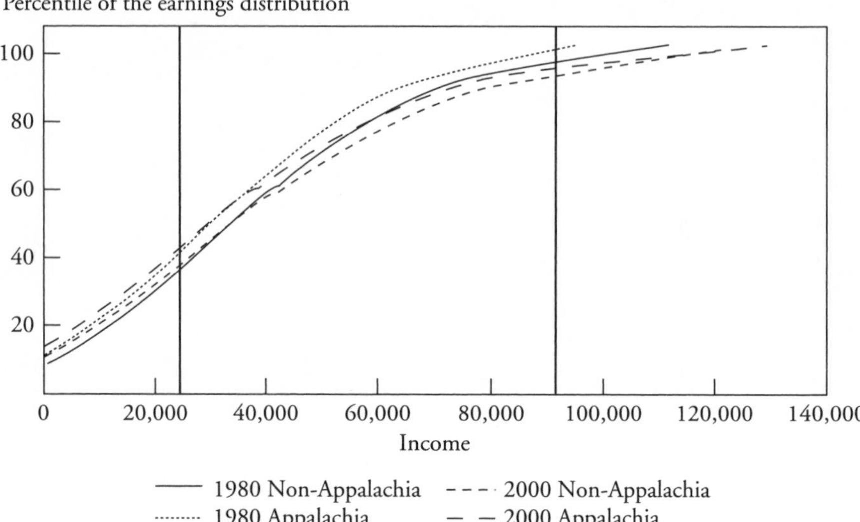

Source: Authors' analysis of the 1960 and 2000 decennial censuses.

a. Vertical lines are 25th and 90th percentile for urban men in 1980.

Links between the Distribution of Earnings and the Level of and Return to Education

Table 3-3 shows the level of education in rural Appalachia, in other rural areas of the country, and in urban areas outside of Appalachia. Table 3-4 shows the growth in the fraction of the population with a given level of education in rural Appalachia relative to urban areas. A primary reason for differential changes in the earnings distribution at a quantile might be because of differential changes in the skill composition of the population.

What is clear is that, in 1980, residents of rural Appalachia had lower levels of education at every point in the earnings distribution. At the 25th percentile, 86 percent of men in rural Appalachia had a high school degree or less. In other rural areas this was 77 percent, and in urban areas, 61percent. What is also clear is that in Appalachia in 1980 it was possible to be at the top of the earnings distribution without a college degree. The fraction of men at the 90th percentile that had a college degree in Appalachia was 19 percent; in urban areas more than 50 percent of men in the 90th percentile of earnings had a college degree.

Table 3-3. *Education, Rural Kentucky and West Virginia, Rural and Urban United States, Selected Years, 1980–2007*
Percent

Percentile	*1980*	*1990*	*2000*	*2007*
	Rural Kentucky and West Virginia			
25th percentile				
Less than high school	57.14	40.05	31.14	23.31
High school	28.59	38.53	42.91	45.13
Some college	7.03	14.13	17.16	20.27
Bachelor's degree or more	7.25	7.29	8.79	11.28
50th percentile				
Less than high school	32.84	24.27	15.69	8.63
High school	41.48	44.88	52.33	58.84
Some college	11.83	20.22	21.76	22.31
Bachelor's degree or more	13.85	10.63	10.23	10.23
75th percentile				
Less than high school	27.58	13.22	7.33	6.83
High school	45.54	45.20	46.31	41.25
Some college	13.40	24.15	28.16	29.95
Bachelor's degree or more	13.47	17.43	18.19	21.98
90th percentile				
Less than high school	24.07	11.18	4.49	3.97
High school	39.79	36.42	36.52	35.52
Some college	16.34	27.49	29.35	29.82
Bachelor's degree or more	19.80	24.91	29.65	30.68
	Rural United States			
25th percentile				
Less than high school	39.55	24.02	18.92	15.09
High school	37.59	44.66	45.12	46.68
Some college	13.48	22.04	25.00	26.27
Bachelor's degree or more	9.38	9.28	10.96	11.96
50th percentile				
Less than high school	25.57	15.25	10.21	8.12
High school	42.84	45.65	46.47	46.69
Some college	15.34	26.21	30.05	31.16
Bachelor's degree or more	16.25	12.89	13.27	14.02

(continued)

Table 3-3. *Education, Rural Kentucky and West Virginia, Rural and Urban United States, Selected Years, 1980–2007* (continued)
Percent

Percentile	*1980*	*1990*	*2000*	*2007*
75th percentile				
Less than high school	19.46	8.54	5.58	5.05
High school	44.22	38.89	37.41	35.65
Some college	16.98	29.06	33.57	34.20
Bachelor's degree or more	19.35	23.51	23.43	25.10
90th percentile				
Less than high school	15.03	5.41	3.22	2.89
High school	39.35	28.88	28.49	25.99
Some college	17.24	28.62	31.79	31.04
Bachelor's degree or more	28.37	37.09	36.50	40.08
	Urban United States			
25th percentile				
Less than high school	24.21	13.43	10.10	8.54
High school	36.87	38.99	38.83	39.36
Some college	19.54	31.34	32.49	31.24
Bachelor's degree or more	19.39	16.24	18.58	20.86
50th percentile				
Less than high school	17.99	8.14	4.68	3.74
High school	38.77	34.48	32.58	33.82
Some college	20.79	32.81	35.35	33.80
Bachelor's degree or more	22.44	24.57	27.38	28.64
75th percentile				
Less than high school	12.19	3.90	2.15	1.45
High school	34.51	23.15	21.05	17.79
Some college	21.16	31.40	32.62	29.78
Bachelor's degree or more	32.15	41.55	44.17	50.98
90th percentile				
Less than high school	7.24	1.99	1.05	0.86
High school	23.40	12.20	9.99	7.68
Some college	18.55	24.41	21.90	17.70
Bachelor's degree or more	50.82	61.41	67.06	73.75

a. Sample is white, non-Hispanic men aged 25 to 64 years. Earnings percentiles are based on wage and salary, farm, and self-employment data. Data are weighted to reflect both sampling and the inverse probability reweighting for missing data.

Table 3-4. *Education, Rural Appalachia and Urban Non-Appalachia, 1980–2000*
Percent

Percentile	*Rural Appalachia*	*Urban non-Appalachia*	*D-in-D*
25th percentile			
Less than high school	−0.260	−0.141	−0.119
High school	0.143	0.020	0.124
Some college	0.101	0.130	−0.028
Bachelor's degree or more	0.015	−0.008	0.024
50th percentile			
Less than high school	−0.172	−0.133	−0.038
High school	0.109	−0.062	0.170
Some college	0.099	0.146	−0.046
Bachelor's degree or more	−0.036	0.049	−0.086
75th percentile			
Less than high school	−0.203	−0.100	−0.102
High school	0.008	−0.135	0.142
Some college	0.148	0.115	0.033
Bachelor's degree or more	0.047	0.120	−0.073
90th percentile			
Less than high school	−0.196	−0.062	−0.134
High school	−0.033	−0.134	0.101
Some college	0.130	0.034	0.097
Bachelor's degree or more	0.099	0.162	−0.064

Some of this difference in the distribution of education across areas stems from urban areas having higher earnings at any percentile of its distribution.

Table 3-3 also shows how the education distribution changed over time by quantiles of the earnings distribution. Table 3-4 focuses specifically on the period between 1980 and 2000. Table 3-4 shows that educational attainment rose in rural Appalachia relative to U.S. urban areas at the bottom of the earnings distribution. There was a precipitous decrease in the fraction of men who were high school dropouts (a decline of 26 percentage points) and a strong gain in the fraction who where high school graduates (an increase of 14.3 percentage points). Of course there was also a drop in the fraction of men who were high school dropouts in urban areas and a small increase in the fraction who were high school graduates. On net, the fraction of men who were high school dropouts at the 25th percentile fell 11.9 percentage points faster in rural Appalachia than in urban areas; the fraction who were high school graduates rose 12.4 percentage points faster. There were smaller relative changes in the fraction of the population who had some college or were college graduates, but the most important trend was a great increase in education among the least educated, a process we term *upskilling*. Because high school graduates earn considerably more than high school dropouts (20 percent more in 1980 and 29–38 percent more in 2000), this shift in relative education is no doubt a primary reason that the low end of the earnings distribution declined less in Appalachia and other rural areas relative to urban areas.

The story at the upper end of the earnings distribution is more complicated. What is remarkable is the fraction of men in 1980 in Appalachia in the 90th percentile of the earnings distribution with very low levels of education. Over time, men in Appalachia at the top of the earnings distribution were more likely to be college graduates. For example, the fraction that were college graduates increased by 9.9 percentage points between 1980 and 2000. But at the same time, the fraction of men who were college graduates at the 90th percentile of the urban earnings distribution increased even faster (16.2 percentage points). Overall, at the 90th percentile, Appalachia had relatively fewer high school dropouts and relatively fewer college graduates at the top of the earnings distribution.

The rise in relative education levels at the bottom of the earnings distribution may help explain why the bottom of the earnings distribution fell faster in urban areas than in rural areas. It still leaves, however, two puzzles. First, if education was rising (for both urban areas and for rural Appalachia), why was the bottom of the earnings distribution falling? Second, if the level of human capital at the upper end of the distribution was not rising substantially more in urban than in rural Appalachia, why was the upper tail of the earnings distribution rising faster in urban areas? Table 3-5 shows earnings of male high school dropouts, men with some college, men with associate's degrees, men with bachelor's degrees, men with master's degrees, and men with professional degrees relative to high school graduates. The table shows that the earnings deficit for not completing high school increased substantially in all areas but particularly in Appalachia. Had it not been for the significant increase in the quantity of education, especially the rapid reduction in the fraction of men who were high school dropouts, it is likely that the bottom of the earnings distribution in rural Appalachia would have fallen relative to urban areas.

The table also shows that the return to college education doubled between 1980 and 2000. And there is also evidence that rural areas in general did not experience the rapid rise in the returns to college education that urban areas did. One notable pattern, however, is that Appalachian rural counties did experience a

Table 3-5. *Earnings Percentile Relative to Education, Rural Kentucky and West Virginia, Rural and Urban United States, Selected Years, 1980–2007*

Education	*1980*	*1990*	*2000*	*2007*
Rural Kentucky and West Virginia				
10th grade	−0.193	−0.316	−0.383	−0.489
Return to some college	—	0.205	0.236	0.253
Return to associate's degree	—	0.253	0.325	0.342
Return to bachelor's degree	0.352	0.597	0.825	0.897
Return to master's degree	—	0.445	0.802	0.964
Return to professional degree	—	2.182	3.110	3.130
Rural United States				
Return to 10th grade	−0.197	−0.259	−0.289	−0.346
Return to some college	—	0.133	0.177	0.169
Return to associate's degree	—	0.179	0.240	0.262
Return to bachelor's degree	0.365	0.516	0.644	0.685
Return to master's degree	—	0.540	0.773	0.863
Return to professional degree	—	1.895	2.649	2.680
Urban United States				
Return to 10th grade	−0.191	−0.249	−0.294	−0.337
Return to some college	—	0.185	0.238	0.249
Return to associate's degree	—	0.211	0.277	0.301
Return to bachelor's degree	0.428	0.627	0.876	1.018
Return to master's degree	—	0.738	1.131	1.345
Return to professional degree	—	1.859	2.587	3.055

a. Sample is white, non-Hispanic men aged 25 to 64 years. Earnings percentiles are based on wage and salary, farm, and self-employment data. Data are weighted to reflect both sampling and the inverse probability reweighting for missing data.

precipitous rise in the return to college education that is similar to the returns for urban areas. But even without a differential rise in the return to college education, the much higher levels of college education in urban areas at the upper end of the earnings distribution mean that the general rise in the return to education raised the upper tail of the earnings distribution in urban areas more than in rural areas.

Conclusion

This chapter shows that working-age men in Appalachia still lag behind the rest of the United States in terms of income and employment—and that on average the relative income differences were only slightly better in 2000 than they were in 1960. This result, however, obscures substantial regional trends and substantial changes in earnings at some points in the earnings distribution. Northern Appalachia, whose average male earnings were 90 percent of male earnings outside of Appalachia in 1960, has had average earnings fall substantially, especially since 1980. Southern Appalachia, on the other hand, has had a substantial improvement in average earnings. Much of this appears to be driven by the fate of the largest cities that either comprise or influence these areas (see chapter 6, this volume). The decline of Pittsburgh, Morgantown, and Wheeling and the growth of Atlanta and Charlotte appear to have had a heavy influence on these patterns. Central Appalachia had a period of relative prosperity in the 1970s, but average earnings now are approximately what they were in 1960 relative to the remainder of the country.

Averages do mask substantial relative progress at the bottom of the earnings distribution for some areas. Rural Appalachia, like other rural areas of the country, has experienced relative growth at the bottom of the income distribution. This growth, however, should be kept in perspective. There was real earnings growth between 1960 and 1980 in rural Appalachia, as there was in other rural areas, a pattern not true in urban areas. But between 1980 and 2000, earnings in urban areas at the bottom of the income distribution fell dramatically, whereas in rural areas they fell only slightly. This is the sense in which there has been relative progress at the bottom of the earnings distribution.

One interesting finding is the changes at the upper end of the earnings distribution. While all areas of the country experienced substantial growth in the fraction of high earners (more than \$91,500) between 1960 and 2000, the growth in this fraction, between 1980 and 2000, in cities was nearly double what it was in rural counties. Skill levels in cities were higher at various percentiles of the earnings distribution and at important levels of income. For example, in rural Appalachia in 1980, 64 percent of men earning in the 90th percentile of Appalachian earnings had a high school education or less; in urban areas in 1980 only 31 percent of men earning in the 90th percentile of urban earnings had only this level of education. Some of this no doubt stems from the 90th percentile of earnings being higher in urban areas than in rural Appalachia. But in 1980, among men who earned \$100,000, 52 percent of rural Appalachian men had a high school education or less, while 27 percent of urban men had only this level of education. Clearly, education has been more important historically in cities for achieving high earnings than it has been in rural areas.

We also find ample evidence of a rising return to education (as has been found elsewhere in the literature). While the return to a high school degree and a college degree in 1980 are similar between rural and urban areas, the return to a college education has risen more in rural than in urban areas (although the return in Appalachia has risen in a way that is similar to urban areas). The combination of urban areas having higher levels of education and a more rapid rise in the return to education likely explains much of the relative rise in earnings at the top of the earnings distribution in cities. Changes in the bottom of the earnings distribution reflect a rise in the penalty for being a high school dropout combined with a shrinking number of high school dropouts. Because the fraction of high school dropouts at the bottom of the earnings distribution fell faster in rural Appalachia than in cities, there was generally a smaller fall in earnings at the bottom of the distribution there.

While it is difficult to predict the future, the scenario we see as most likely is that Appalachia will continue to be integrated in and influenced by the cities on its borders. Especially in the South, these cities continue to have robust economies, and their growth yields economic opportunities for Appalachians on their borders. The prospects for Southern Appalachia are likely increasingly tied to the economic success of Charlotte, Atlanta, and Memphis; that of Northern Appalachia to Pittsburgh, Washington, Baltimore, Columbus, and Cleveland. Central Appalachia remains a vexing issue, as there are no cities within reasonable distances, especially given the topology. And cities appear to be a main driver of economic growth. Ironically, for much of Appalachia the best development policies may be those that promote the growth and physical expansion of its border cities. But this is unlikely to help Central Appalachia, which may require more targeted policies to encourage economic growth or at least to alleviate prevailing levels of poverty.

Appendix A. Calculating Income Inequality, Appalachia and other U.S. Regions, Using County-Level Data

There is a straightforward way to estimate the income level at a given percentile of earnings in Appalachia. Let $F_{ct}(i) = \Pr(I \leq i) = P_i$ be the cumulative distribution function (CDF) for county c in year t. A specific percentile of the earnings distribution, x, for that county is defined as the value of i such that $F_{ct}(i) = x$. For example the 25th percentile is defined as the value of i such that $F_{ct}(i) = 0.25$. If this value of i is denoted i_{25}, then $i_{25} = F_{ct}^{-1}(0.25)$. Now for any collection of counties, A, the CDF is equal to $F_{At}(i) = \sum_{c \in A} w_{ct} F_{ct}(i)$, where w_{ct} is the fraction of the relevant population (men ages twenty-five through sixty-four) in county c in year t. Therefore for any collection of counties, A, the x percentile of the earnings distribution is $i_x = F_{At}^{-1}(x)$. This gives a straightforward way of calculating the level of earnings at each percentile of the earnings distribution in Appalachia; first calculate the CDF for Appalachia by calculating a (weighted) average at each *i;* then invert this CDF at specific percentiles of interest.

Unfortunately we do not have the entire CDF for each county in each year. What we do have is the level of earnings at the 10th, 25th, 50th, 75th, and 90th percentiles; we also know the fraction of men that are zero earners. That is, for each county and year, we potentially observe six points on the CDF but do not observe the CDF at income levels between any known percentiles. We need to know the CDF for each county at all levels of *i* in order to calculate the CDF for the collection of counties.

We estimate the CDF for each county for each year using a five-part spline. We allow the CDF to have a different slope between the intercept (fraction of the population with earnings equal to zero) and the income level at the 10th percentile; between the income level at the 10th percentile and the income level at the 25th percentile, and so on. Specifically we model:

$$\log\left(\frac{P_i}{1-P_i}\right)=\begin{cases}\gamma_{ct}+\beta_{0-10}*i \text{ if } i<i_{10}, \\ \gamma_{ct}+\beta_{0-10}*i_{10}+\beta_{10-25}*(i-i_{10}) \text{ if } i<i_{25}, \\ \vdots \\ \gamma_{ct}+\beta_{0-10}*i_{10}+\beta_{10-25}*(i_{25}-i_{10})+\beta_{25-50}*(i_{50}-i_{25}) \\ \quad +\beta_{50-75}*(i_{75}-i_{50})+\beta_{75-90}*(i-i_{75}) \text{ if } i\geq i_{75}.\end{cases} \tag{A-1}$$

Because we have six points on the CDF for each county and each year, we solve for the six parameters above. Clearly when $i = 0$, $\gamma_{ct} = \log(P_0/1 - P_0)$ or the log of the fraction of zero earners over positive earners; when $i = i_{10}$, $\beta_{0-10} = [\log(P_0/1 - P_0) - \log(0.10/1 - 0.10)]/i_{10}$, and so on. This method ensures that the level of income at the known points on the CDF lie by definition on our estimated CDF; the points in between are interpolated by assuming that between each known percentile, the function follows a log linear form in income.

We report the changes in the earnings distribution over time inside and outside of Appalachia in two ways. One way answers the question, What are the earnings at a given percentile for one area relative to another area? For example, in 1960, what were the earnings at the 25th percentile of the earnings distribution in Appalachia versus in the remainder of the United States? This statistic is calculated as

$$D_{x,t}^{A,B} = i_{x,t,A} \Big/ i_{x,t,B}, \tag{A-2}$$

where A and B are specific areas of comparison and x is a percentile of interest, in this case $x = 0.25$. A complementary statistic is the growth rate in a percentile within an area: $D_{x,t,t-1}^{A} = i_{x,t} / i_{x,t-1}$, where t and $t - 1$ are specific years of comparison.

A second way of reporting our results answers a slightly different question: How much has the fraction of the population below (or above) some specified level of earnings changed over time, and has it changed differently across areas? This statistic is calculated as

$$P_{At,t-1}(i*) = F_{At}(i*) \Big/ F_{At-1}(i*), \tag{A-3}$$

where i^* is the level of income of interest.

Appendix B. Calculating Nonparametric Weights to Compare the Effect of Education on the Earnings Distribution: Balancing Sex and Age and Accounting for Nonresponse

The microdata from the censuses and American Community Survey provide challenges for researchers because of item nonresponse on the long-form data. Respondents will occasionally not answer questions about their age, sex, or education and will much more frequently not answer questions about their hours worked or, even more frequently, about their wages and salaries. Our approach is to drop respondents who do not answer questions about their sex, age, education, or earnings but then reweight the data to impose the identical distribution of age, sex, and education as observed in the public use microdata within that state (or city, for the urban analysis). To be precise, we estimate the probably of a nonresponse, or

$$\Pr(NR = 1 | X = x^0) = F(x^0), \tag{B-1}$$

where x indexes the age-race-education-location cell, and then we construct weights, w_1,

$$w_1(x^0) \equiv \frac{w_0}{1 - F(x^0)}, \tag{B-2}$$

where w_0 are the initial census weights. Thus if half the people in a cell do not respond to at least one of the earnings, education, sex, or age questions, the responders within the cell have their weights doubled.[18] This procedure implicitly assumes that data are, conditional on the age-sex-education-location cell, missing at random.[19]

In addition, there is considerable evidence of substantial measurement error in these data. Focusing on the 1990 census, a 2003 study documents that the census educational degree questions have such measurement error.[20] For instance, they report that among men who report holding a bachelor's degree in the 1990 census, 91.2 percent confirm holding a bachelor's degree in a subsequent report, only 86.1 reconfirm holding a master's degree, and only 77.4 percent confirm holding a professional's degree. Thus the data are quite noisy.

If we wish to know how people with a bachelor's degree fare relative to those with a high school diploma with the same distribution of observables, we need only calculate

$$\Delta = \int \left(E\left(y_{BA,i} \middle| X \right) - E\left(y_{HS,i} \middle| X \right) \right) dF_{BA}\left(X \right), \tag{B-3}$$

where $F_{BA}(X)$ is the distribution of observables (age and location within area) for a given area. The parameter Δ answers the question, What are the earnings of bachelor-degree holders in the data compared to the earnings of high school graduates with the same distribution of observables within an area? It is important to keep in mind that the estimate contains not only the impact of the observables but also the impact of unobservables. Given the paucity of covariates, it seems inconceivable that the distribution of the unobservables would be the same across these education levels.

In principle, one could directly estimate equation B-3 by calculating the conditional means at each point in the distribution of covariates. We implement a somewhat easier estimator. Consider the conditional probability of being a bachelor-degree holder (BA) given by

$$p\left(x^0\right) = \Pr\left(BA \middle| X = x^0\right). \tag{B-4}$$

This probability can be calculated for each point in the data, and then we may define the weights

18. Wooldridge (2007).

19. Bollinger and Hirsch (2006) document the problem with using the imputed data in the Current Population Survey; they, too, advocate using reweighting as a means of dealing with the imputed data.

20. Black, Sanders, and Taylor (2003).

$$w_2(x^0) \equiv w_1(x^0) \equiv \frac{w_0}{1-F(x^0)},$$

if the worker has a bachelor's degree; and

$$w_2(x^0) = w_1(x^0)\frac{p(x^0)}{1-p(x^0)} = \frac{w_0}{1-F(x^0)}\frac{p(x^0)}{1-p(x^0)}, \tag{B-5}$$

if the worker has a high school diploma.

Thus high school graduates who have characteristics more like the bachelor-degree holders in the sample are weighted more highly, and high school graduates who, based on their observed characteristics are unlikely to be bachelor-degree holders, are weighted less.

References

Autor, David, and Mark Duggan. 2006. "The Growth in the Social Security Disability Rolls: Crisis Unfolding." *Journal of Economic Perspectives* 20, no. 3: 71–96.

Autor, David, Lawrence Katz, and Alan Kruger. 1998. "Computing Inequality: Have Computers Changed the Labor Market?" *Quarterly Journal of Economics* 113, no. 4: 1169–213.

Berman, Eli, John Bound, and Zvi Griliches. 1994. "Changes in the Demand for Skill within the U.S. Manufacturing Industries: Evidence from the Annual Survey of Manufacturers." *Quarterly Journal of Economics* 109, no. 2: 367–97.

Black, Dan, Kermit Daniel, and Seth Sanders. 2002. "The Impact of Economic Conditions on Disability Program Participation: Evidence from Coal Boom and Bust." *American Economic Review* 92, no. 1: 27–50.

Black, Dan A., and Seth G. Sanders. 2004. "Labor Market Performance and Income Inequality in Appalachia." In *Demographic and Socioeconomic Change in Appalachia.* Washington: Population Reference Bureau and Appalachian Regional Commission.

Black, Dan, Seth Sanders, and Lowell Taylor. 2003. "Measurement of Higher Education in the Census and CPS." *Journal of the American Statistical Association* 98 (September): 545–54.

Black, Dan, and others. 2006. "Why Do Minority Men Earn Less? A Study of Wage Differentials among the Highly Educated." *Review of Economics and Statistics* 88, no. 1: 300–13.

Black, Dan, and others. 2008. "Gender Wage Disparities among the Highly Educated." *Journal of Human Resources* 42, no. 3: 630–59.

Bollinger, Christopher, and Barry Hirsch. 2006. "Match Bias in the Earnings Imputations in Current Population Survey: The Case of Imperfect Matching." *Journal of Labor Economics* 24, no. 3: 483–520.

Bollinger, Christopher, James Ziliak, and Kenneth Troske. 2011. "Down from the Mountain: Skill Upgrading and Wages in Appalachia." *Journal of Labor Economics* 29, no. 4: 819–57.

Borjas, George, Richard Freeman, and Lawrence Katz. 1992. "On the Labor Market Effects of Immigration and Trade." In *Immigration and the Work Force: Economic Consequences for the United States and Source Areas,* edited by G. Borjas and R. Freeman, pp. 213–44. University of Chicago Press.

Card, David, and Thomas Lemieux. 2001. "Can Falling Supply Explain the Rising Return to College for Younger Men? A Cohort-Based Analysis." *Quarterly Journal of Economics* 116, no. 2: 705–46.

DiNardo, John, Nicole M. Fortin, and Thomas Lemieux. 1996. "Labor Market Institutions and the Distribution of Wages, 1973–1992: A Semiparametric Approach." *Econometrica* 64, no. 5: 1001–44.

Edelman, Peter, Harry J. Holzer, and Paul Offner. 2006. *Reconnecting Disadvantaged Young Men.* Washington: Urban Institute.

Freeman, Richard. 1996. "Labor Market Institutions and Earnings Inequality." *New England Economic Review,* special issue (May/June): 157–72.

Hirano, Keisuke, Guido Imbens, and Gert Ridder. 2003. "Efficient Estimation of Average Treatment Effects Using the Estimated Propensity Score." *Econometrica* 71, no. 4: 1161–89.

Juhn, Chinhui. 1992. "Decline of Male Labor Market Participation: The Role of Declining Market Opportunities." *Quarterly Journal of Economics* 107, no. 1: 79–121.

Juhn, Chinhui, and Simon Potter. 2006. "Changes in Labor Force Participation in the United States." *Journal of Economic Perspectives* 20, no. 3: 27–46.

Katz, Lawrence, and David Autor. 1999. "Changes in the Wage Structure and Earnings Inequality." In *Handbook of Labor Economics,* edited by Orley Ashenfelter and David Card, vol. 3A, pp. 1463–555. Amsterdam: Elsevier–North Holland.

Katz, Lawrence, and Kevin Murphy. 1992. "Changes in Relative Wages, 1963–1987: Supply and Demand Factors." *Quarterly Journal of Economics* 107, no. 1: 35–78.

Lee, David. 1999. "Wage Inequality in the US during the 1980s: Rising Dispersion of Falling Minimum Wage." *Quarterly Journal of Economics* 114, no. 3: 977–1023.

Murphy, Kevin, and Robert Topel. 1997. "Unemployment and Nonemployment." *American Economic Review* 87, no. 2: 295–300.

Pollard, Kelvin M. 2003. "Appalachia at the Millennium: An Overview of Results from Census 2000." *Demographic and Socioeconomic Change in Appalachia* (Washington: Population Reference Bureau and Appalachian Regional Commission).

Topel, Robert. 1994. "Regional Labor Markets and the Determinants of Wage Inequality." *American Economic Review* 84, no. 2: 17–22.

Wheeler, Christopher. 2001. "Search, Sorting, and Urban Agglomeration." *Journal of Labor Economics* 19, no. 4: 879–99.

Wood, Adrian. 1994. *North-South Trade, Employment and Inequality.* Oxford. Clarendon Press.

Wood, Lawrence E., and Gregory A. Bischak. 2000. "Progress and Challenges in Reducing Economic Distress in Appalachia: An Analysis of National and Regional Trends since 1960." Washington: Appalachian Regional Commission.

Wooldridge, Jeffrey M. 2007. "Inverse Probability Weighted Estimation for General Missing Data Problems." *Journal of Econometrics* 141, no. 2: 1281–301.

DANIEL T. LICHTER
LISA A. CIMBALUK

4

Family Change and Poverty in Appalachia

On April 24, 1964, President Lyndon Baines Johnson visited Inez, Kentucky, where he announced the War on Poverty from the front porch of Tommy Fletcher, a father of eight children, who epitomized the squalid conditions of rural Appalachia. Appalachia has become an iconic symbol of America's struggle against persistent poverty and economic hardship in rural areas. Although poverty rates in Appalachia have plummeted at a faster rate than in the nation as a whole over the past several decades, chronic poverty nevertheless persists in many parts of Appalachia, especially its geographically remote rural areas. Nearly two-thirds of Appalachian counties have unemployment rates that exceed the U.S. average.[1]

Most efforts to reduce poverty in Appalachia (and the nation as a whole) have focused on job growth and human resource development.[2] More recently, however, the federal government's healthy marriage initiative has sought to balance policies that promote economic development with a commitment to strengthen America's fragile families and to reduce out-of-wedlock

The authors acknowledge financial support from the University of Kentucky Center for Poverty Research as well as the helpful comments of Steve Martin, Sharon Sassler, Richard Turner, and James Ziliak.

1. ARC (2011).
2. Tickamyer and Henderson (2010).

childbearing.[3] To its critics, the emphasis on marriage promotion seemingly puts the cart (a healthy marriage) before the horse (stable employment at decent wages). For people living in Appalachia, especially its remote rural parts, the national economic crisis is nothing new or unusual; coping with high unemployment and poverty has been a way of life.[4] In Appalachia, the family is alternatively viewed as a source of strength and social support during economic hard times or as a casualty of employment dislocations and chronic poverty.

The goal of this chapter is to take stock of recent changes in family structure and to evaluate the implications for changing patterns of rural and regional family poverty in Appalachia and the rest of the nation. Is there any link between family poverty and the so-called retreat from marriage? Specifically, we estimate regression models that evaluate the effects of changing county compositional characteristics, including female headship and marital status, on changing rates of family poverty while controlling for state fixed effects. We update recent studies of spatial variation in Appalachian poverty rates over the post-2000 period.[5] This objective is accomplished using county data from the 1990 and 2000 decennial censuses and from the 2005–09 American Community Survey.[6] We then simulate subregional family poverty rates in the absence of post-1990 changes in family patterns and compare them with observed rates over the period 2005–09. The analysis of new data provides an empirical benchmark for research on changing patterns of family poverty in Appalachia vis-à-vis the rest of the nation.

Family Structure, Poverty, and Public Policy

The current economic and political climate provides a vivid contrast with circumstances of the 1990s, when passage of the 1996 Personal Responsibility and Work Opportunity Reconciliation Act (PRWORA) ushered in welfare reform during a period of unprecedented economic expansion and job growth.[7]

3. The October 2009 unemployment rate was 10.1 percent, its highest level since June 1983 (U.S. Bureau of Labor Statistics, 2009). Equally disquieting is that this figure undoubtedly underestimates labor force hardship. For example, it does not account for unemployed workers who have given up looking for work or who are working involuntarily at part-time jobs. The policies of the Obama administration have focused on job growth and the national economy (stimulus package, bailouts, and "cash for clunkers") rather than marriage promotion.

4. McLaughlin, Lichter, and Matthews (1999).

5. Billings and Blee (2000); Mather (2004); Werner and Badagliacco (2004).

6. U.S. Census Bureau (1990, 2000, 2005–09).

7. Blank (2002); Ziliak (2009). In September 2011, the U.S. Census Bureau announced that the official 2010 poverty rate was 15.1 percent, up significantly from 14.3 percent in 2009 (DeNavas-Walt, Proctor, and Smith 2011). 46.2 million people are below the government poverty line, which is the largest number in the fifty-two years for which poverty estimates have been published.

This legislation sought to "end the dependence of needy parents on government benefits by promoting job preparation, work, and marriage." Among PRWORA's goals were to reduce out-of-wedlock births and to encourage the formation of two-parent families. For most states, much of the initial emphasis on self-sufficiency was placed on "work first" programs—that is, moving poor single mothers into the labor force—rather than on marriage promotion.[8] However, with the 2006 reauthorizing legislation (the Deficit Reduction Act of 2005), the federal government provides $150 million annually for healthy marriage initiatives and fatherhood programs. An explicit goal is to increase the share of children living with both biological parents in a "healthy" marriage. A stable marriage is often viewed as a pathway from poverty and welfare dependency.[9]

Marriage is on the public policy agenda for several reasons. Fewer people are getting married, and those who marry do so at later ages.[10] Divorce rates have remained at historically high levels over the past two decades.[11] A report by the National Center for Health Statistics indicates that 41 percent of all U.S. births are to unmarried women.[12] The number of out-of-wedlock births—over 1.7 million—hit an all-time high in 2008. Moreover, cohabitation has transformed recent patterns of partnering and parenting in the United States.[13] The share of women who have ever cohabited increased from 45 percent to 54 percent between 1995 and 2002.[14] In 2009, roughly 25 percent of all families with children were headed by single mothers.[15] Only 62.5 percent of U.S. children lived with both biological parents.[16] Recent changes in family structure have placed upward demographic pressure on poverty rates nationally and represent a behavioral mechanism that sometimes links poverty between parental and filial generations.[17] Poverty rates among single-parent families (with children) are exceptionally high.[18]

The economic implications of changing family structure nationally have been large. One approach to establishing this statistical relationship is shift-share

8. Blank (2002); Lichter and Jayakody (2002).

9. Lichter, Graefe, and Brown (2003); Roberts and Martin (2010). For reviews, see Dion (2005); Burstein (2007); and Kane and Lichter (2006).

10. Lichter and Qian (2004).

11. Teachman (2002).

12. Hamilton, Martin, and Ventura (2010).

13. Cherlin (2009); Seltzer (2000).

14. Kennedy and Bumpass (2008).

15. U.S. Census Bureau (2010d).

16. U.S. Census Bureau (2010c).

17. Martin (2006); McLanahan and Percheski (2008); McLanahan (2009).

18. Snyder, McLaughlin, and Findeis (2006); U.S. Census Bureau (2010a).

analysis, a form of demographic standardization in which the distributions of families or children across family types (single-parent and married-couple families, for example) are held constant at some baseline year and rates of poverty by family type are allowed to vary over time.[19] The difference between observed and expected poverty rates reveals the effects of changing family structure on poverty trends. For example, a 1991 study shows that child poverty rates would have declined from 25.7 percent in 1960 to 13.8 percent in 1988 if the distribution of children across family types had remained at 1960 levels.[20] Instead, the observed poverty rate among children in 1988 was 20.8 percent. Changing family structure slowed reductions in child poverty over this period. More recently, in 2002, a study reports that the 1998 child poverty rate would have been 4.4 percentage points lower than the observed rate if the percentage of children living in female-headed families had remained unchanged since 1970.[21] A later study similarly finds that changes in family structure between 1969 and 2006 increased the family poverty rate by 3.1 percentage points.[22] Like previous studies, it concludes that changes in family structure are "poverty-increasing."

A second approach is based on estimating place-based or areal (such as county or state) regression models of poverty.[23] The emphasis on places (over people or populations) reflects the fact that poverty varies substantially over geographic space and that it is often highly concentrated in inner-city neighborhoods and in isolated or remote rural communities and regions (such as Appalachia and the Mississippi Delta). Ecological studies also reflect a particular public policy orientation, one that emphasizes the need for *place-based* public policies that target economically distressed communities and regions rather than *person-based* policies.[24] The White House, through the Office of Management and Budget, issued a memorandum to all heads of executive departments and agencies "to increase the impact of government dollars by leveraging place-conscious planning and place-based programming."[25] Now, as in the past, much of the emphasis centers on the role of labor demand (unemployment, job growth, and so on) and labor

19. Other scholars use regression standardization or decomposition methods to accomplish similar heuristic objectives and to highlight the implications of family change for poverty. See Duncan and Rodgers (1991); Ross, Danziger, and Smolensky (1987).

20. Eggebeen and Lichter (1991).

21. Thomas and Sawhill (2002).

22. Cancian and Reed (2009).

23. Albrecht, Albrecht, and Albrecht (2000); Gundersen and Ziliak (2004); Rodgers and Payne (2007).

24. Crandall and Weber (2004); Partridge and Rickman (2006).

25. Orszag and others (2009).

supply (such as education) rather than on the changing marital status and family structure of poor neighborhoods, counties, and states.[26]

A 2006 study, for example, finds that state employment growth during the 1990s reduced the poverty rate by about 0.5 percent, while industrial composition (such as high-wage employment share) significantly affected state-to-state variation in poverty rates as well.[27] The teen birth rate, however, was unrelated to state poverty rates in models controlling for state and year fixed effects. No other family-related variables were considered. Data at the state level are useful for identifying state policy effects, but they arguably mask considerable within-state heterogeneity, especially between populous metropolitan areas (which dominate estimates) and rural pockets of poverty. An earlier study, using county data from the 1980 and 1990 censuses, finds that spatial differences and relative increases in county poverty are most strongly associated with women's employment and headship status.[28] This study reports that each 1 percent increase in female headship in nonmetropolitan counties is associated with roughly a 0.5 percent increase in the poverty rate.

Other county-level analysis implicitly controls for the state policy environment by focusing on counties within a specific state or on a small number of states. For example, a study of counties in Georgia finds that the percentage share of families headed by mothers in 2000 was highly correlated ($r = 0.70$) with county-to-county variation in child poverty rates.[29] The model, however, does not include county economic indicators (such as unemployment) that are commonly linked to both family structure and poverty. Another study compares the effects of employment and human capital (such as schooling) on poverty rates of married-couple and single-parent families in counties of the Lower Mississippi Delta and the Texas Borderland.[30] Regional poverty differences could largely be explained by differences in economic factors. Like Appalachia, most poor families in the Texas Borderland are married-couple families.

Both approaches—shift-share analysis and place-based regression modeling—document wide disparities in poverty rates across family types and strong statistical relationships between changing family structure and poverty. But none of these studies focuses specifically on the economically depressed region of Appalachia.

26. Mencken and Tolbert (2005).
27. Partridge and Rickman (2006).
28. Lichter and McLaughlin (1995).
29. Ferriss (2006).
30. Slack and others (2009).

Appalachian Families and Poverty

Appalachia has always been one of America's most distinctive cultural regions, one with a fascinating history and an uneasy relationship with the rest of the country.[31] "The image of Appalachia's people has been one of a fiercely independent lot, who were strongly committed to family, and ultimately to the land they called home," notes one study.[32] Historically, generation after generation of social and cultural isolation bred both suspicion of outsiders (including the government) and elaborate support networks rooted in interdependent family kinship structures, cross-cutting friendship networks, strong faith traditions, entrenched political and job patronage systems, and a common cultural heritage (Scots-Irish).[33]

Negative stereotypes of the Appalachian region as a cultural backwater persist. It is sometimes viewed as a region saturated with uneducated hillbillies and feuding family clans, prone to ill temper and violence, and dependent on illegal activities and a vibrant underground economy (such as making illegal liquor, or moonshine). Today, geographic and cultural isolation may be less relevant in Appalachia as advances in transportation (interstate highways) and telecommunication systems (fiber optics and the Internet) have continued apace. Characterizations of Appalachia as remote and isolated echo late nineteenth- and early twentieth-century depictions of a region untouched by modernity, not the complexity of persistent poverty in a zone of natural resource extraction.[34] Indeed, coal mining areas are among the poorest in the region. Capital-intensive mountaintop mining, which employs few workers, is particularly associated with high levels of poverty.

Ethnographic accounts of Appalachia often point to family strength in the face of severe economic hardship.[35] Perhaps paradoxically, decades of economic hardship may have made Appalachian families more resilient to economic conditions, including economic downturns, than families living outside of Appalachia. But family change has not bypassed Appalachia.[36] Nor have Appalachian families and children been immune to the economic consequences of declining marriage,

31. Billings and Blee (2000); Tickamyer and Henderson (2010).
32. McLaughlin, Lichter, and Matthews (1999, p. 9).
33. Billings (1974); Porter (1981).
34. Lewis (1998).
35. Hennon and Photiadis (1979); Keefe (1971); Schwarzweller, Brown, and Magalam (1971).
36. Mather (2004); Werner and Badagliacco (2004).

high rates of nonmarital fertility, and rising numbers of female-headed families, especially in rural areas.[37]

Regional differences (Appalachia versus non-Appalachia) in family structure nevertheless are not entirely responsible for the higher poverty rates in Appalachia than elsewhere. In 2000, a slightly smaller percentage of all households in Appalachia (6.2 percent) than of those in non-Appalachia (7.3 percent) were headed by at-risk single mothers. But in 1999, the poverty rate of female-headed households with children was higher in Appalachia (39.8 percent) than in non-Appalachia (35.7 percent). Poverty rates were also higher among married-couple families with children (7.7 percent versus 5.6 percent outside Appalachia).[38] The similarities, both in poverty and family structure, between Appalachia and non-Appalachia are more apparent than the differences.

The demographic backdrop of changes in family and poverty in rural Appalachia nevertheless makes it an interesting regional case study. For example, despite changing family patterns since the 1960s, poverty rates have declined more rapidly in Appalachia than elsewhere in the country.[39] Compared with other regions in the nation, an accelerated pattern of spatial inequality now characterizes Appalachia, especially between Central Appalachia and the rest of Appalachia, and between its isolated rural areas and its burgeoning metropolitan regions (like Atlanta and its northern suburbs).[40] Family disruption and single parenthood are usually viewed as big-city problems, which prey disproportionately and perhaps most visibly on America's racial and ethnic minorities.[41] Unlike the nation as a whole, as well as in the Lower Mississippi Delta, the majority of Appalachian families living in poverty are headed by married couples.[42] The highest poverty rates in Appalachia also are found in remote rural areas (such as the isolated hollows of Eastern Kentucky and West Virginia), where the overwhelming share of the population, including its poor families, is white. Appalachian poverty is highly concentrated and persistent over time and generations.[43] The exodus of the best and brightest from rural areas to cities has left the undereducated, the unemployed, and the poor behind and has reinforced patterns of concentrated and persistent rural poverty.

37. McLaughlin, Lichter, and Matthews (1999); Newsome and others (2008).
38. Werner and Badagliacco (2004).
39. Newsome and others (2008).
40. McLaughlin, Lichter, and Matthews (1999).
41. Lichter, Qian, and Crowley (2008).
42. U.S. Census Bureau (2010b); Slack and others (2009); Mather (2004).
43. Brown and Warner (1991); Peters (2009).

Recent Family Poverty Trends in Appalachia

County data for the analysis conducted in this chapter come from the summary files of the 1990 and 2000 decennial censuses and from the 2005–09 American Community Survey (ACS).[44] Appalachia, as defined by the Appalachian Regional Commission, includes all or parts of thirteen states, encompassing roughly 205,000 square miles stretching from southern New York to northern Mississippi. Appalachia includes 428 of the nation's 3,108 contiguous counties. The region is disproportionately rural (42 percent), compared with 20 percent rural for the United States overall. We also give special attention to Central Appalachia, which includes 83 counties in much of eastern Kentucky and in parts of southwestern West Virginia and Virginia and north-central Tennessee.

Poverty income levels for families (and the individuals who live in families) are defined by the Office of Management and Budget, and poverty rates are based on family income reported by all family members in the years preceding the 1990 and 2000 decennial censuses. In 1999, the average poverty threshold for a family of four was $17,029. Poverty rates for 2005–09 are based on family income over the previous twelve-month period. The 2005–09 ACS poverty estimates are based on income data collected in 2005, 2006, 2007, 2008, and 2009. The ACS is an ongoing monthly survey, which in practice means that the income accounting period for a specific year covers a different twelve-month period for each family. The five-year data provide larger sample sizes than annual data; this fact alone reduces sampling variability and problems of data suppression for small population groups in the least-populated counties.

Our analysis begins with table 4-1, which reports mean and median family poverty rates for counties over the study period 1990–2009. The data indicate a reduction in average family poverty during the 1990s followed by a small uptick over the 2000s in each of the broad geographic categories considered here: Central Appalachia, all of Appalachia, non-Appalachia, and the continental United States. One notable exception to this trend is Central Appalachia, whose average family poverty rate did not change over the 2000s. However, change in the 1990s was especially large in Central Appalachia, where the family poverty rate declined on average across counties from 25 percent to 20 percent. This finding compares to smaller absolute decreases in Appalachian and non-Appalachian counties over the 1990–2000 period. For each period considered here, the average Central Appalachia family poverty rate is nearly twice the average across non-Appalachia.

44. U.S. Census Bureau (1990, 2000, 2005–09).

Table 4-1. *County Family Poverty, Central Appalachia, Appalachia, Non-Appalachia, and Total United States, Selected Years, 1990–2009*[a]
Percent

Year	*Central Appalachia*	*Appalachia*	*Non-Appalachia*	*U.S. total*
1990	25.0 (23.9)	15.3 (13.1)	12.7 (11.3)	13.1 (11.5)
2000	20.0 (19.1)	12.6 (10.9)	10.4 (9.2)	10.7 (9.5)
2005–09	20.0 (18.9)	13.8 (12.8)	11.0 (10.1)	11.4 (10.5)
N	83	428	2,680	3,108

Source: U.S. Census Bureau (1990, 2000, 2005–09).

a. Figures are means; medians are in parentheses. Sample includes all counties in the continental United States plus the District of Columbia (excludes Alaska and Hawaii).

Evidence of regional convergence over time between Central Appalachia and the rest of the nation is limited.

These are the average rates of family poverty for counties. Nonpoor families, however, may live disproportionately in highly populated counties—that is, those with a larger number of families, such as metropolitan areas, which may have comparatively lower poverty rates. County averages may thus misrepresent the poverty experience of the typical Appalachian county. Table 4-2 therefore provides weighted mean and median family poverty rates for Central Appalachia, Appalachia overall, non-Appalachia, and the continental United States. These family poverty rates are lower than the unweighted county averages for each of the three time periods but still remain higher than family poverty rates for the non-Appalachian United States. Furthermore, the average county (identified as the median county if counties are arrayed by family poverty rates from low to

Table 4-2. *Weighted County Family Poverty, Central Appalachia, Appalachia, Non-Appalachia, and Total United States, Selected Years, 1990–2009*[a]

Year	*Central Appalachia*	*Appalachia*	*Non-Appalachia*	*U.S. total*
1990	23.4 (23.0)	12.0 (10.5)	9.8 (8.9)	10.0 (9.2)
N	517,463	6,031,644	58,613,344	64,644,988
2000	19.0 (18.4)	10.2 (9.1)	9.1 (8.0)	9.2 (8.2)
N	544,211	6,482,928	65,335,098	71,818,026
2005–09	18.6 (17.3)	11.3 (10.7)	9.7 (9.3)	9.9 (9.4)
N	522,258	6,571,248	68,032,433	74,603,681

Source: U.S. Census Bureau (1990, 2000, 2005–09).

a. Figures are means; medians are in parentheses. Sample includes all counties in the continental United States plus the District of Columbia (excludes Alaska and Hawaii).

high) has an even lower poverty rate than the weighted county average and the unweighted family poverty rate. This result simply reflects the fact that family poverty rates are lower in highly populated areas than in remote rural areas.

Modeling Changes in Family Poverty for 1990–2009

County rates of poverty are influenced by economic growth, decline, and other county-level processes, such as racial and ethnic change. County-level processes are influenced by governmental and legislative activities at the state level, such as welfare programs and economic development strategies.[45] Panel county data are amenable to estimation methods that correct for state heterogeneity bias: the confounding effects of unmeasured state-level variables that are county-invariant within a state and omitted from the regression model. Heterogeneity bias can affect ordinary least squares estimates and the independence of the error term. This analysis implements state fixed effects regression modeling to address the issue of state heterogeneity. The standard errors of the estimates are corrected to account for the clustering of observations in counties.

To illustrate the modeling approach, we begin with estimates from a pooled county-level cross-sectional regression model of the family poverty rate. Let $y_{ij}(t)$ denote the family poverty rate in county i in state j in year t. Let $x_{ij}(t)$ denote the set of observed county- and year-specific economic and demographic variables (such as female headship), and let $d(t)$ be a dummy variable indicating the year of the observation (2000 or 2005–09). The year dummy, $d(t)$, is used to account for "global" effects that alter the trend in family poverty. With this notation, a standard regression equation of the relationship between family poverty and local economic and demographic conditions can be written as

$$y_{ij}(t) = \beta_0 + \beta_x' x_{ij}(t) + \beta_D d(t) + e_{ij}(t), \qquad (4\text{-}1)$$

where $e_{ij}(t)$ represents unobserved county-specific determinants of family poverty. This specification is estimated by applying ordinary least squares to the pooled county-level sample.

Estimates of the coefficients in equation 4-1 are biased if the error term, $e_{ij}(t)$, includes unobserved state factors that are correlated with the variables in $x_{ij}(t)$. To control for unobserved time-invariant factors at the state level, we estimate a

45. Lobao and Kraybill (2009).

model that incorporates state-specific fixed effects. Using the notation from the specification above, such a model can be expressed as

$$y_{ij}(t) = \beta_0 + \beta_x' x_{ij}(t) + \beta_D d(t) + \mu_j + e_{ij}(t), \tag{4-2}$$

where μ_j represents a state-specific effect (with β_0 suppressed, a state-specific intercept). The inclusion of state fixed effects mitigates biases associated with unobserved state variables. This factor is important in understanding the "effects" between the various observed indicators, including family variables and family poverty.

The county-based regression models in equations 4-1 and 4-2 include several independent variables (see box 4-1) that measure different aspects of the demographic and economic climate of counties. These variables are largely identified from previous county-level studies.[46] Based on previous studies, we expect that Appalachian family poverty rates will be affected by county racial and ethnic composition (percent nonwhite), age structure (percent under eighteen and over sixty-four), educational attainment (as an indicator of human capital), foreign-born inhabitants (who often migrate to economically advantaged counties), employment level (percent unemployed and percent females employed), and industrial structure (dependence on low-wage industries). We expect that poverty will be higher in nonmetropolitan than in metropolitan areas.[47]

Given our objectives, the analysis focuses on two family-related variables measured at the county level: percent of all families that are female-headed with children and percent never married. These variables measure the effects of delayed marriage, high divorce rates, and out-of-wedlock childbearing, and are expected to be associated with higher rates of family poverty. For each family variable, table 4-3 provides descriptive results for 1990, 2000, and 2005–09.

These preliminary results provide some useful insights about Central Appalachia, Appalachia overall, and non-Appalachia differences in family structure. In 1990, Central Appalachia had a higher percentage of female-headed families with children than did Appalachia overall and than the non-Appalachian United States. However, this trend reversed in 2000 and 2005–09.[48] For the entire 1990–2009 period, Central Appalachia had smaller shares of percent never

46. Lichter and McLaughlin (1995); Partridge and Rickman (2006); Slack and others (2009).

47. Crandall and Weber (2004); Lichter and McLaughlin (1995); Weber and others (2005).

48. This conclusion is reinforced with some additional analyses of state nonmarital fertility in 2006. Kentucky (35.3 percent) and West Virginia (37.9 percent)—two states at the heart of Central Appalachia and part of its poorest subregion—had lower shares of nonmarital births (that is, nonmarital births as a percentage of all births) than the nation overall (38.5 percent).

Box 4-1. *Definitions of Variables*

Variable	*Definition*
Appalachia	Counties in Appalachia as of November 2009
Central Appalachia	Counties in Central Appalachia as of November 2009
Nonmetropolitan	Counties with rural-urban continuum code 4-9
Family	Householder and one or more other persons living in same household related to householder by birth, marriage, or adoption
Percent families in poverty	Percentage of families with income below poverty level
Percent nonwhite	Percentage of population not non-Hispanic white
Percent foreign-born	Percentage of population foreign-born
Percent aged under 18	Percentage of population younger than 18
Percent aged 65 and over	Percentage of population 65 or older
Percent with bachelor's degree	Percentage of population 25 or older with bachelor's degree only
Percent in manufacturing industry	Percentage of civilian employed population 16 or older working in manufacturing
Percent in extractive industry	1990: percentage of civilian employed population 16 or older working in agriculture, forestry, fishing, or mining 2000, 2005–09: percentage of civilian employed population 16 or older working in agriculture, forestry, fishing, hunting, or mining
Percent in service industry	1990: percentage of civilian employed population 16 or older working in business and repair services, personal services, entertainment and recreation services, or professional services 2000, 2005–09: percentage of civilian employed population 16 or older working in professional, scientific, management, administrative, or waste management services; education, health, or social services; arts, entertainment, recreation, accommodation, or food services; or other services
Percent unemployed	Percentage of civilian labor force 16 or older unemployed
Percent females employed	Percentage of females 16 or older employed in civilian labor force
Percent female-headed families with children	Percentage of female-headed families with children younger than 18
Percent never married	Percentage of population 15 or older never married

Table 4-3. *County Family Variables, Central Appalachia, Appalachia, Non-Appalachia, and Total United States, Selected Years, 1990–2009*[a]
Percent

Year and variable[b]	*Central Appalachia*	*Appalachia*	*Non-Appalachia*	*U.S. total*
1990				
Percent female-headed families with children	6.0 (1.4)	5.7 (1.6)	4.7 (2.6)	4.9 (2.5)
Percent never married	19.9 (2.8)	21.5 (5.1)	22.0 (5.7)	22.0 (5.6)
2000				
Percent female-headed families with children	9.6 (1.7)	9.8 (2.9)	10.5 (4.5)	10.4 (4.4)
Percent never married	19.0 (2.5)	21.1 (5.1)	22.6 (5.6)	22.4 (5.6)
2005–09				
Percent female-headed families with children	10.9 (2.7)	10.9 (3.2)	11.3 (5.0)	11.3 (4.8)
Percent never married	22.6 (4.4)	24.3 (6.0)	25.6 (7.0)	25.4 (6.9)
N	83	428	2,680	3,108

Source: U.S. Census Bureau (1990, 2000, 2005–09).

a. Figures are means; standard deviations are in parentheses. Sample includes all counties in the continental United States plus the District of Columbia (excludes Alaska and Hawaii).

b. See box 4-1 for definition of variables.

married than all of Appalachia and non-Appalachia. In general, these data suggest that family structure may be less strongly associated with poverty—or with changing poverty—in Appalachia than in the rest of the nation. The regression model results that follow test whether this association holds once we control for other confounding factors.

National County Estimates of Family Poverty

The initial results (reported in the first column of table 4-4) provide national estimates from a pooled regression model including county data for 1990, 2000, and 2005–09 for the continental United States. No state fixed effects are included. This conventional analysis illustrates that average family poverty in Central Appalachia is 3.91 percentage points higher than in counties outside of Central Appalachia, even after controlling for observed social, economic, and demographic factors, including changes in family structure. In addition, family poverty is particularly high on average in nonmetropolitan counties in

Table 4-4. *Model for Continental United States, 1990–2009*[a]

Variable[b]	*No area effects*	*State fixed effects*[c]
Intercept	12.49***	8.90***
Year 2000	–2.46***	–2.48***
Year 2005–09	–2.14***	–2.41***
Central Appalachia	3.91***	2.62***
Nonmetropolitan	1.30***	1.15***
Central Appalachia*nonmetropolitan	2.77***	3.08***
Percent nonwhite	0.09***	0.08***
Percent foreign-born	–0.14***	–0.03
Percent aged under 18	0.18***	0.17***
Percent aged 65 and over	–0.03	0.01
Percent with bachelor's degree	–0.09***	–0.13***
Percent in manufacturing industry	0.03***	0.02*
Percent in extractive industry	0.15***	0.12***
Percent in service industry	0.07***	0.08***
Percent unemployed	0.33***	0.39***
Percent females employed	–0.29***	–0.25***
Percent female-headed families with children	0.31***	0.25***
Percent never married	0.05***	0.08***
N	9,324	9,324
R^2	0.78	0.82

Source: U.S. Census Bureau (1990, 2000, 2005–09).

***$p \leq 0.001$, **$p \leq 0.01$, *$p \leq 0.05$.

a. Sample includes all counties in the continental United States plus the District of Columbia (excludes Alaska and Hawaii). Estimates are unstandardized coefficients.

b. See box 4-1 for definition of variables. Dependent variable is percent families in poverty.

c. State fixed effects are jointly significant at 0.001 level.

comparison to their metropolitan counterparts (b = 1.30). The Central Appalachia by nonmetropolitan interaction (b = 2.77) indicates especially high average rates of family poverty in the rural parts of Central Appalachia as opposed to metropolitan areas of Central Appalachia and the rural parts of other regions.

Percent female-headed families with children (b = 0.31) and percent never married (b = 0.05) are positively and significantly associated with average county family poverty. According to the descriptive statistics in table 4-3, in the continental United States, the county average percentage of families that are female-headed with children grew by 6.4 percent between 1990 and 2009. This finding means that the rise in female-headed households with children nationally is associated with a 1.98 (0.31 * 6.4) percentage point increase in the average family poverty rate during that period. The effect of changing marital status composition is more modest, however. The growth in the average percent never married of 3.4 percent affects the decline in family poverty by only 0.17 (0.05 * 3.4) percentage points between 1990 and 2009. Changing family structure, on balance, mutes downward trends in family poverty rates over the 1990s and 2000s. As expected, counties with higher shares of foreign born ($b = -0.14$), adults with a college education ($b = -0.09$), and employed women ($b = -0.29$) have lower average rates of family poverty. In contrast, counties with a larger percentage of nonwhites ($b = 0.09$), children ($b = 0.18$), manufacturing employment ($b = 0.03$), extractive employment ($b = 0.15$), service employment ($b = 0.07$), and the unemployed ($b = 0.33$) have higher average family poverty rates. The percent elderly is not significantly associated with variation in county levels of family poverty.

If the year dummy variables are not significant (table 4-4), the usual inference would be that declines in average family poverty are due entirely to changes in the county compositional characteristics considered here. But as shown in the first column of the table, the net year effects of −2.46 for 2000 and −2.14 for 2005–09 are statistically significant in the model. The descriptive statistics in table 4-1 indicate that the percentage of families in poverty actually declined by 2.4 percentage points on average between 1990 and 2000, and by 1.7 percentage points over 1990 to 2005–09 in the continental United States. Because the time coefficients are larger than the observed reduction in family poverty, most of the 1990s and 2000s decrease in family poverty cannot be explained by variables included in the model.

A criticism of previous research is that estimates of family structure effects may be spurious, a result of excluding state-level policy or sociocultural variables associated with both family structure and poverty, from the model. The model presented in the second column of table 4-4 addresses this concern by including forty-eight state dummy variables as controls for unmeasured time-invariant state-level effects. Specification tests reveal that the state dummy variables are jointly significant at the 0.001 level. The inclusion of state fixed effects leads to only a small absolute decrease in the estimated effect of female headship (0.31 to 0.25) and a slight increase in the estimated effect of percent never married (0.05 to 0.08). The other variables previously discussed are similar in sign, magnitude, and significance to the no area effects model, with one exception: percent foreign-born is reduced to statistical insignificance with the inclusion of state fixed effects. On balance, any concerns about potential biases from omitted state-level variables, even in models such as these that are augmented by a relatively rich and detailed set of observed control variables, do not appear to be well founded in this case.

Appalachian County Estimates of Family Poverty

We next turn to the estimates from our pooled regression model of 1990, 2000, and 2005–09 county data for all Appalachian counties (table 4-5). As before, we estimate models without and with state fixed effects. These models also distinguish Central Appalachia from the rest of Appalachia.

The model without state fixed effects indicates that the average family poverty in Central Appalachia is 1.83 percentage points higher than counties in North and South Appalachia. Nonmetropolitan counties in Appalachia have higher average rates of family poverty ($b = 0.98$) than metropolitan counties after controlling for the county variables considered here. The large Central Appalachia-by-nonmetropolitan interaction ($b = 3.28$) illustrates that average family poverty

Table 4-5. *Model for Appalachia, 1990–2009*[a]

Variable[b]	*No area effects*	*State fixed effects*[c]
Intercept	22.09***	9.62**
Year 2000	−3.30***	−2.77***
Year 2005–09	−2.35***	−2.19***
Central Appalachia	1.83**	−0.12
Nonmetropolitan	0.98***	0.73***
Central Appalachia*nonmetropolitan	3.28***	2.51**
Percent nonwhite	0.07***	0.02
Percent foreign-born	−0.07	−0.02
Percent aged under 18	0.17**	0.41***
Percent aged 65 and over	−0.22***	0.04
Percent with bachelor's degree	−0.24***	−0.30***
Percent in manufacturing industry	0.07***	0.02
Percent in extractive industry	0.05	0.07
Percent in service industry	0.17***	0.15***
Percent unemployed	0.29***	0.25***
Percent females employed	−0.38***	−0.33***
Percent female-headed families with children	0.36***	0.32***
Percent never married	−0.10***	0.07
N	1,284	1,284
R^2	0.81	0.84

Source: U.S. Census Bureau (1990, 2000, 2005–09).
$^{***}p \leq 0.001$, $^{**}p \leq 0.01$, $^{*}p \leq 0.05$.
a. Sample includes all 428 Appalachian counties. Estimates are unstandardized coefficients.
b. See box 4-1 for definition of variables. Dependent variable is percent families in poverty.
c. State fixed effects are jointly significant at 0.001 level.

is especially high in nonmetropolitan areas of Central Appalachia in comparison to metropolitan parts of Central Appalachia and the rural areas of non-Central Appalachia.

The results also demonstrate, as with the country as a whole, the large effects of changing family structure. Female headship has a statistically significant positive effect ($b = 0.36$) on average county changes in family poverty. This demographic effect of changing female headship is slightly larger than the size of the effect for the continental United States ($b = 0.31$) (see table 4-4). The observed increase in average female headship in Appalachia between 1990 and 2009 of 5.2 percent has dampened the downward slide in poverty by 1.87 (0.36 * 5.2) percentage points. As we note below, these conclusions are affected by the inclusion of state fixed effects (column 2, table 4-5).

Appalachian counties with higher shares of elderly ($b = -0.22$) and adults with a bachelor's degree ($b = -0.24$) have lower average rates of family poverty. Furthermore, counties with a larger percentage of nonwhites ($b = 0.07$), children ($b = 0.17$), manufacturing employment ($b = 0.07$), and service employment ($b = 0.17$) have higher average family poverty rates. The percentage of foreign-born and the percentage of employment in extractive industries are not significantly associated with family poverty. The results also suggest that unemployment leads to higher average county rates of family poverty in Appalachia; a 1 percentage point increase in the unemployment rate contributes to a 0.29 percentage point rise in family poverty. Growing women's employment has the salutary effect of decreasing average poverty ($b = -0.38$). As in previous studies, the effect of female employment is large, which possibly points to the poverty-reducing impacts of recent increases in female employment associated with welfare reform and perhaps a growing economy.[49]

The year 2000 dummy variable in the first column of table 4-5 shows a −3.30 percentage point decline in the average Appalachian family poverty rate over the 1990s, independent of observed county changes in the social and economic variables considered. Similarly, the 2005–09 dummy variable indicates a −2.35 percentage point reduction in average family poverty in comparison with the base year, 1990. However, average family poverty in Appalachia actually decreased by 2.7 percent between 1990 and 2000 and by 1.5 percent over 1990–2009, as shown by the descriptive statistics in table 4-1. The large magnitude of the time coefficients indicates that, like the nation as a whole, most of the 1990s and 2000s decrease in average family poverty within Appalachia cannot be

49. See Lichter and McLaughlin (1995).

explained by variables included in the model. Nonetheless, the size of the time coefficients decreases for the state fixed effects model to −2.77 for 2000 and to −2.19 for 2005–09. This finding also reflects the fact that some county compositional changes in Appalachia have been poverty-increasing while other changes have been poverty-decreasing, essentially canceling each other out.

Next, we move on to the state fixed effects model shown in the second column of table 4-5. As with the country overall, state fixed effects are jointly significant at the 0.001 level. In this case, their inclusion leads to some substantive changes in several of the coefficients of interest. Concerning the family variables, the inclusion of state fixed effects decreases the estimated effect of female headship (0.36 to 0.32) and renders the estimated effect of percent never married as insignificant.[50] Most of the other variables analyzed are close in sign, size, and significance to the no area effects model, with three exceptions: the effects of percent nonwhite, percent elderly, and percent manufacturing employment are reduced to statistical insignificance. Unlike estimates for the nation as a whole, estimates of family poverty in Appalachia appear to be influenced by unobserved state-level factors.

Simulations of Appalachian County Family Poverty

As a final exercise, the effects of changing family structure in Appalachia are simulated for the two family variables considered here (female headship and never married). First, we estimated a 2005–09 cross-sectional regression model (not shown) using the same variables as the previous model for Appalachia reported in the first column of table 4-5. For simplification, the simulations are based on the model without state fixed effects.[51] Next, to produce the observed average family poverty rate, we entered the 2005–09 mean of each variable for Appalachia into the 2005–09 prediction equation. That is, we multiplied each variable's estimated coefficient by its mean in 2005–09 and then summed all of these terms together. To compute the counterfactual family poverty rate, we replaced the 2005–09 means for both family variables with their means in 1990 but held all of the other variables at their 2005–09 levels. The counterfactual predicts what the average family poverty rate would have been in 2005–09 if the means of the two family

50. In some additional analysis (not reported), we also fit models with county fixed effects. The effect size for female headship is further reduced to 0.14 but remains statistically significant at the 0.001 level.

51. Simulations based on the state fixed-effects model would require reporting observed and counterfactual family poverty rates for each of the thirteen Appalachian states separately (that is, if we reported simulations based on the state fixed-effects model).

variables had not changed since 1990 (that is, there had been no family change over the 1990–2009 period). By comparing the counterfactual with the observed average family poverty rate, we can identify the implications of changing family structure in Appalachia.

The findings in table 4-6 demonstrate the effects of family change in Appalachia over the 1990 to 2009 period. We distinguish between counties that are in Central Appalachia from those in non-Central Appalachia as well as counties that are nonmetropolitan or metropolitan. At a minimum, regardless of area, the observed average family poverty rate in 2005–09 is larger than the counterfactual, where we assume family mean values to be at 1990 levels. For counties that are in Central Appalachia and are nonmetropolitan, the counterfactual family poverty rate of 14.3 percent is 15.9 percent lower than the observed rate of 17.0 percent. In metropolitan counties located within Central Appalachia, the counterfactual rate of 10.8 percent is 19.4 percent lower than the observed rate of 13.4 percent. The effects are slightly larger in non-Central Appalachia. For nonmetropolitan counties in non-Central Appalachia, the counterfactual family poverty rate of 10.9 percent is 19.3 percent lower than the observed rate of 13.5 percent. In metropolitan counties located within non-Central Appalachia, the counterfactual rate of 10.0 percent is 20.6 percent lower than the observed rate of 12.6 percent.

To place these results in comparative perspective, we also set the percentage of adults with a bachelor's degree at its 1990 level and calculated the counter-

Table 4-6. *Observed and Counterfactual County Family Poverty, Appalachia, 2005–09*[a]

		Counterfactual poverty		
County type	*Observed poverty*	*No family change*	*No BA change*	*N*
Nonmetropolitan				
Central Appalachia	17.0	14.3	17.8	71
Non-Central Appalachia	13.5	10.9	14.4	213
Metropolitan				
Central Appalachia	13.4	10.8	14.3	12
Non-Central Appalachia	12.6	10.0	13.5	132

Source: U.S. Census Bureau (1990, 2000, 2005–09).

a. Figures are means. Sample includes all 428 Appalachian counties. Counterfactual family poverty obtained by substituting 1990 Appalachia sample mean into 2005–09 Appalachia prediction equation.

factual family poverty rate in the third column of table 4-6. In nonmetropolitan counties in Central Appalachia, the counterfactual poverty rate is 17.8 percent, a figure only 4.7 percent higher than the observed rate of 17.0 percent. By comparing the observed compositional changes in family structure and educational attainment between 1990 and 2009, the analysis suggests that family change had larger absolute and relative impacts on average family poverty in Appalachia over this period.

These findings highlight the poverty-increasing implications of family change since 1990. Moreover, some additional analysis (not shown) suggests that much of this effect is driven by the growth of female-headed families with children. This result can be shown by setting the female headship variable to its 1990 mean value but allowing each of the means for the other variables (including percent never married) to vary over time. The counterfactual family poverty rate is almost identical to the rate if both family variables are set at their 1990 means. These simulations have heuristic value, but they also raise new questions about the causes of Appalachian family change, including the rise in female-headed families with children.

Conclusion

Nearly fifty years have passed since the War on Poverty was first declared in Appalachia during the mid-1960s. This chapter has a singular goal, to balance the current preoccupation with employment and income growth by focusing instead on the poverty implications of changing family structure in Appalachia. This topic is especially salient today, when promoting marriage has become an important part of the welfare dialogue about how to improve the economic circumstances of low-income, welfare-dependent mothers and their children. Marriage and a stable family life are increasingly viewed as a panacea to poverty and welfare dependence.[52]

The results confirm the fact that average family poverty rates in Appalachia, especially rural areas in Central Appalachia, are higher than in the rest of the nation. Central Appalachia, however, experienced a comparatively more rapid decline in poverty during the 1990s and no increase during the post-2000 period. The analysis highlights the poverty-increasing effects of changing family structure, especially the growth of female-headed families with children. In this respect, the findings replicate conventional results of other demographic studies

52. See Lichter, Graefe, and Brown (2003).

using either shift-share analysis or place-based regression modeling.[53] Changes in family structure have dampened the pace of post-1990 declines in family poverty, both nationally and in Appalachia.

The important new lessons from this analysis are twofold. First, the implications of family change for family poverty appear to be larger in Appalachia than in non-Appalachia parts of the continental United States, independent of regional differences in employment opportunities, industrial structure, demographic variables, and unobserved state variables. Issues of family change cannot be ignored in policy discussions of poverty reduction strategies in Appalachia.[54] Policies aimed at strengthening families need a place at the policy table, even in a region with a long history of chronic unemployment.

Second, family effects, notably those associated with changing female headship, are estimated to be larger than those for conventional economic and human capital variables. This finding is perhaps surprising in light of studies that emphasize employment and wages, often to the exclusion of changing family patterns. The simulations suggest that average family poverty in Appalachia would have been roughly 15–20 percent lower than the observed rate of 2005–09 if Appalachian families had not changed in structure since 1990.

The interpretation of these baseline results nevertheless requires some caveats. For example, the data do not include the entirety of the economic recession and therefore may misrepresent the significance of family change vis-à-vis employment change on family poverty. The analyses also cannot support strong causal claims, although state fixed effects provide stronger evidence of links between family change and family poverty than many previous analyses have provided. The findings are nonetheless subject to simultaneity bias (that is, poverty may be a cause of family change rather than an effect). Finally, changes in family structure may mediate the effects of changing economic conditions on family poverty. Much of the effect of changing employment and economic conditions may be indirect. Family change may be a proximate "cause" of poverty, but employment and wages may be a "first cause," or fundamental cause, of changing poverty rates. Our statistical approach cannot fully adjudicate these competing claims about the mechanisms that ultimately serve to increase or reduce poverty. The results nevertheless highlight the need for a better accounting of how family change has exacerbated the deleterious consequences of job instability and low wages for family poverty.

53. Cancian and Reed (2009); Lichter and McLaughlin (1995).
54. Werner and Badagliacco (2004).

References

Albrecht, Don E., Carol Mulford Albrecht, and Stan L. Albrecht. 2000. "Poverty in Nonmetropolitan America: Impacts of Industrial, Employment, and Family Structure Variables." *Rural Sociology* 65, no. 1: 87–103.

ARC (Appalachian Regional Commission). 2009. *Subregions in Appalachia.* Washington (www.arc.gov/research/MapsofAppalachia.asp?MAP_ID=31).

———. 2011. *FY 2012 Performance Budget Justification.* Washington.

Billings, Dwight B. 1974. "Culture and Poverty in Appalachia: A Theoretical Discussion and Empirical Analysis." *Social Forces* 53, no. 2: 315–23.

Billings, Dwight B., and Kathleen M. Blee. 2000. *The Road to Poverty: The Making of Wealth and Hardship in Appalachia.* Cambridge University Press.

Blank, Rebecca M. 2002. "Evaluating Welfare Reform in the United States." *Journal of Economic Literature* 40, no. 4: 1105–66.

Brown, David L., and Mildred E. Warner. 1991. "Persistent Low-Income Nonmetropolitan Areas in the United States: Some Conceptual Challenges for Development Policy." *Policy Studies Journal* 19, no. 2: 22–41.

Burstein, Nancy R. 2007. "Economic Influences on Marriage and Divorce." *Journal of Policy Analysis and Management* 26, no. 2: 387–429.

Cancian, Maria, and Deborah Reed. 2009. "Family Structure, Childbearing, and Parental Employment: Implications for the Level and Trend in Poverty." In *Changing Poverty, Changing Policies,* edited by Maria Cancian and Sheldon H. Danziger, pp. 92–121. New York: Russell Sage.

Cherlin, Andrew J. 2009. *The Marriage-Go-Round: The State of Marriage and the Family in America Today.* New York: Knopf.

Crandall, Mindy S., and Bruce A. Weber. 2004. "Local Social and Economic Conditions, Spatial Concentrations of Poverty, and Poverty Dynamics." *American Journal of Agricultural Economics* 86, no. 5: 1276–81.

DeNavas-Walt, Carmen, Bernadette D. Proctor, and Jessica C. Smith. 2011. "Income, Poverty, and Health Insurance Coverage in the United States: 2010." Current Population Reports P60-239. U.S. Census Bureau.

Dion, M. Robin. 2005. "Healthy Marriage Programs: Learning What Works." *Future of Children* 15, no. 2: 139–56.

Duncan, Greg J., and Willard Rodgers. 1991. "Has Children's Poverty Become More Persistent?" *American Sociological Review* 56, no. 4: 538–50.

Economic Research Service. 1993. *1993 Rural-Urban Continuum Codes* (www.ers.usda.gov/Briefing/Rurality/RuralUrbCon/).

———. 2003. *2003 Rural-Urban Continuum Codes* (www.ers.usda.gov/Briefing/Rurality/RuralUrbCon/).

Eggebeen, David J., and Daniel T. Lichter. 1991. "Race, Family Structure, and Changing Poverty among American Children." *American Sociological Review* 56, no. 6: 801–17.

Ferriss, Abbott L. 2006. "Social Structure and Child Poverty." *Social Indicators Research* 78, no. 3: 453–72.

Gundersen, Craig, and James P. Ziliak. 2004. "Poverty and Macroeconomic Performance across Space, Race, and Family Structure." *Demography* 41, no. 1: 61–86.

Hamilton, Brady E., Joyce A. Martin, and Stephanie J. Ventura. 2010. "Births: Preliminary Data for 2009." *National Vital Statistics Reports* 59, no. 3: 1–19.
Hennon, Charles B., and John Photiadis. 1979. "The Rural Appalachian Low-Income Male: Changing Role in a Changing Family." *Family Coordinator* 28, no. 4: 608–15.
Kane, Andrea, and Daniel T. Lichter. 2006. "Reducing Unwed Childbearing: The Missing Link in Efforts to Promote Marriage." Center on Children and Families Brief 37. Brookings.
Keefe, Susan Emily. 1971. "Appalachia Family Ties." In *Appalachia's Children: The Challenge of Mental Health,* edited by David H. Looff. University of Kentucky Press.
Kennedy, Sheela, and Larry L. Bumpass. 2008. "Cohabitation and Children's Living Arrangements: New Estimates from the United States." *Demographic Research* 19, no. 47: 1663–92.
Lewis, Ronald L. 1998. *Transforming the Appalachian Countryside: Railroads, Deforestation, and Social Change in West Virginia, 1880-1920.* University of North Carolina Press.
Lichter, Daniel T., Deborah R. Graefe, and J. Brian Brown. 2003. "Is Marriage a Panacea? Union Formation among Economically Disadvantaged Unwed Mothers." *Social Problems* 50, no. 1: 60–86.
Lichter, Daniel T., and Rukmalie Jayakody. 2002. "Welfare Reform: How Do We Measure Success?" *Annual Review of Sociology* 28: 117–41.
Lichter, Daniel T., and Diane K. McLaughlin. 1995. "Changing Economic Opportunities, Family Structure, and Poverty in Rural Areas." *Rural Sociology* 60, no. 4: 688–706.
Lichter, Daniel T., and Zhenchao Qian. 2004. *Marriage and Family in a Multiracial Society.* New York: Russell Sage.
Lichter, Daniel T., Zhenchao Qian, and Martha L. Crowley. 2008. "Poverty and Economic Polarization among Children in Racial Minority and Immigrant Families." In *Handbook of Families and Poverty,* edited by D. Russell Crane and Tim B. Heaton, pp. 119–43. Los Angeles: Sage.
Lobao, Linda M., and David S. Kraybill. 2009. "Poverty and Local Governments: Economic Development and Community Service Provision in an Era of Decentralization." *Growth and Change* 40, no. 3: 418–51.
Martin, Molly A. 2006. "Family Structure and Income Inequality in Families with Children, 1976 to 2000." *Demography* 43, no. 3: 421–45.
Mather, Mark. 2004. *Households and Families in Appalachia.* Washington: Population Reference Bureau and Appalachian Regional Commission.
McLanahan, Sara S. 2009. "Fragile Families and the Reproduction of Poverty." *Annals of the American Academy of Political and Social Sciences* 621, no. 1: 111–31.
McLanahan, Sara S., and Christine Percheski. 2008. "Family Structure and the Reproduction of Inequalities." *Annual Review of Sociology* 34: 257–76.
McLaughlin, Diane K., Daniel T. Lichter, and Stephen A. Matthews. 1999. *Demographic Diversity and Economic Change in Appalachia.* Washington: Appalachian Regional Commission.
Mencken, F. Carson, and Charles M. Tolbert II. 2005. "Federal Public Investment Spending and Economic Development in Appalachia." *Rural Sociology* 70, no. 4: 514–39.
Newsome, Sean W., and others. 2008. "Appalachian Families and Poverty: Historical Issues and Contemporary Economic Trends." In *Handbook of Families and Poverty,* edited by D. Russell Crane and Tim B. Heaton, pp. 104–18. Los Angeles: Sage.

Orszag, Peter R., and others. 2009. *Memorandum for the Heads of Executive Departments and Agencies: Developing Effective Place-Based Policies for the FY 2011 Budget.* White House (http://courses.washington.edu/geog464/Obama_administration_place-based_policy.pdf).

Partridge, Mark D., and Dan S. Rickman. 2006. *The Geography of American Poverty: Is There a Need for Place-Based Policies?* Kalamazoo: W. E. Upjohn Institute for Employment Research.

Peters, David J. 2009. "Typology of American Poverty." *International Regional Science Review* 32, no. 1: 19–39.

Porter, Julia Damron. 1981. "Appalachians: Adrift in the Mainstream." *Theory into Practice* 20, no. 1: 13–19.

Roberts, Tracy E., and Steven P. Martin. 2010. "Welfare Exit, Marriage, and Welfare Recidivism: A Reevaluation of Patterns of the 1980s and 1990s." *Population Research and Policy Review* 29, no. 2: 105–25.

Rodgers, Harrell R., Jr., and Lee Payne. 2007. "Child Poverty in the American States: The Impact of Welfare Reform, Economics, and Demographics." *Policy Studies Journal* 35, no. 1: 1–21.

Ross, Christine, Sheldon H. Danziger, and Eugene Smolensky. 1987. "The Level and Trend of Poverty in the United States, 1939–1979." *Demography* 24, no. 4: 587–600.

Schwarzweller, Harry K., James S. Brown, and J. J. Magalam. 1971. *Mountain Families in Transition: A Case Study of Appalachian Migration.* Pennsylvania State University Press.

Seltzer, Judith A. 2000. "Families Formed outside of Marriage." *Journal of Marriage and Family* 62, no. 4: 1247–68.

Slack, Tim, and others. 2009. "Poverty in the Texas Borderland and Lower Mississippi Delta: A Comparative Analysis of Differences by Family Type." *Demographic Research* 20, no. 15: 353–76.

Snyder, Anastasia R., Diane K. McLaughlin, and Jill L. Findeis. 2006. "Household Composition and Poverty among Female-Headed Households with Children: Differences by Race and Residence." *Rural Sociology* 71, no. 4: 597–624.

Teachman, Jay D. 2002. "Stability across Cohorts in Divorce Risk Factors." *Demography* 39, no. 2: 331–51.

Thomas, Adam, and Isabel V. Sawhill. 2002. "For Richer or for Poorer: Marriage as an Antipoverty Strategy." *Journal of Policy Analysis and Management* 21, no. 4: 587–99.

Tickamyer, Ann R., and Debra A. Henderson. 2010. "Devolution, Social Exclusion, and Spatial Inequality in U.S. Welfare Provision." In *Research in Rural Sociology and Development,* edited by Paul Milbourne, pp. 41–59. Bingley, U.K.: Emerald Group.

U.S. Bureau of Labor Statistics. 2009. "The Employment Situation, October 2009." USDL-09-1331. U.S. Department of Labor (www.bls.gov/news.release/archives/empsit_11062009.pdf).

U.S. Census Bureau. 1990. *1990 Census of Population and Housing, Summary Files 1 and 3.*

———. 2000. *2000 Census of Population and Housing, Summary Files 1 and 3.*

———. 2005–09. *2005–09 American Community Survey.*

———. 2010a. *People in Families by Family Structure, Age, and Sex, Iterated by Income-to-Poverty Ratio and Race: 2009 (All Races).* POV02 (www.census.gov/hhes/www/cpstables/032010/pov/new02_100_01.htm).

———. 2010b. *Families by Age of Householder, Number of Children, and Family Structure: 2009 (All Races).* POV04 (www.census.gov/hhes/www/cpstables/032010/pov/new04_100_01.htm).

———. 2010c. *Children by Presence and Type of Parent(s), Race, and Hispanic Origin: 2009 (All Races).* C9 (www.census.gov/population/www/socdemo/hh-fam/cps2009.html).

———. 2010d. *Family Groups: 2009 (All Races).* FG10 (www.census.gov/population/www/socdemo/hh-fam/cps2009.html).

Weber, Bruce A., and others. 2005. "A Critical Review of Rural Poverty Literature: Is There Truly a Rural Effect?" *International Regional Science Review* 28, no. 4: 381–414.

Werner, Tammy, and Joanna Badagliacco. 2004. "Appalachian Households and Families in the New Millennium: An Overview of Trends and Policy Implications." *Journal of Appalachian Studies* 10, no. 3: 373–88.

Ziliak, James P. 2009. *Welfare Reform and Its Long-Term Consequences for America's Poor.* Cambridge University Press.

PART II

Future Challenges for Appalachia

JANET CURRIE
MARIESA HERRMANN

5

Socioeconomic Status, Child Health, and Future Outcomes: Lessons for Appalachia

While there are clearly many things about a person's background that might matter for future outcomes, research increasingly implicates health as a major factor. Given the importance of "health capital" for education and earnings, poor health in childhood may be an important mechanism for intergenerational transmission of education and economic status.[1]

This link is disturbing in light of the poor health of Appalachians, both relative to national samples and in relation to other residents of Appalachian states. Figure 5-1 shows age-adjusted mortality rates from all causes for the whole population and by race for four geographical groups: Central Appalachian counties, all Appalachian counties, other regions of Appalachian states (excluding New York City and Philadelphia), and the entire United States. The figure clearly shows higher death rates in Appalachia, and particularly in Central Appalachia, than in the rest of the country. However, death rates for blacks and whites are very different. These figures suggest that the disparity between Appalachia and other regions is mostly due to whites; mortality rates for blacks are high but are very similar between Appalachia and elsewhere.

Mariesa Herrmann gratefully acknowledges the financial support of the National Science Foundation's Graduate Research Fellowship Program. All opinions expressed are those of the authors and not those of the NSF. The authors also thank Gary Burtless, Hilary Hoynes, Mark Schweitzer, James Ziliak, and others for helpful comments.

1. Grossman (2000); Case, Fertig, and Paxson (2005); Currie and Madrian (1999); Smith (2009).

Figure 5-1. *Mortality, by Area, 1989–2006*

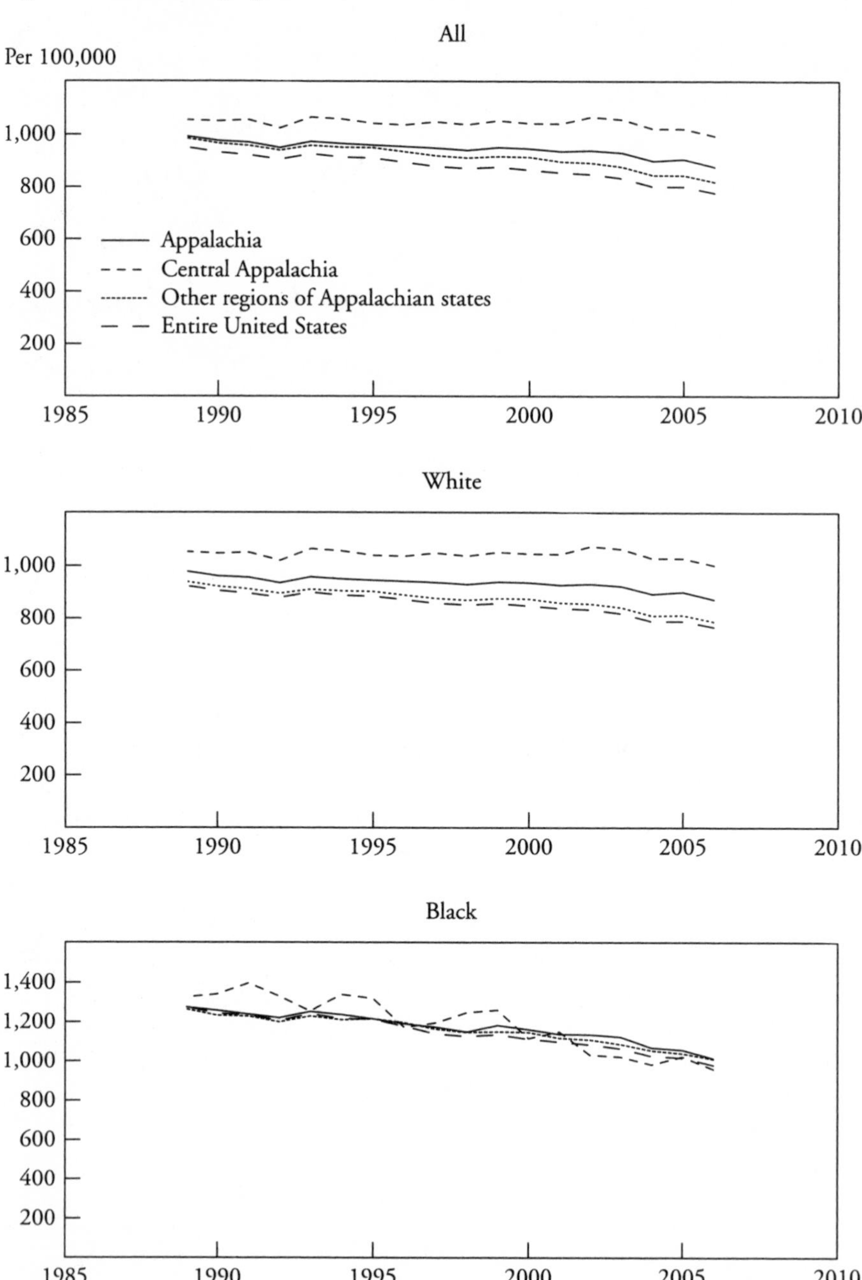

Source: Authors' calculations from Vital Statistics datasets from the U.S. National Center for Health Statistics. See appendix for details.

This chapter asks whether higher death rates among adults in Appalachia might possibly be due to poorer health in childhood. Lack of longitudinal data makes it difficult to test this hypothesis, but evidence presented below suggests that it is at least a plausible scenario. If it is indeed the case that current disparities are likely to have important future health effects, then the case for ameliorating these disparities becomes even stronger.

Why Might Poverty in Appalachia Yield Poor Health?

In the standard model of child health production, parents are assumed to maximize an intertemporal utility function, in which parental utility depends on child health (among other things).[2] Parents face budget constraints that limit the time and money they can invest in child health as well as constraints that dictate how their time and money inputs can be converted into child health.

Health inputs are valued by consumers not for their own sake but because they affect child health, which in turn has a direct effect on parental utility. Nonmarket time is an input into both health production and the production of other valued nonmarket goods (like leisure activities). This model is dynamic in the sense that the stock of child health today depends on past investments in health and on the rate of depreciation of health capital. This model yields several insights into why parental poverty might matter for child health. For example, the budget constraint will be less binding in wealthier families, and these families will be able to purchase more or better quality material health inputs. Inputs include better quality medical care and food as well as safer toys, housing, and neighborhoods. Set against this is the possibility that parents with a higher value of time in market work will invest less time in child health production, though to the extent that parents can purchase substitute care of adequate quality, this may not have any negative consequence.

Lower socioeconomic status (SES) is, however, not only a matter of what inputs one can afford to buy but also a matter of what one can do and chooses to do with the inputs one has at hand. Parents of lower SES may have different past experiences with the health care system, or different health beliefs (for example, about whether it is normal for a child to have coughing or wheezing), or different preferences. Victor Fuchs (1992) emphasizes the rate of time preference and a sense of self-efficacy as two things that are related to socioeconomic status but that might have independent effects on the way parents choose to combine inputs in order to produce child health. David Cutler and Adriana Lleras-Muney (2006)

2. Grossman (2000).

also emphasize the effect of education on decisionmaking about health behaviors. Parental education is often highlighted as something that determines how productively parents can invest in child health.

In their models of capacity formation, F. Cunha, J. Heckman, and S. Schennach (2006) and James Heckman (2007) focus on the dynamic aspects of the human capital investment model. They argue that a model in which there are "dynamic complementarities" and "self-productivity" fits the available evidence well. Dynamic complementarities imply that investments in period t are more productive when there is a high level of capability in period $t-1$. Self-productivity implies that higher levels of capacity in one period create higher levels of capacity in future periods. Studies by David Barker show that poor fetal conditions are related to a higher adult risk of disease, especially cardiovascular disease and diabetes.[3] This relationship has come to be known as the fetal origins hypothesis. There is also recent literature discussing the fetal origins of cancer.[4] Thus differences in health at birth may affect disparities in health later in life.

Evidence Linking Parent's SES and Child Health

Many authors show that children born to low SES parents have worse health at birth than children born to high SES parents.[5] In an important study Anne Case, Darren Lubotsky, and Christina Paxson (2002) show that in the United States these gaps in health status tend to grow as children age. Janet Currie and Mark Stabile (2003) show that this is also true in Canada, where children have access to universal health insurance, though the rate at which the relationship between income and health strengthens with age is lower in Canada. Their results suggest that variations in the incidence of health problems are important explanations of the gap in health status between rich and poor and that equalizing access to palliative care is not likely to eliminate these gaps.

Poor children suffer more insults to their health than richer ones. For example, Paul Newacheck (1994), Jeanne Brooks-Gunn and Greg Duncan (1997), Paul Newacheck and Neil Halfon (1998), Case, Lubotsky, and Paxson, and Janet Currie and Wanchuan Lin (2007) all show that poor children are more likely to have many chronic conditions and that poor children are more likely to have their daily activities limited by their conditions. Using data from the Third National Health and Nutrition Examination Surveys, Jayanta Bhattacharya and

3. See for example Barker (1998).
4. See Stiller (2004).
5. See Currie (2009) for a summary.

Janet Currie (2001) show that family income below 1.3 times the U.S. poverty line is a significant predictor of high blood cholesterol and of high body mass index among adolescents, conditional on other demographic variables.

The theory sketched above suggests that persistent poverty is likely to have worse effects on health than transitory poverty, since health is a stock that will be affected by past investments, and children with low "capacities" may be less able to parlay new investments in their health capital into good outcomes. Several authors use data from the National Longitudinal Survey of Youth to address this issue, although its health measures are rather limited. Sanders Korenman and Jane Miller (1997) find that children in persistently poor families have lower height for their age than other children. J. McLeod and M. Shanahan (1993, 1996) and Lisa Strohschein (2005) find that child mental health, and particularly aggressive behavior, may be affected more by persistent poverty than by current poverty alone.

The literature conclusively demonstrates that children of poor or less educated parents are in worse health on average than other children, even in a rich country like the United States. But this does not necessarily imply that low SES causes poor child health. It is possible, for example, that a third factor causes both poverty and poor child health. Since parents who are in poor health are likely to have lower earnings, and may have achieved less education, perhaps parents' poor health, rather than parents' low earnings or education, is causally related to poor child health. Alternatively, poor child health may reduce parental earnings. The limited evidence on this point does not suggest large effects, however.[6]

It is important to identify causal effects, because if parental SES does not affect child health (at least when SES is above some minimum level) then interventions to increase parental SES will not necessarily improve child health. However, the literature attempting to identify causal impacts of parental SES on child health in a developed country context is small. It is difficult to find interventions that affect parental SES that are not also likely to have a direct effect on children's health.

Janet Currie and Enrico Moretti (2003) use the great expansion in the number of colleges that occurred in the United States in the 1960s and 1970s as an instrument for measuring college going among American women. They show that higher rates of college attendance are related to improved infant health. College attendance also increases the probability that a new mother is married, reduces parity, increases the use of prenatal care, and substantially reduces maternal smoking, suggesting that these may be important pathways through which college attendance affects health.

6. See Powers (2001); Wolfe and Hill (1995).

Pedro Carneiro, Costas Meghir, and Matthias Parey (2007) examine the effect of maternal education using data from the National Longitudinal Survey of Youth. They instrument maternal education, using local labor market conditions, the presence of a four-year college, and college tuition at age seventeen in the county where the mother resided when she was fourteen years old. They find strong effects on measures of cognitive outcomes and even stronger medium-term effects on a measure of behavior problems, which might be regarded as a proxy for, or a correlate of, mental health. They also find strong effects of maternal education on the home environment, measured using variables such as whether the child is read to and whether the child has special lessons. They conclude that the effects of increases in maternal education are large relative to the effects of other interventions designed to affect child outcomes.

A few studies attempt to look at the effects of exogenous changes in household income. The problem here is to find exogenous sources of variation in household income that do not also affect other conditions in the household. For example, some welfare-to-work experiments increase household income, but these interventions also encourage maternal employment, so they cannot be regarded as purely income interventions. Eugene Smolensky and Jennifer Gootman (2003) and Rebecca Blank (2009) summarize the welfare-to-work literature and find that, overall, these interventions have surprisingly little impact on children, positive or negative.

There is some evidence that changes in family circumstances affect childhood mental health conditions. In particular, the Moving to Opportunity experiment, which randomly assigned some public housing residents to move to low-poverty neighborhoods while control households stayed in public housing projects, found improvements in the mental health of girls. Specifically, the experimental group experienced reductions in generalized anxiety disorders and psychological distress. Curiously, there was no such positive effect for boys.[7]

Jane Costello and others (2003) discuss the Great Smoky Mountains Study, a natural experiment involving the opening of a casino on an Indian reservation in western North Carolina. As a result of the opening, every family on the reservation received a cash transfer, but not every family was raised out of poverty by this transfer. Costello and her colleagues compare families before and after the casino opening and whether or not they were raised from poverty by the opening. They find that, before the opening, poor children had higher levels of psychiatric symptoms than nonpoor children. After the opening, children in families that were

7. Orr and others (2003).

raised above poverty had larger declines in conduct and oppositional disorders (though there was no effect on anxiety and depression) than children in families who were never poor or who remained poor. However, the families that were raised out of poverty were also less likely to be single headed and reported that they were better able to supervise their children after the change, suggesting that there may have been other factors at work than money.

Several studies attempt to control for unobserved family characteristics that might be associated with both low income and low birth weight by estimating models with sibling fixed effects. Dalton Conley and Neil Bennett (2000, 2001), using data from the Panel Study of Income Dynamics (PSID), find that income during pregnancy has no effect on the risk of low birth weight either when the mother's birth weight is controlled or when family fixed effects are included in the model. However, they suggest that if the mother was low birth weight, then income at the time of the birth has a significant impact on the probability that her child is low birth weight in models that include mother fixed effects. Similarly, Rucker Johnson and Robert Schoeni (2007) estimate sibling fixed-effects models using PSID data and show that increases in income increase birth weight by much more if the mother was low birth weight herself.

Currie and Moretti (2007) examine intergenerational transmission of low birth weight using a much larger data set based on birth records from California. They define the mother's birth socioeconomic status by examining income in the zip code of the hospital where the mother was born. They find that mothers who were born in poor areas were both more likely to be low birth weight and more likely to eventually deliver a low birth weight baby themselves (by 6 percent), even in models comparing mothers who were sisters (that is, models including grandmother fixed effects).

In summary, there is a strong and exceedingly robust correlation between various measures of parental background and child health and some evidence that suggests that the relationship is causal. Hence, given persistent poverty in Appalachia, it would not be surprising to see poor infant and child health.

Child Health in Appalachia

It is remarkably difficult to document differences in child health between Appalachia and other regions with the publicly available health data, because most health data sets do not provide data on counties. Many data sets, such as the National Health Interview Survey and the National Health and Nutrition Examination Surveys, do not even provide information about state of residence in their public use files. Other data files, such as hospital discharge records or Medicaid claims data, are difficult to access and are maintained at the state level, which means that there is no uniform national database to draw on.

In this section, we draw on the vital statistics natality and mortality data sets in order to compare Appalachian counties to non-Appalachian counties in the same states as well as to other areas of the United States. Vital statistics data have the advantage of being comprehensive, since they include virtually all U.S. births and deaths. In addition to vital events, they contain a great deal of information about parental background as well as parent and child health conditions. (For further information about the data sources for this chapter, see the appendix to the chapter.)

How Does Appalachia Compare to the Rest of the United States?

Figure 5-2 presents data on infant mortality rates, one of the most commonly used summary measures of child health, for all races and for whites and blacks separately. The figure shows a pattern very similar to that of figure 5-1. Although mortality rates fall over the period shown, they are higher for whites in Appalachia, and particularly in Central Appalachia, than elsewhere. It is remarkable that in non-Appalachian regions of Appalachian states, white infant (and child) mortality rates in general are almost identical to national rates, so the disparity between Appalachia and elsewhere is not due to anything that is happening at the state level. For blacks the rates are somewhat noisy, but there is little evidence that Appalachian rates exceed those for the country as a whole. However, rates for blacks are so much higher than those for whites that adding the two groups together obscures the very clear pattern for whites.

Figure 5-3 shows the incidence of low birth weight, the most widely used summary measure of infant health at birth. The figure suggests that the seeds of poor health are sown before children are born. Among whites, rates are persistently higher in Appalachia than elsewhere, and these rates seem to be not only increasing but also diverging somewhat from the U.S. average over time. Among blacks, rates of low birth weight are quite similar in Appalachia and the rest of the United States at the beginning of the sample period but begin to diverge in 1995. This pattern does not auger well for the future health of black Appalachians. Note that one might expect some mechanical correlation between falling infant death rates and rising rates of low birth weight if it is primarily low birth weight infants who are saved by improvements in medical care. However, the relative rates are such that falling death rates can explain only a small part of the increasing incidence of low birth weight.

Figure 5-2. *Infant Mortality, by Area, 1989–2006*

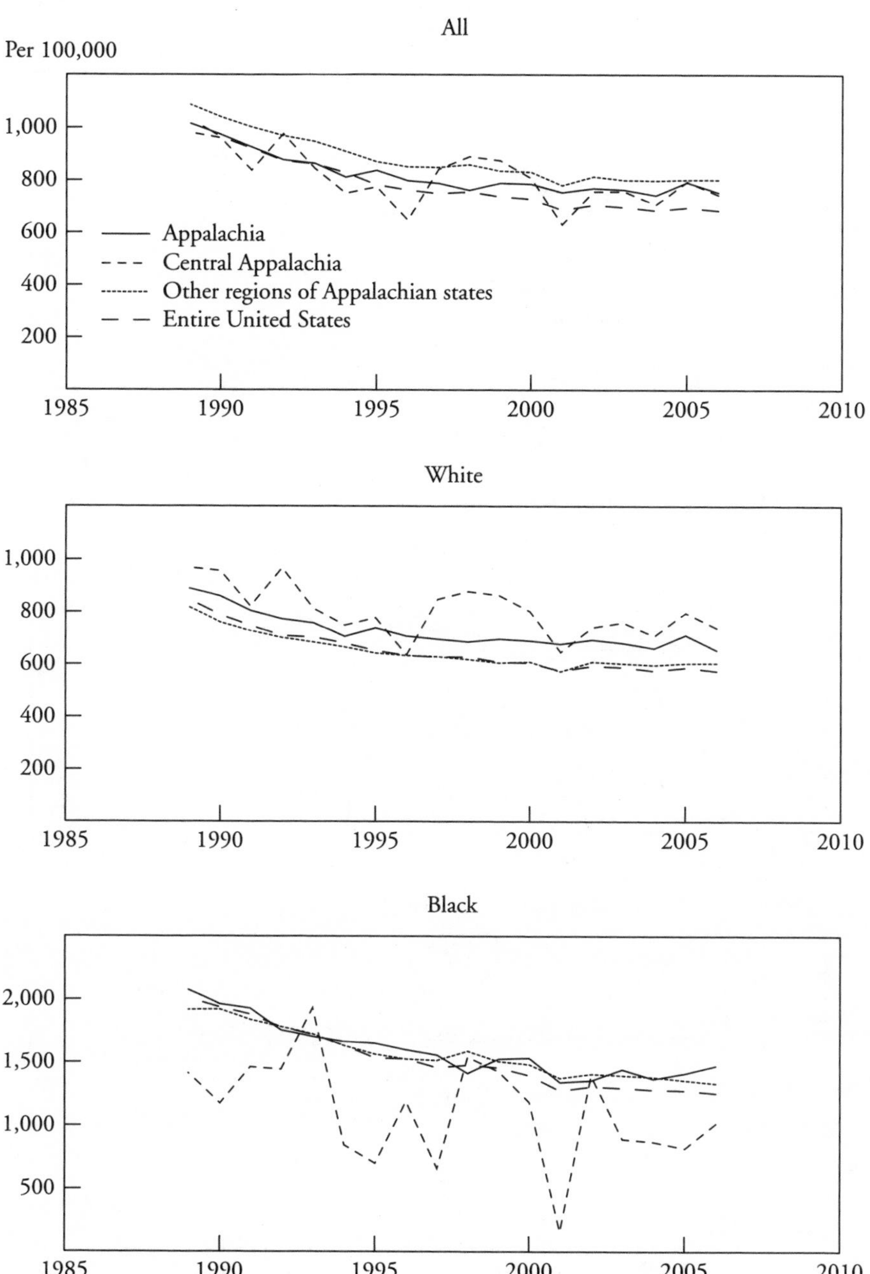

Source: Authors' calculations from Vital Statistics datasets from the U.S. National Center for Health Statistics. See appendix for details.

Figure 5-3. *Low Birth Weight, by Area, 1989–2006*

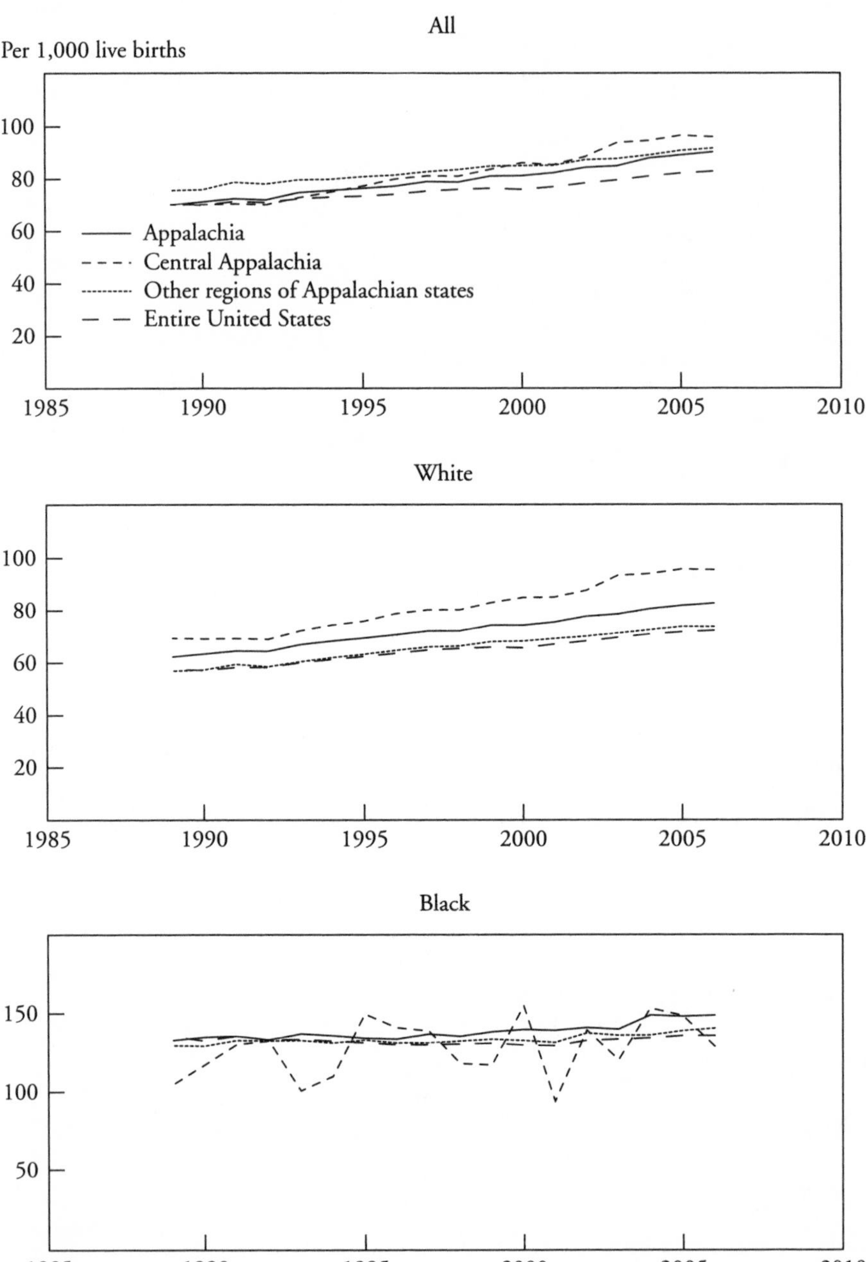

Source: Authors' calculations from Vital Statistics datasets from the U.S. National Center for Health Statistics. See appendix for details.

The natality data can also be used to shed some light on the reasons for these trends. For example, is poor infant health in Appalachia due to lack of access to medical care, to maternal background, or to maternal behaviors? Measures of access that we can examine include whether the child was born in the same county the mother resides in or a different one; whether the mother received prenatal care starting in the first trimester; and whether or not she had a Caesarian section. The first two outcomes are plotted in figures 5-4 and 5-5 for all mothers and separately for white and black mothers.

As shown in figure 5-4, it is striking how many women in Central Appalachia must travel out of their county to give birth—roughly 60 percent. Other regions of Appalachian states have rates of approximately 30 percent, compared to a U.S. rate of about 25 percent, while rural America outside of Appalachia has rates of about 45 percent. Figure 5-5 shows that the fraction of women beginning prenatal care in the first trimester is generally at least as high in Appalachia as elsewhere and only slightly lower in Central Appalachia. Rates of C-section (not shown) are almost identical in Appalachia to those in the rest of the United States (and are rising steadily).

On the whole, and perhaps surprisingly, the evidence regarding access to care suggests that, while Appalachian women generally have poorer access to hospitals in their county of residence, delivery of prenatal care and obstetrical care may not be greatly affected. This relatively good access to prenatal and obstetrical care may reflect the impact of expansions of Medicaid to poor pregnant women that took place over the late 1980s. In any case, trends in these variables are unlikely to explain increases in the incidence of low birth weight over time.

If differential access to medical care cannot explain the trends, perhaps the trends can be at least partially explained by maternal characteristics and maternal behaviors. Figures 5-6 and 5-7 show the fraction of mothers who have less than a high school education and the fraction of mothers who are less than nineteen years old. Figure 5-6 shows that Central Appalachian mothers are considerably less likely than other mothers to have a high school education. It is striking that mothers in non-Appalachian areas of Appalachian states are actually more likely to have at least this much education than the average U.S. mother, so there is a large disparity in levels of education within these states. Figure 5-7 indicates that Central Appalachian mothers are also much more likely to be teenagers than mothers in other areas, though the proportion of teen births is falling over time in Appalachia as in the rest of the country. Since the children of teenage, high school dropout, mothers would be expected to have poorer outcomes than other children, these differences in the composition of who is giving birth may explain some of the poorer birth outcomes.

Figure 5-4. *Infants Born outside County of Residence, by Area, 1989–2006*

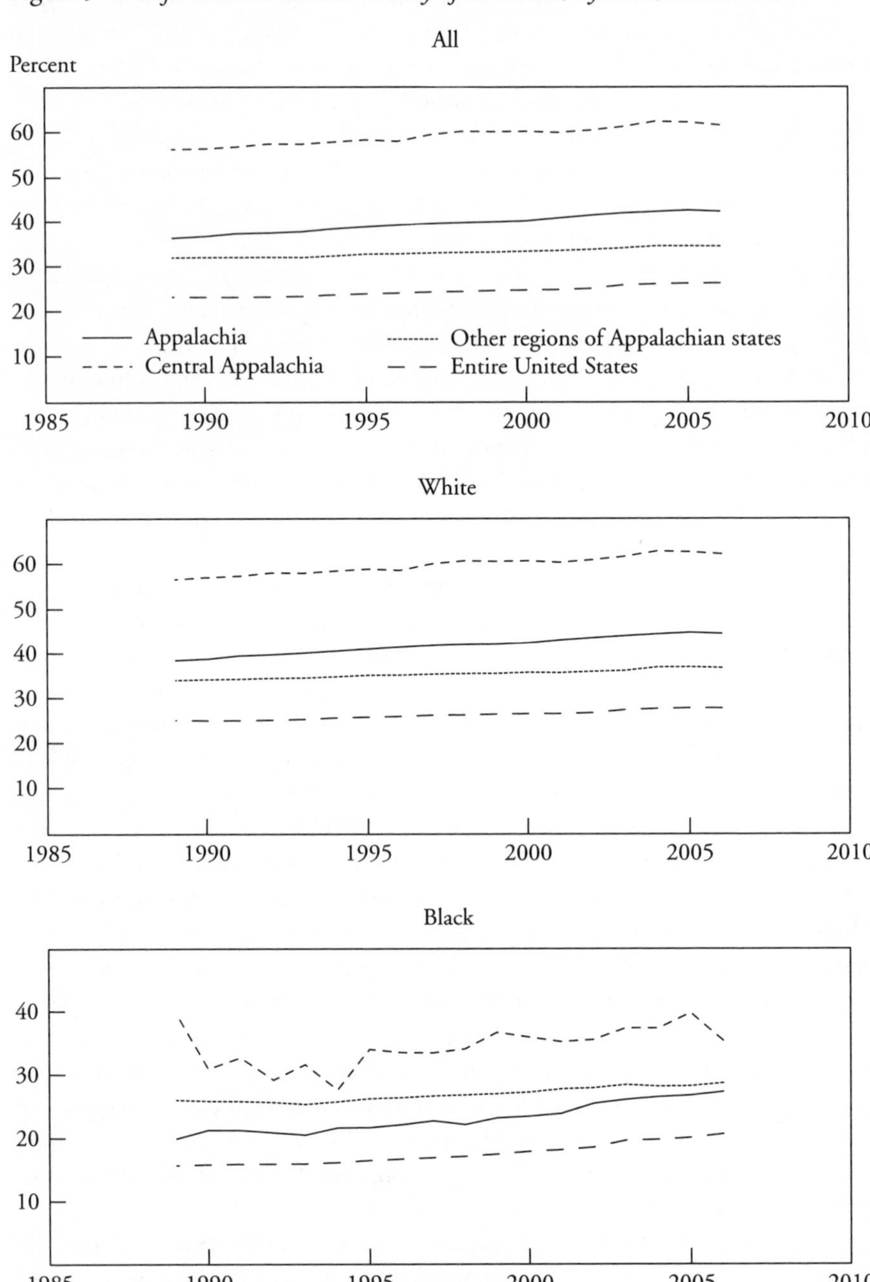

Source: Authors' calculations from Vital Statistics datasets from the U.S. National Center for Health Statistics. See appendix for details.

Figure 5-5. *Infants Receiving Prenatal Care in First Trimester, by Area, 1989–2006*

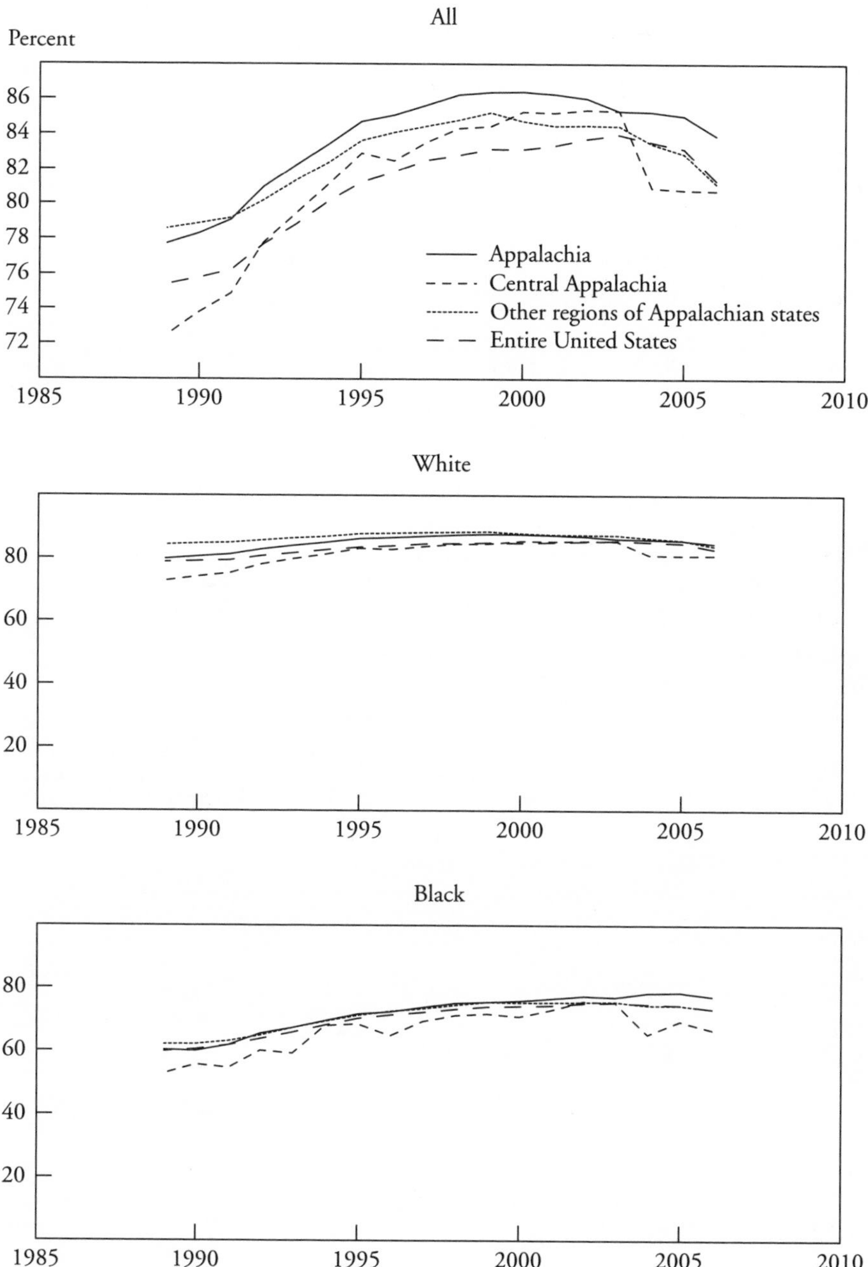

Source: Authors' calculations from Vital Statistics datasets from the U.S. National Center for Health Statistics. See appendix for details.

Figure 5-6. *Mothers with Less than High School Education, by Area, 1989–2006*

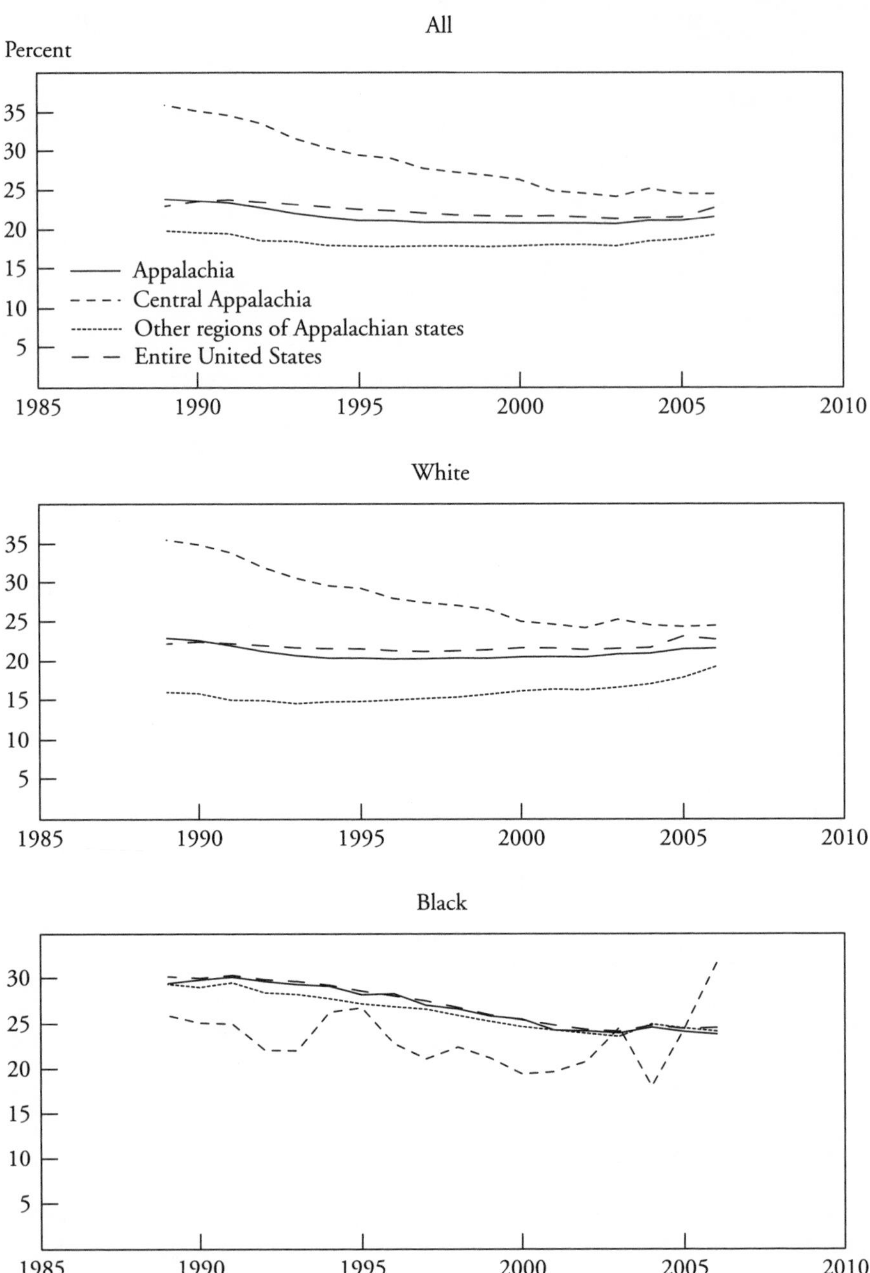

Source: Authors' calculations from Vital Statistics datasets from the U.S. National Center for Health Statistics. See appendix for details.

Figure 5-7. *Mothers Less than Nineteen Years of Age, by Area, 1989–2006*

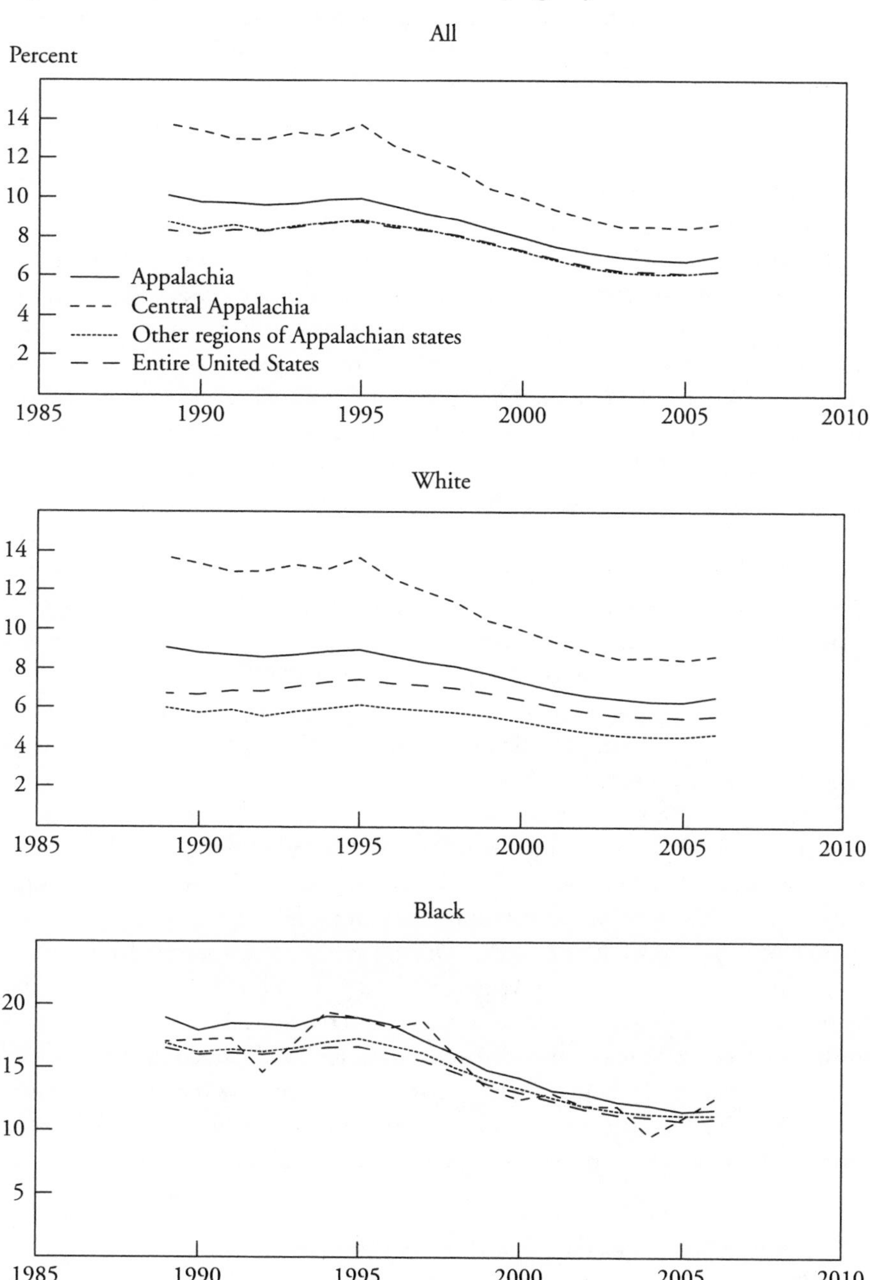

Source: Authors' calculations from Vital Statistics datasets from the U.S. National Center for Health Statistics. See appendix for details.

Moreover, the natality data suggest that differences in maternal behaviors are likely to be responsible for much of the differences in infant outcomes between Appalachia and elsewhere. Figure 5-8 demonstrates that smoking is a significant problem for both whites and blacks. In Central Appalachia over 30 percent of mothers smoked during pregnancy in 2005, a rate that has changed little since 1990. In contrast, in the United States as a whole about 12 percent of mothers smoked during pregnancy in 2005, a rate that fell from about 20 percent in 1990. Thus the growing disparity in smoking rates could very well explain the widening disparity in outcomes, since smoking is a leading cause of low birth weight.

Increasing rates of maternal obesity may also be a factor. Obese women are at higher risk for many complications of pregnancy and delivery, and their infants are more likely to be high birth weight. High birth weight (often defined as birth weight over 4,000 grams) has become increasingly prevalent and is an increasing concern since it is linked to higher body weight later in life as well as metabolic disorders such as diabetes.[8] There is increasing interest in the idea that high maternal weight may program the fetus for higher weight gain both in pregnancy and after birth, with the result that the obesity epidemic may tend to accelerate over time.[9] Certainly, childhood obesity is an important concern, with 31 percent of children ages six to nineteen being overweight or at risk of being overweight.[10] While the natality data do not record maternal prepregnancy weight, they do record the incidence of conditions such as diabetes and chronic hypertension that are often caused by obesity and that are risk factors in pregnant women. For example, the incidence of chronic hypertension is higher in Central Appalachia than elsewhere, especially for whites.

Table 5-1 presents the results of a regression analysis that compares the proportions of low birth weight infants in Appalachia and in the rest of the United States between 1989 and 2006. To avoid composition effects caused by the high prevalence of low birth weight among twins and other higher order births, we restrict attention to singleton births. During this period, about 6.1 percent of singleton births were low birth weight nationally. In column 1 of table 5-1, the fraction of low birth weight infants was regressed on controls for state, month of birth, year, race, ethnicity, maternal education, and an interaction between the controls for state and whether the state had adopted the new version of the birth certificate. This regression shows that children in Appalachia were 0.5 percent more likely to be low birth weight than other U.S. children. When controls for

8. Cedergren (2004); Watkins and others (2003); Sorenson and others (1997).

9. Ludwig and Currie (2010).

10. Hedley and others (2004).

Figure 5-8. *Mothers Smoking during Pregnancy, by Area, 1989–2006*

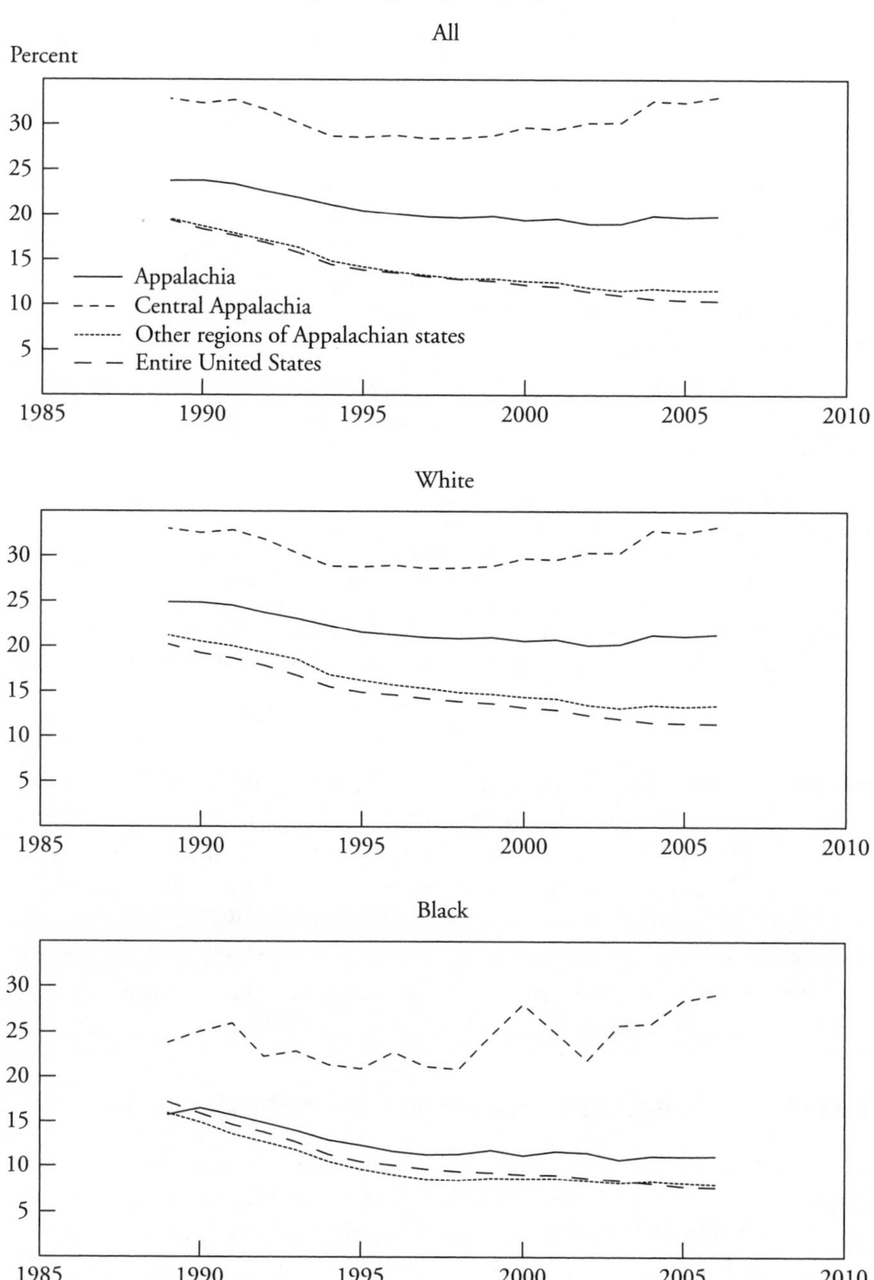

Source: Authors' calculations from Vital Statistics datasets from the U.S. National Center for Health Statistics. See appendix for details.

Table 5-1. *Low Birth Weight, Appalachia*[a]

	Low birth weight (< 2,500 g) regressions		
	1	*2*	*3*
Appalachia	0.0047***	0.0033***	0.0032***
	(0.0007)	(0.0005)	(0.0005)
Controls for maternal demographics	Yes	Yes	Yes
Controls for maternal choices/behaviors	No	Yes	Yes
Controls for access to care	No	No	Yes
State and state*new birth certificate fixed effects	Yes	Yes	Yes
Birth month and year fixed effects	Yes	Yes	Yes
R-squared			
Number of observations	667,983	667,983	667,983

Source: Authors' calculations from Vital Statistics datasets from the U.S. National Center for Health Statistics. See appendix for details.

***Significant at 1 percent level.

a. These regressions were estimated using county-year cells of singleton births for the years 1989–2006 and were weighted by the number of births in each cell. Specifications that control for maternal demographics include controls for black, Hispanic, maternal education (less than HS, HS, some college, college plus). Specifications that control for maternal choices/behaviors include controls for maternal age (19–24, 25–34, 35–44, 45+), parity (1, 2, 3, 4, 5+), married, smoking, and maternal weight gain (0–15, 16–30, 31–45, 46–60, 60+). Specifications that control for access to care control for prenatal care in the first trimester, whether the birth was in a hospital, and whether the birth was in the county of residence. Standard errors (in parentheses) are clustered by county.

mother's age, birth order of the child, mother's marital status, weight gain during pregnancy, and whether the mother smoked during pregnancy were added to the regression, the "Appalachia effect" dropped to 0.3 percent (column 2). Thus these relatively crude indicators of maternal background and behaviors explain a third of the differential in low birth weight between Appalachia and elsewhere. Adding controls for prenatal care in the first trimester, whether the birth was in a hospital, and whether the birth was in the county of residence has little impact on these estimates (column 3).

How Does Central Appalachia Compare to Rural America?

The previous section documents that Appalachians, particularly Central Appalachians, are in poor health relative to other Americans. Since Appalachia and Central Appalachia are comparatively rural, it is important to understand whether the health trends seen above are unique to Appalachia or are characteristic of rural America.

In figures not depicted, we compare two summary measures of health trends—age-adjusted, all cause, mortality rates and infant mortality rates—for four groups: Central Appalachian counties, rural Appalachian counties, other rural counties in the United States, and the entire United States. We find that the high mortality rates in Appalachia are not explained by the generally higher mortality rates in rural areas. The mortality rates in Central and rural Appalachia dwarf the mortality rate for other rural counties, which is only slightly higher than the national average. Once again, there are clear racial patterns in health disparities between Appalachia and the rest of the United States; large disparities exist for whites but not for blacks. We also find similar trends for infant mortality; the gaps between white infant mortality in Central and rural Appalachia and rural America are at least as large as the gaps between rural and nonrural America. However, there are no differences in infant mortality between blacks living in Appalachia and those living elsewhere in America.

Taken together, these findings suggest that the poor health outcomes in Appalachia are not merely a rural phenomenon; Appalachians are in poor health not only relative to other Americans but also relative to other rural Americans.

Effects of Child Health on Future Outcomes

The fetal origins hypothesis strongly suggests that conditions in utero affect not only birth weight but also features such as basic metabolism, which in turn affect future health outcomes. Since adult health is strongly linked to adult economic well-being, this suggests a relationship between health in utero and future outcomes.[11]

Figures 5-9 and 5-10 examine patterns in two important causes of death that have been linked to fetal and child health: cancer and diabetes. Figure 5-9 indicates that while death rates due to cancer are falling over time in the United States, they are not falling as fast in Appalachia; in particular, the rate for whites in Central Appalachia has been relatively constant. We also find that, although the incidence of cardiovascular disease, heart disease, and stroke has been declining over time, rates are higher in Appalachia, and especially in Central Appalachia, than elsewhere. Overall, trends in cardiovascular disease and cancer are similar to those shown in figure 5-1. That is, among whites there are much

11. Currie and Madrian (1999) summarize the evidence linking health and labor market outcomes among working-age adults. The relationship between SES and outcomes may be weaker for older adults.

Figure 5-9. *Mortality from Cancer, by Area, 1989–2006*

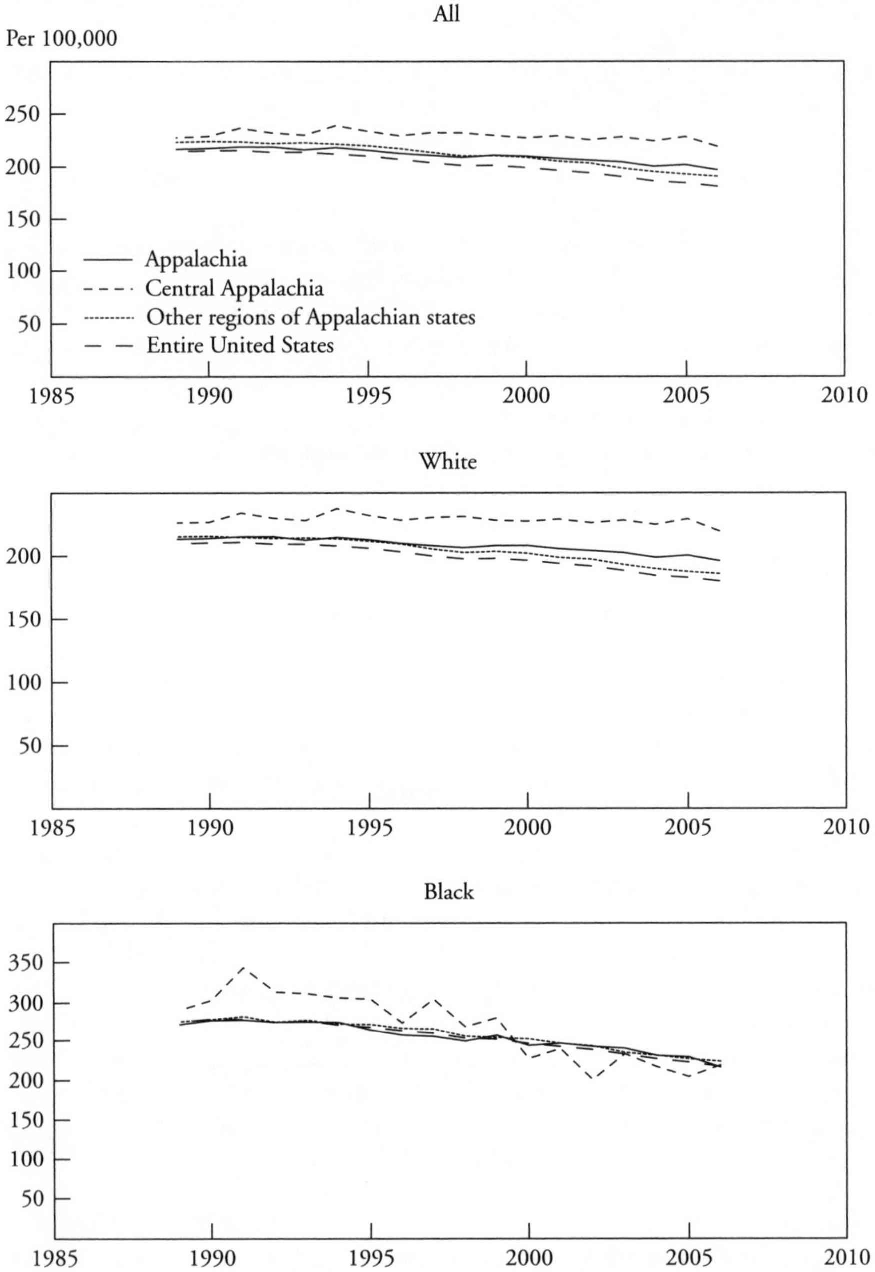

All

Per 100,000

250
200
150
100
50

Appalachia
Central Appalachia
Other regions of Appalachian states
Entire United States

1985 1990 1995 2000 2005 2010

White

200
150
100
50

1985 1990 1995 2000 2005 2010

Black

350
300
250
200
150
100
50

1985 1990 1995 2000 2005 2010

Source: Authors' calculations from Vital Statistics datasets from the U.S. National Center for Health Statistics. See appendix for details.

Figure 5-10. *Mortality from Diabetes, by Area, 1989–2006*

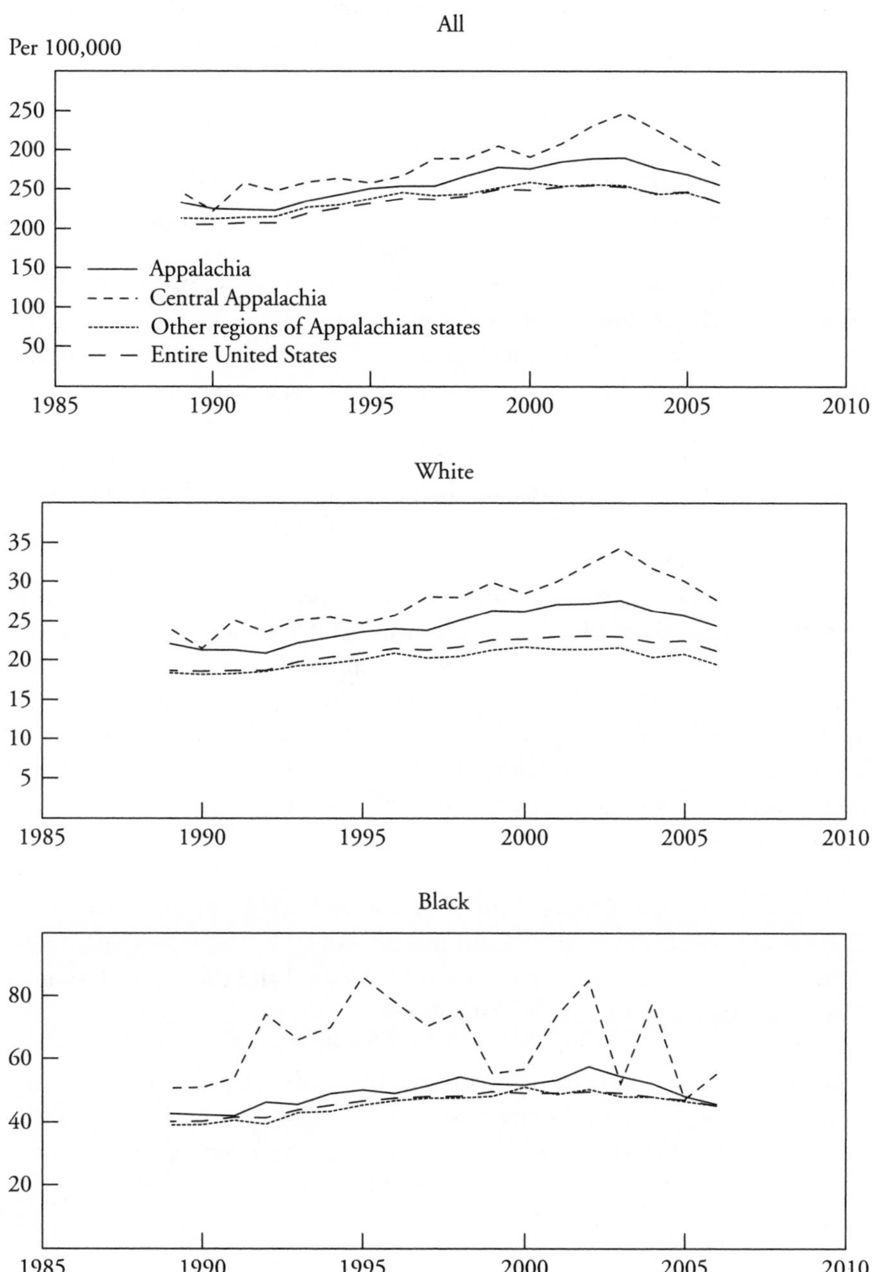

Source: Authors' calculations from Vital Statistics datasets from the U.S. National Center for Health Statistics. See appendix for details.

higher death rates in Appalachia, and especially in Central Appalachia, than elsewhere, while for blacks, there are high overall rates but little evidence of disparity between Appalachia and elsewhere. In contrast, figure 5-10 shows that death rates from diabetes are higher for blacks in Appalachia as well as for whites. Given the evidence of small disparities in black child health between Appalachian and non-Appalachian counties, this result may suggest the importance of differences in access to medical care for this specific condition rather than differences in underlying disease prevalence.

Of course, adult death rates today potentially reflect child health conditions many years ago. But if the patterns for child health were similar in the past to what we see today (that is, if child health was poorer among whites in Appalachia than among whites elsewhere, which seems quite likely) then this would at least be consistent with the patterns in adult health that are observed today.

Poor fetal and child health can also have direct effects on the acquisition of skills. For example, maternal alcohol consumption can lead to permanent fetal brain damage, as can trauma during the birth itself. Thus we know that severe insults in utero or in early childhood can cause permanent cognitive impairments. The question is really how sensitive these "sensitive periods" are and whether damage due to less extreme deprivation is noteworthy or widespread. Some commentators focus on school absences as a measure of the effect of health on education.[12] However the mean number of days absent is generally quite small for both poor and nonpoor children. Hence if poor health among school-aged children has an effect on the acquisition of skills, it is more likely to come through impairing children's ability to learn while they are in school. Conditions such as anemia and lead poisoning would have this effect. Conditions such as dental caries and ear infections are much more common, so they might have a greater overall impact.

The most compelling examinations of the fetal origins hypothesis look for sharp exogenous shocks in fetal health that are caused by conditions outside the control of the mother. For example, Douglas Almond and Bhashkar Mazumder (2005) use data from the U.S. Census Bureau's Survey of Income and Program Participation to follow cohorts affected by the influenza epidemic of 1918. The epidemic struck suddenly in the fall of 1918 and was largely over by January 1919. Approximately a third of women of childbearing age were infected. These researchers show that, compared to cohorts in utero either just before or just after the epidemic, the affected cohorts were more likely to suffer from diabetes, stroke,

12. Grossman and Kaestner (1997).

activity limitations, cancer, hypertension, and heart problems and that they reported poorer general health status as adults.

Douglas Almond (2006), examining the effects of the influenza epidemic on education and labor market outcomes of people affected by the disease in utero, finds that children of infected mothers were 15 percent less likely to graduate from high school and that the wages of affected men were lowered by 5–9 percent. Moreover, affected individuals were more likely to be poor and to be receiving transfer payments (in part because they were more likely to be too disabled to work). Thus this natural experiment provides compelling evidence that negative shocks to health in utero can have very significant effects on future economic outcomes.

An alternative way to demonstrate the importance of fetal conditions is to look at the long-term effects of low birth weight using sibling/twin comparisons. Several recent studies use large samples drawn from vital statistics records in Scotland, Norway, Canada, and the United States. All show a link between low birth weight and lower educational attainment. For example, Sandra Black, Paul Devereux, and Kjells Salvanes (2007) find (using twin fixed effects) that a 10 percent increase in birth weight leads to a 1 percentage point increase in the probability of graduating from high school and a 1 percent increase in earnings.

In addition to examining the effects of mother's SES on birth weight, Currie and Moretti (2007) use California birth certificate data to examine the long-term effect of maternal low birth weight. When they compare mothers who are sisters they find that the sister who was low birth weight is 3 percent more likely to live in a poor area at the time she delivers her own child and 3 percent less likely to be married when she gives birth. The low birth weight sister also has about a tenth of a year less education on average.

Johnson and Schoeni (2007), examining the long-term effects of low birth weight using data from the PSID and sibling fixed-effects models, find that low birth weight is strongly related to poorer adult health and that it lowers adult annual earnings by 17.5 percent. Siblings who are low birth weight are less likely to have any earnings (by 4.8 percentage points). A relatively small part of this reduction in earnings is mediated by lower educational attainment: low birth weight siblings are 4.8 percentage points more likely to drop out of school, and completed education is a tenth of a year lower.

Douglas Almond and Kenneth Chay (2006) examine the effect of a mother's health at birth (and in early childhood) on the health of her children, using an identification strategy based on the comparison of cohorts. They build on previous work showing that the civil rights movement had a large effect on the health of black infants in certain southern states, especially Mississippi (one of the Appalachian states), due to desegregation of hospitals and increased access to medical care.[13] For example, there was a large decline in deaths due to infectious disease and diarrhea in these cohorts.

Because birth records include the mother's state of birth, it is possible to identify black women who benefited from these changes (the 1967–69 cohorts) and to compare the outcomes of their infants to the outcomes of infants born to black women in the 1961–63 birth cohorts. The birth outcomes of white women in the same cohorts are examined as a control. Almond and Chay conclude that the infants of black women who had healthier infancies as a result of the civil rights movement show large gains in birth weight relative to the infants of black women born just a few years earlier; these gains are largest for women from Mississippi, the most affected state. The estimates indicate that the black-white gap in the incidence of very low birth weight was 40 percent lower in children of mothers from the 1967–69 cohort compared to the earlier cohort.

Although this is a historical study, the results may be particularly relevant for Appalachia today, given the evidence (discussed above) that Appalachian mothers continue to have poorer access to health care than other mothers in their states. Unfortunately, birth records do not include county of birth, so it is impossible to do a similar study focusing on women born in Appalachian counties.

In summary, there is a great deal of evidence that fetal health affects future child outcomes. Hence if fetal health was poorer in rural Appalachia then elsewhere over the past fifty years (as seems likely), it is not surprising that many Appalachians remain poor and subject to higher death rates years later.

Child Health Problems

Relative to the many recent studies examining health at birth, there are few studies examining other health measures or measures for older children. James Smith (2009) investigates the relationship between child health and future outcomes using data from the 1999 PSID. The adult children of the PSID respondents (who were twenty-five to forty-seven years old) were asked a retrospective question about the state of their health when they were sixteen years old: Was it excellent, very good, good, fair, or poor? Smith estimates sibling fixed-effects models and shows that better health in childhood is related to higher incomes, higher wealth, more weeks worked, and a higher growth rate in income in adult-

13. Almond, Chay, and Greenstone (forthcoming).

hood. The estimates imply that, within families, a sibling who enjoyed excellent or very good health in childhood earns 24 percent more than a sibling who was not in good health. Much of this effect on earnings appears to come through effects on adult health, which reduce work effort.

Janet Currie and others (2010) use Canadian administrative data to look at the effects of health conditions in childhood on future outcomes using sibling fixed-effects models. Data on all contacts with health care providers from the public health insurance system were merged with data on future health, educational attainment, and welfare use. The authors examine asthma, serious injuries, an aggregate composed of all other physical health problems, and mental health problems at different stages of childhood. Their main finding is that other physical health problems in early life predict poorer educational attainment and higher welfare use, because they predict future health problems. That is, once health problems in young adulthood are controlled for, measures of physical health in childhood have little predictive value. This finding is striking in view of claims that poor health in childhood can reduce human capital accumulation by, for example, causing school absences.

Currie and her colleagues pay particular attention to injuries, given that injuries, rather than illnesses, are the leading cause of death among children in developed countries.[14] They present some evidence that injuries in adolescence are predictive of poor future outcomes. However, they find that early childhood injuries do not affect future outcomes unless they have lasting effects on health.

Perhaps surprisingly in view of the large literature focusing on asthma, which is the most prevalent chronic condition of childhood, these researchers find little evidence that asthma in childhood is predictive of either lower educational attainments or an increased probability of welfare use. Previous studies report an effect of asthma on school absences, the probability of having learning disabilities, and grade repetition. For example, M. Fowler, M. Davenport, and R. Garg (1992), using data from the 1988 National Health Interview Survey for children in grades 1–12, find that asthmatic children averaged 7.6 days absent compared to 2.5 days for well children. Nine percent of the asthmatic children had learning disabilities, compared to 5 percent of the well children; 18 percent repeated a grade, compared to 15 percent of the well children.

In the only study to explicitly examine the effect of asthma on school readiness, Jennifer Halterman and others (2001) examine 1,058 children entering

14. Bonnie, Fulco, and Liverman (1999).

kindergarten in urban Rochester and find that asthmatic children have lower scores on a test of school readiness skills and that their parents are three times more likely to report that their child needed extra help with learning. There are no differences, however, on tests of language, motor skills, and socioemotional skills. The negative effects of asthma are concentrated among children whose asthma caused activity limitations (suggesting that it was not adequately controlled). Boys are more likely to be in this group than girls.

A difficulty with all of these studies is that, since asthma is more prevalent among poor and minority children than among other children, the apparent connection between asthma and outcomes could reflect omitted third factors. The studies from the medical literature discussed above are typically correlational studies, which control for few potential confounders.

In contrast to the results for physical health problems, Currie and colleagues report that mental health problems have an independent effect on educational attainment and welfare use, even after conditioning on future health problems. Relative to their own healthy siblings, children with an early diagnosis of ADHD or conduct disorders were 1.6 percentage points more likely to end up on welfare immediately after becoming eligible at age eighteen (on a baseline of 5.5 percent). They were also 4.4 percent less likely to be in grade 12 by age seventeen.

More about the Importance of Mental Health Conditions

The MECA study (Methodology for Epidemiology of Mental Disorders in Children and Adolescents), cited in the 1999 U.S. Surgeon General's report on mental health, finds that approximately one in five children and adolescents in the United States exhibit some impairment from mental or behavioral disorders, 11 percent have significant functional impairments, and 5 percent suffer extreme functional impairment.[15] These are very large numbers of children. Moreover, as Janet Currie and Bridget Madrian (1999) discuss, mental health problems are leading causes of days lost in the work place, because they strike many people of working age.

In one of the few studies to examine the issue, Jane Costello and her colleagues (1996) find that the rates of mental illness (including anxiety, conduct disorders, and hyperactivity) in Appalachian children aged nine to thirteen were quite similar to national rates. However, mental health problems may be a particular concern in Appalachia because of a lack of services for mental health con-

15. Shaffer and others (1996); U.S. Department of Health and Human Services (1999).

ditions. One study finds that, compared to 58 percent of rural non-Appalachian counties in Appalachian states, 70 percent of rural Appalachian counties lacked mental health services.[16] Several longitudinal studies find that children with "externalizing" mental health conditions, such as attention deficit/hyperactivity disorder (ADHD) or conduct disorders have significantly poorer mental health and schooling outcomes as teens or young adults than children without these conditions.[17] Some studies find that effects are particularly pronounced in children of young or less educated mothers, which would mean that Appalachian children are particularly at risk, given that their mothers are more likely to fall into these categories.[18]

Currie and Stabile (2006, 2009) use sibling fixed-effects models estimated on data from the National Longitudinal Survey of Youth and a similar Canadian survey. All children in these surveys were administered "screener questions" that can be used to form a scale for ADHD. The researchers focus on four-to-eleven-year-olds with ADHD and examine outcomes six years later. They find that children with initial high scores on the ADHD screener have lower cognitive test scores than other children for math and reading (by approximately a third of a standard deviation) and much higher probabilities of being in special education or repeating a grade. The effects of ADHD are larger than those of other mental problems and are quite similar in the United States and Canada. Finally, the effects of ADHD are large relative to those of physical chronic conditions.

These findings suggest that mental health conditions may form an important component of the noncognitive skills that are stressed by authors such as James Heckman, Jora Stixrud, and Sergio Urzua (2006). These authors distinguish between measures of children's cognitive skills (such as IQ scores) and measures of their noncognitive skills (such as the presence of behavior problems) and argue that the latter are at least as important as the former in explaining future success in life.

Toxic Exposures

Toxic exposure is an area of particular concern in Appalachia, given the prevalence in the region of heavy industries such as coal mining. Coal mining generates particulates and may lead to exposures to toxins such as arsenic, cadmium,

16. Hendryx (2007).

17. See Caspi and others (1998); Miech and others (1999); McLeod and Kaiser (2004); Mannuzza and Klein (2000).

18. Nagin and Tremblay (1999).

lead, and mercury. There has been little study of the extent to which pollution due to coal mines or other heavy industries is associated with poor health.

Michael Hendryx (2007) uses county-level data about hospitalizations from the Healthcare Cost and Utilization Project to examine the way that hospitalizations for "coal-sensitive" and "non coal-sensitive" conditions vary with levels of coal production in West Virginia. He finds some evidence of an effect on coal-sensitive conditions and finds that the effects are as large for women (who are less likely than men to work in the mines) as for men. He interprets this as evidence that coal production may have effects on townspeople as well as on workers.

Exposures to heavy metals in childhood have serious consequences: For example, lead has been shown to decrease IQ by two to five points for each 10–20 micrograms per deciliter of blood above the current standard.[19] However, the government tracks lead poisoning by looking for areas with a combination of older housing stock and low-income households (since these markers are predictive of exposure to lead paint), so that surveillance is not especially precise. Lead may also have negative effects on children's mental health, making them more prone to antisocial behavior.[20] Before the regulation of lead, children were exposed to lead from paints, water pipes, gasoline, and canned food. Evidence from the National Health and Nutrition Examinations Survey shows that 88.2 percent of children aged one to five had lead levels above 10 micrograms per deciliter of blood during 1976–80, 8.6 percent had lead levels above the threshold in 1988–91, and only 2.2 percent had levels this high in 1999–2000. These figures imply that the number of children with unsafe lead levels declined from 13.5 million to less than 0.5 million over this period.[21]

Lead poisoning hot spots persist, however, and some of them are in Appalachia.[22] Practices such as coal mining via mountaintop removal and failures of coal ash sludge ponds (like the one that recently occurred in Tennessee) are alleged to contaminate drinking water with heavy metals, including lead.[23]

There is little research on the question of whether exposure to toxic releases at the level that now generally occurs in the population has negative health effects. Data on possible human health effects often come either from animal studies or

19. Pocock, Smith, and Baghurst (1994).

20. Needleman and Gatsonis (1991).

21. U.S. Centers for Disease Control (2003).

22. See www.cdc.gov/nceh/lead/data/state.htm for maps showing counties with elevated lead in 2006. Note that no such data are available for Tennessee, South Carolina, or Alabama.

23. Charles Duhigg, "Clean Water Laws Are Neglected, at a Cost in Suffering," *New York Times*, September 12, 2009, p. A1.

from disastrous accidental releases. Tracey Woodruff (1998), by running 1990 data from the U.S. Environmental Protection Agency's Toxic Release Inventory through a dispersion model, calculates that 90 percent of census tracts have concentrations of several chemicals greater than cancer benchmarks. This suggests that American children (and others) may be at risk from toxic releases, but it does not establish any direct relationship between releases and health effects.

Janet Currie and Johannes Schmieder (2009) use data from the Toxic Release Inventory and compare chemicals known to have developmental effects to those not known to have such effects. They also compare the effects of "fugitive air releases" (in which chemicals escape from a plant in to the surrounding environment) to those of "stack air releases" (in which chemicals are funneled up a tall smoke stack and hence disperse over a further area). They show that fugitive releases of developmental chemicals are associated with higher infant death rates. The effects are particularly large for heavy metals such as cadmium but are also significant for commonly released volatile organic compounds such as toluene.

Martine Vrijheid (2000) looks at the question of whether residence near a hazardous waste site has health effects and highlights some of the methodological weaknesses of existing studies. Residents of areas near hazardous waste sites are more likely to be poor and have lower levels of education than people in the remainder of the country.[24] That means that their children's health outcomes are likely to differ even in the absence of negative health effects from exposure. Some studies control for some observable confounding factors, but there is still a possibility that there are unobservable characteristics of people who live close to hazardous waste sites that would tend to cause bad outcomes. An additional problem is that the number of hazardous waste sites analyzed in many of the previous studies is small, so that some "results" may actually be due to sampling variability. These problems plague much of the literature on toxic effects, so that it is quite difficult to measure effects of pollution on health, let alone show that there are long-term consequences of exposures.

In two important and innovative works, Kenneth Chay and Michael Greenstone (2003a, 2003b) use changes in regulation to identify pollution's effects on infant mortality. They argue that the 1970 and 1977 Clean Air Acts caused exogenous changes in pollution levels and that the changes were different in different areas. These changes can be used to examine pollution's effects on housing markets and infant mortality. They find that a one $\mu g/m^3$ reduction in total suspended particulates (a common measure of overall pollution at that time) resulted

24. Currie and Neidell (2005); Greenstone and Gallagher (2008).

in five to eight fewer deaths per 100,000 live births. Jessica Reyes (2005) uses variation in prenatal lead exposure caused by the Clean Air Acts on infant health outcomes and finds that even small amounts of lead are associated with adverse outcomes.

Janet Currie and Matthew Neidell (2005) examine the effects of air pollution on infant deaths in the 1990s. They use individual-level data and within-zip-code variation in pollution over time to identify the effects of pollution. They include zip code fixed effects to account for omitted characteristics like ground water pollution and socioeconomic status and find that reductions in two pollutants—carbon monoxide and particulate matter—in the 1990s saved over 1,000 infant lives in California. Pollution may also have many negative health effects without causing deaths. Matthew Neidell (2004) also uses within-zip-code variation in pollution levels in California to provide evidence that air pollution affects child hospitalizations for asthma. Janet Currie, Matthew Neidell, and Johannes Schmieder (2009) conduct a similar analysis for New Jersey, using individual panel data, and show that in models with mother fixed effects increases in exposure to carbon monoxide are predictive of lower birth weight and prematurity.

Exposure to pesticides may also be an important concern, particularly in rural Appalachia. Virginia Rauth and others (2006) examine children who were prenatally exposed to pesticide (chlorpyrifos) and find that children in a high-exposure group are five times more likely to be developmentally delayed than those in a lower exposure group. This is not an experimental study, but the results suggest that differential exposure to toxic substances might be a significant problem for poor children.

These studies show that pollution can have causal effects on child health, but there has been little investigation of whether these negative health effects have long-term consequences for children's outcomes. The National Children's Study, which was authorized by the Children's Health Act of 2000, will attempt to remedy this situation by examining the effects of environmental exposures on 100,000 children who will be followed from birth to age twenty-one.[25]

Acute Conditions

That mothers in Appalachia must frequently travel to neighboring counties to give birth and that there is a shortage of mental health professionals in Appalachia may be indicative of a general lack of access to care for acute conditions. Poor

25. See www.nationalchildrensstudy.gov.

children are more likely to suffer from acute illnesses, such as dental caries and ear infections, than richer ones. Poor dental health in particular seems to be a significant problem in Appalachia, and groups such as the Remote Area Medical Corps make it a special focus.[26] Richard Crout and others (2008) report that, by the age of eight, one-third of children in West Virginia have untreated dental decay and that one-third of West Virginians under age thirty-five have lost at least six permanent teeth.

Ear infections (otitis media) affect most young children at one time or another and are the most common reason children visit a doctor. Ear infections can be extremely painful, though more than 80 percent of infections resolve themselves within three days if untreated. Among children who have had acute otitis media, almost half have persistent effusion after one month, a condition that can cause hearing loss. Researchers estimate that at any given time roughly 5 percent of two- to four-year-old children have hearing loss because of middle-ear effusion lasting three months or longer.[27] Hearing loss can delay language development.

The prevalence of acute conditions is not well monitored in national data, so it is difficult to ascertain how conditions such as ear infections compare between Appalachia and the rest of the country.

Conclusion

Health is a multidimensional concept, and ideally we would like to account for the effects of all of the health problems suffered by a child and the possible interactions among them. As we see above, long-term effects of low birth weight on education, though relatively small (on the order of a tenth of a year of education, on average), are statistically significant and are found in many different settings. However, this is just one of a number of health insults that a child may be exposed to. For many important categories of health problems, such as injuries and environmental exposures, we do not have accurate evidence regarding the likely long-term effects or the extent of the disparity in exposures.

Moreover, several studies suggest that poor health in childhood may have large effects on future earnings or employment probabilities, even if it has relatively little effect on completed education. Completed education is a crude proxy (with relatively little variation) for the possibly more subtle effects of health in child-

26. See www.ramusa.org/learn/media.html.

27. O'Neill (1999).

hood on cognitive functioning. Further, childhood health may affect adult outcomes through its effect on noncognitive skills and through its effect on adult health.

In contrast to the estimates for most conditions routinely observed at birth or later, the fetal injuries investigated by Almond and his collaborators appear to have very large effects on future outcomes. Recall that children of U.S. mothers infected during the flu epidemic were 15 percent less likely to graduate from high school. Further, Swedish children exposed to low-level radiation after Chernobyl were 5.6 percent less likely to qualify for high school. These results raise the possibility that the best way to safeguard children's health may be to protect the health of their pregnant (or prepregnant) mothers. They also suggest that our standard measures of child health after birth (such as birth weight) are inadequate, since they do not appear to fully capture the effects of these fetal health insults.

As discussed above, several studies demonstrate that there are intergenerational correlations in health status and that there may be interactions between parental health status and parental economic status that affect child health. The fetal origins literature provides a natural explanation of why this might be. But thus far few researchers have attempted to directly assess the intergenerational effects: that is, the effect of parent income on child health and the subsequent effects of child health on that child's adult outcomes.

What are the implications of these findings for Appalachia? First, as we see above, Appalachian adults are in relatively poor health and are more likely to die of cardiovascular disease, stroke, cancer, and diabetes than other U.S. adults. It is common to blame such disparities in outcomes on disparities in access to medical care. However, the research summarized above suggests that these disparities may have their roots in childhood deprivation rather than current deprivation. This observation further suggests that it will be difficult to eradicate adult health disparities in the short run.

While death rates for blacks are higher than for whites, black Appalachians do not appear to be disadvantaged relative to other U.S. blacks. These patterns may reflect the fact that all blacks were disadvantaged relative to whites fifty or sixty years ago and that the gap between Appalachian blacks and other blacks at that time may not have been very large.

The results discussed above suggest that it is important to work to eliminate child health disparities if adult health in Appalachia is ever to be brought up to national levels. The large numbers of pregnant women who smoke or who have obesity-related conditions are of particular concern. Since both smoking and obesity are better treated through prevention than after the fact, a larger role for public health campaigns targeting these health behaviors would seem to be warranted.

Appendix

The data used in this chapter come from National Vital Statistics natality and mortality files. Public-use files do not contain county identifiers, but these are available by permission from the National Center for Health Statistics.

Geographic Category Definitions

—Appalachia: any county in Appalachia. The Appalachian Regional Commission, which was established in 1965 by President Johnson, defines Appalachia based on counties. As of fall 2009 Appalachia contained 420 counties, which span from southern New York to northern Mississippi. It covers all of West Virginia and parts of twelve other states. A map of the region is available at www.arc.gov/research/MapsofAppalachia.asp?MAP_ID=31.

—Central Appalachia: A region in Appalachia composed of all of Kentucky and parts of West Virginia, Virginia, and Tennessee.

—Rural Appalachia: Any county in Appalachia that was not a metropolitan county in 2006. Note that while researchers commonly refer to areas that are "not metropolitan" as "rural," the census definition is much more limited; it defines rural areas as comprising open county and settlements with fewer than 2,500 residents.

—Metropolitan Appalachia: Since 2003 the Office of Management and Budget has defined metropolitan areas as either central counties with one or more urbanized areas or outlying counties that are economically tied to core counties as measured by work commuting. Outlying counties are included if 25 percent of workers living in the county commute to the central county or if 25 percent of the employment in the county consists of workers coming out from the central county—the so-called reverse commuting pattern. The 2006 classifications are used to avoid composition effects due to the change in definition. More information about these definitions can be found at www.ers.usda.gov/Briefing/Rurality/NewDefinitions.

—Other regions of Appalachian states: Appalachia and "other regions of Appalachian states" are mutually exclusive categories. An Appalachian state contains one or more counties that are in Appalachia. "Other regions" are the areas of these states that are not in Appalachia. New York City and Philadelphia are excluded from this group even though they are technically in

Appalachian states. Central Appalachia and rural Appalachia are proper subsets of Appalachia.

Calculation of Age-Adjusted Death Rates

It is important when examining trends in death rates over time to adjust for the age composition of the population. This was done following the procedures in www.health.state.pa.us/hpa/stats/techassist/ageadjusted.htm, except that the year 2000 standard population is used, which is the population that the National Center for Health Statistics and the Centers for Disease Control use for any data from 2003 or later. This procedure involves the following steps:

—Calculate the crude death rates for each of the year 2000 standard population age categories.

—Multiply the population for each age group by its crude death rate to obtain the expected number of deaths for each age group.

—Divide the total number of expected deaths by the total year 2000 standard population (274,633,642).

—Multiply by 100,000 to obtain the age-adjusted rate per 100,000 population.

The following is the result:

All ages	274,633,642	35–44 years	44,659,185
Under 1 year	3,794,901	45–54 years	37,030,152
1–4 years	15,191,619	55–64 years	23,961,506
5–14 years	39,976,619	65–74 years	18,135,514
15–24 years	38,076,743	75–84 years	12,314,793
25–34 years	37,233,437	85 years and over	4,259,173

Procedures for Using Natality Data

The variable means for the geographic categories are constructed from a data set of county-year-month means. Means by geographic category are constructed by taking the means over the cells in those categories, weighting by the number of births in each cell.

Since the county-year-month means are taken over the nonmissing values of variables in the cell, it is possible for means to be assigned based on a very small fraction of births in the cell. This can happen because some residents of one state that does not report a particular variable could give birth in another state that does report that variable. Therefore, if 90 percent or more of births in the cell have missing values for a variable, a missing value for that cell is created. Then the means by geographic category are constructed from the nonmissing cell means, weighting by the number of births in the cell.

Prenatal Care Figures

Beginning in 2003 states began to adopt the Center for Disease Control's recommended 2003 revised birth certificate. Unfortunately, the question about prenatal care differs between the 1989 birth certificate and the 2003 revised birth certificate. The wording of the prenatal care item was changed from "Month prenatal care began" to "Date of first prenatal visit." Also, the 2003 revision process resulted in a recommendation that the prenatal care information be gathered from the prenatal care or medical records, whereas the 1989 revision did not recommend a source for these data. Accordingly, prenatal care data for the two revisions are not directly comparable. The prenatal care figures are thus corrected for the changes in the question in the following way:

Let *Y* be observed first trimester prenatal care. Let *X* be the proportion of first trimester prenatal care under 1989 birth certificate. Let *X*_hat be the proportion of first trimester prenatal care under the 2003 revised birth certificate. If the change in the question is assumed to just result in a mean shift, then

$$X\_\text{hat} = X + \text{beta}\left(\text{New\_birth\_certificate}\right).$$

Then

$$Y = X$$

if New_birth_certificate = 0, and

$$Y = X\_\text{hat}$$

if New_birth_certificate = 1. So

$$Y = X + \text{beta}\left(\text{New\_birth\_certificate}\right).$$

This implies that

$$Y = X - \text{beta}\left(\text{New\_birth\_certificate}\right).$$

The observed value of prenatal care is regressed on a constant and an interaction between the state dummy and new birth certificate. This allows us to obtain a beta_hat_*s* for each state, *s*, that changed birth certificates, effectively allowing the mean shift to differ by state. We then substract beta_hat_*s**state_dummy*New_birth_certificate from *Y* to obtain estimates of *X* and then averaged these *X*s over the geographic areas.

Regressions

Three sets of regression models are estimated, which include the variables listed below plus dummies for state and dummies for changes to the birth certificate described above. The regressions are weighted by the number of births in each cell, and standard errors are clustered by county.

Model 1 controls for black, Hispanic, maternal education (<HS, HS, some college, college plus), state, birth month, year and (state*after adopting new certificate). The latter is included to deal with the measurement problem having to do with the revision of the birth certificate. Model 2 adds maternal age (19–24, 25–34, 35–44, 45+), parity (1, 2, 3, 4, 5+), married, smoking, weight gain (0–15, 16–30, 31–45, 46–60, 60+). These variables reflect maternal choices and behaviors. Model 3 adds indicators that might have to do with access to care: prenatal care in first trimester, birth in a hospital, birth in county of residence.

The variables are

—Low birth weight: less than 2,500 grams

—White (includes Hispanic whites)

—Black (includes Hispanic blacks)

—Hispanic: Hispanic origin, includes Hispanic whites and Hispanic blacks

—Non-Hispanic white: whites, excluding Hispanic whites

—Education: The education variable changed between the 1989 and the 2003 birth certificates. In 1989, years of education were reported, while in 2003 the highest completed degree is reported. We mapped 0–11 years to "Less than High School," 12 years to "High School," 13–15 years to "Some College," and 16+ to "Bachelor's Degree or More."

—Smoking during pregnancy: There is a change from the 1989 to the 2003 revised birth certificate; for the 1989 birth certificate, smoking is 1 if the mother reported tobacco use during pregnancy. For the 2003 birth certificate, the mother is asked how many cigarettes she smoked daily in the first trimester, how many cigarettes she smoked daily in the second trimester, how many cigarettes she smoked daily in the third trimester, and a recode designates whether she is a smoker.

References

Almond, Douglas. 2006. "Is the 1918 Influenza Pandemic Over? Long-Term Effects of In Utero Influenza Exposure in the Post-1940 U.S. Population." *Journal of Political Economy* 114, no. 4: 672–712.

Almond, Douglas, and Kenneth Chay. 2006. "The Long-Run and Intergenerational Impact of Poor Infant Health: Evidence from Cohorts Born during the Civil Rights Era." University of California at Berkeley.

Almond, Douglas, Kenneth Chay, and Michael Greenstone. Forthcoming. "Civil Rights, the War on Poverty, and Black-White Convergence in Infant Mortality in Mississippi." *American Economic Review.*

Almond, Douglas, and Bhashkar Mazumder. 2005. "The 1918 Influenza Pandemic and Subsequent Health Outcomes: An Analysis of SIPP Data." *American Economic Review: Papers and Proceedings* 95, no. 2: 258–62.

Barker, D. J. P. 1998. *Mothers, Babies, and Health in Later Life.* 2d ed. Edinburgh: Churchill Livingston.

Bhattacharya, Jayanta, and Janet Currie. 2001. "Youths at Nutritional Risk: Malnourished or Misnourished?" In *Risky Behavior among Youths: An Economic Analysis,* edited by Jonathan Gruber, pp. 483–522. University of Chicago Press.

Black, Sandra E., Paul J. Devereux, and Kjells G. Salvanes. 2007. "From the Cradle to the Labor Market? The Effect of Birth Weight on Adult Outcomes." *Quarterly Journal of Economics* 122, no. 1: 409–39.

Blank, Rebecca. 2009. "What We Know, What We Don't Know, and What We Need to Know about Welfare Reform." In *Welfare Reform and Its Long-Term Consequences for America's Poor,* edited by J. Ziliak, pp. 22–58. Cambridge University Press.

Bonnie, R. J., C. E. Fulco, and C. T. Liverman. 1999. *Reducing the Burden of Injury.* Washington: Institute of Medicine.

Brooks-Gunn, Jeanne, and Greg Duncan. 1997. "The Effects of Poverty on Children." *Future of Children* 7: 55–71.

Carneiro, Pedro, Costas Meghir, and Matthias Parey. 2007. "Maternal Education, Home Environments, and the Development of Children and Adolescents." Working Paper 15/07. London: Institute of Fiscal Studies.

Case, Anne, Angela Fertig, and Christina Paxson, 2005. "The Lasting Impact of Childhood Health and Circumstance." *Journal of Health Economics* 24, no. 2: 365–89.

Case, Anne, Darren Lubotsky, and Christina Paxson. 2002. "Economic Status and Health in Childhood: The Origins of the Gradient." *American Economic Review* 92, no. 5: 1308–34.

Caspi, Avshalom, and others. 1998. "Early Failure in the Labor Market: Childhood and Adolescent Predictors of Unemployment in the Transition to Adulthood." *American Sociological Review* 63: 424–51.

Cedergren, M. I. 2004. "Maternal Morbid Obesity and the Risk of Adverse Pregnancy Outcome." *Obstetrics and Gynecology* 103: 219–24.

Chay, Kenneth Y., and Michael Greenstone. 2003a. "The Impact of Air Pollution on Infant Mortality: Evidence from Geographic Variation in Pollution Shocks Induced by a Recession." *Quarterly Journal of Economics* 118, no. 3: 1121–67.

———. 2003b. "Air Quality, Infant Mortality, and the Clean Air Act of 1970." Working Paper 10053. Cambridge: National Bureau of Economic Research.

Conley, Dalton, and Neil Bennett. 2000. "Is Biology Destiny? Birth Weight and Life Chances." *American Sociological Review* 65 (June): 458–67.

———. 2001. "Birth Weight and Income: Interactions across Generations." *Journal of Health and Social Behavior* 42: 450–65.

Costello, Jane E., and others. 1996. "The Great Smoky Mountains Study of Youth: Goals, Design, Methods, and the Prevalence of DSM-III-R Disorders." *Archives of General Psychiatry* 53, no. 12: 1129–36.

———. 2003 "Relationships between Poverty and Psychopathology: A Natural Experiment." *JAMA* 290, no. 15: 2023–28.

Crout, Richard, and others. 2008. "Gum Disease in Appalachia." Paper prepared for the 94th Annual Meeting of the American Academy of Periodontology, Seattle, September 8.

Cunha, F., J. J. Heckman, and S. M. Schennach. 2006. "Estimating the Technology of Cognitive and Noncognitive Skill Formation." Department of Economics, University of Chicago.

Currie, Janet. 2009. "Healthy, Wealthy, and Wise? Socioeconomic Status, Poor Health in Childhood, and Human Capital Development." *Journal of Economic Literature* 47, no. 1: 87–122.

Currie, Janet, and Wanchuan Lin. 2007. "Chipping away at Health: More on the Relationship between Income and Child Health." *Health Affairs* 26, no. 2: 331–44.

Currie, Janet, and Bridget Madrian. 1999. "Health, Health Insurance, and the Labor Market." In *Handbook of Labor Economics,* vol. 3, edited by Orley Ashenfelter and David Card. Amsterdam: North Holland.

Currie, Janet, and Enrico Moretti. 2003. "Mother's Education and the Intergenerational Transmission of Human Capital: Evidence from College Openings." *Quarterly Journal of Economics* 118, no. 4: 1495–532.

———. 2007. "Biology as Destiny? Short- and Long-Run Determinants of Intergenerational Transmission of Birth Weight." *Journal of Labor Economics* 25, no. 2: 231–63.

Currie, Janet, and Matthew Neidell. 2005. "Air Pollution and Infant Health: What Can We Learn From California's Recent Experience?" *Quarterly Journal of Economics* 120, no. 3: 1003–30.

Currie, Janet, Matthew Neidell, and Johannes Schmieder. 2009. "Air Pollution and Infant Health: Lessons from New Jersey." *Journal of Health Economics* 28, no. 3: 688–703.

Currie, Janet, and Johannes Schmieder. 2009. "Fetal Exposure to Toxic Releases and Infant Health." *American Economic Association Papers and Proceedings* 99, no. 2: 177–83.

Currie, Janet, and Mark Stabile. 2003. "Socioeconomic Status and Health: Why Is the Relationship Stronger for Older Children?" *American Economic Review* 93, no. 5: 1813–23.

———. 2006. "Child Mental Health and Human Capital Accumulation: The Case of ADHD." *Journal of Health Economics* 25, no. 6: 1094–118.

———. 2009. "Mental Health in Childhood and Human Capital." In *An Economic Perspective on the Problems of Disadvantaged Youth,* edited by Jonathon Gruber. University of Chicago Press.

Currie, Janet, and Johannes Schmieder. 2009. "Fetal Exposure to Toxic Releases and Infant Health," *American Economic Association Papers and Proceedings* 99, no. 2: 177–83.

Currie, Janet, and others. 2010. "Child Health and Young Adult Outcomes." *Journal of Human Resources* 45, no. 3: 517–48.

Cutler, David, and Adriana Lleras-Muney. 2006. "Education and Health: Evaluating Theories and Evidence." Working Paper 12352. Cambridge: National Bureau of Economic Research.

Fowler, M. G., M. G. Davenport, and R. Garg. 1992. "School Functioning of U.S. Children with Asthma." *Pediatrics* 90, no. 6: 939–44.

Fuchs, Victor R. 1992. "Poverty and Health: Asking the Right Questions." In *Medical Care and the Health of the Poor,* edited by D. E. Rogers and E. Ginzberg, pp. 9–20. Boulder: Westview.

Greenstone, M., and J. Gallagher. 2008. "Does Hazardous Waste Matter? Evidence from the Housing Market and the Superfund Program." *Quarterly Journal of Economics* 123, no. 3: 951–1003.

Grossman, Michael. 2000. "The Human Capital Model." In *The Handbook of Health Economics,* edited by Anthony Culyer and Joseph P. Newhouse. Amsterdam: North Holland.

Grossman, Michael, and Robert Kaestner. 1997. "Effects of Education on Health." In *The Social Benefits of Education,* edited by Jere Behrman and Nevzer Stacey, pp. 69–123. University of Michigan Press.

Halterman, Jennifer S., and others. 2001. "School Readiness among Urban Children with Asthma." *Ambulatory Pediatrics* 1, no. 4: 201–05.

Heckman, James J. 2007. "The Technology and Neuroscience of Capacity Formation." *Proceedings of the National Academy of Sciences* (PNAS) 104, no. 33: 13250–55.

Heckman, James, Jora Stixrud, and Sergio Urzua. 2006. "The Effects of Cognitive and Noncognitive Abilities on Labor Market Outcomes and Social Behavior." *Journal of Labor Economics* 24, no. 3: 411–82.

Hedley, A., and others. 2004. "Overweight and Obesity among U.S. Children, Adolescents, and Adults, 1999–2002." *Journal of the American Medical Association* 291: 2847–50.

Hendryx, Michael. 2007. "Appalachian Health Disparities: Recent Research and Policy Implications." *Public Health Grand Rounds.* West Virginia University.

Johnson, Rucker C., and Robert F. Schoeni. 2007. "The Influence of Early-Life Events on Human Capital, Health Status, and Labor Market Outcomes over the Life Course." Research Report 07-616. Population Studies Center, Institute for Research on Labor and Employment.

Korenman, Sanders, and Jane Miller. 1997. "Effects of Long-Term Poverty on Physical Health of Children in the National Longitudinal Survey of Youth." In *Consequences of Growing Up Poor,* edited by Gregg Duncan and Jeanne Brooks-Gunn. New York: Russell Sage.

Ludwig, David, and Janet Currie. 2010. "The Relationship between Gestational Weight Gain and Birthweight: A Within-Family Comparison." *Lancet* 376: 984–90.

Mannuzza, Salvatore, and Rachel Klein. 2000. "Long-Term Prognosis in Attention-Deficit/Hyperactivity Disorder." *Child and Adolescent Psychiatric Clinics of North America* 9, no. 3: 711–26.

McLeod, Jane D., and Karen Kaiser. 2004. "Childhood Emotional and Behavioral Problems and Educational Attainment." *American Sociological Review* 69: 636–58.

McLeod, J. D., and M. J. Shanahan. 1993. "Poverty, Parenting, and Children's Mental Health." *American Sociological Review* 58, no. 3: 351–66.

———. 1996. "Trajectories of Poverty and Children's Mental Health." *Journal of Health and Social Behavior* 37: 207–20.

Miech, Richard, and others. 1999. "Low Socioeconomic Status and Mental Disorders: A Longitudinal Study of Selection and Causation during Young Adulthood." *American Journal of Sociology* 104: 1096–131.

Nagin, Daniel, and Richard E. Tremblay. 1999. "Trajectories of Boys' Physical Aggression, Opposition, and Hyperactivity on the Path to Physically Violent and Nonviolent Juvenile Delinquency." *Child Development* 70: 1181–96.

Needleman, H., and B. Gatsonis. 1991. "Meta-Analysis of 24 Studies of Learning Disabilities due to Lead Poisoning." *JAMA* 265: 673–78.

Neidell, Matthew. 2004. "Air Pollution, Health, and Socio-Economic Status: The Effect of Outdoor Air Quality on Childhood Asthma." *Journal of Health Economics* 23, no. 6: 1209–36.

Newacheck, Paul. 1994. "Poverty and Childhood Chronic Illness." *Archives of Pediatric and Adolescent Medicine* 148, no. 11: 1143–49.

Newacheck, Paul, and Neil Halfon. 1998. "Prevalence and Impact of Disabling Chronic Conditions in Childhood." *American Journal of Public Health* 88, no. 4: 610–17.

O'Neill, Paddy. 1999. "Acute Otitis Media." *British Medical Journal* 319: 833–35.

Orr, Larry, and others. 2003. "Moving to Opportunity: Interim Impacts Evaluation." U.S. Department of Housing and Urban Development.

Pocock, S. J., M. Smith, and P. Baghurst. 1994. "Environmental Lead and Children's Intelligence: A Systematic Review of the Epidemiological Evidence." *British Medical Journal* 309: 1189–97.

Powers, Elizabeth T. 2001. "New Estimates of the Impact of Child Disability on Maternal Employment." *American Economic Review: Papers and Proceedings* 91, no. 2: 135–39.

Rauh, Virginia, and others. 2006. "Impact of Prenatal Chlorpyrifos Exposure on Neurodevelopment in the First 3 Years of Life among Inner-City Children." *Pediatrics* 118, no. 6: 1845–59.

Reyes, Jessica. 2005. "The Impact of Prenatal Lead Exposure on Health." Working Paper. Department of Economics, Amherst College.

Shaffer, D., and others. 1996. "The NIMH Diagnostic Interview Schedule for Children Version 2.3 (DISC-2.3): Description, Acceptability, Prevalence Rates, and Performance in the MECA Study. Methods for the Epidemiology of Child and Adolescent Mental Disorders Study." *Journal of the American Academy of Child and Adolescent Psychiatry* 35: 865–77.

Smith, James P. 2009. "The Impact of Childhood Health on Adult Labor Market Outcomes." *Review of Economics and Statistics* 91, no. 3: 478–89.

Smolensky, Eugene, and Jennifer A. Gootman, eds. 2003. *Working Families and Growing Kids: Caring for Children and Adolescents.* Washington: National Academies Press.

Sorenson, H. T., and others. 1997. "Relation between Weight and Length at Birth and Body Mass Index in Young Adulthood: Cohort Study." *British Medical Journal* 315: 1137.

Stiller, Charles A. 2004. "Epidemiology and Genetics of Childhood Cancer." *Oncogene* 23: 6429–44.

Strohschein, Lisa. 2005. "Household Income Trajectories and Child Mental Health Trajectories." *Journal of Health and Social Behavior* 46, no. 4: 359–75.

U.S. Centers for Disease Control. 2003. *Children's Blood Lead Levels in the United States.*

U.S. Department of Health and Human Services. 1999. *Mental Health: A Report to the Surgeon General.*

Vrijheid, Martine. 2000. "Health Effects of Residence Near Hazardous Waste Landfill Sites: A Review of Epidemiologic Literature." *Environmental Health Perspectives Supplements* 108(S1): 101–12.

Watkins, M. L., and others. 2003. "Maternal Obesity and Risk for Birth Defects." *Pediatrics* 111: 1152–58.

Wolfe, Barbara L., and Steven C. Hill. 1995. "The Effects of Health on the Work Effort of Single Mothers." *Journal of Human Resources* 30, no. 1: 42–62.

Woodruff, Tracey J. 1998. "Public Health Implications of 1990 Air Toxics Concentrations across the United States." *Environmental Health Perspectives* 106, no. 5: 245–51.

MATTHEW E. KAHN

6

Cities, Economic Development, and the Role of Place-Based Policies: Prospects for Appalachia

Cities are the key engine of economic growth because they economize on the transportation cost of goods, workers, and ideas. Cities facilitate learning and accelerate the diffusion of new ideas. Through encouraging specialization and trade, cities raise per capita income.[1]

In a similar spirit as that of the enormous cross-country empirical growth literature, urban economists estimate countless cross-city growth regressions to uncover the correlates of urban growth. While legitimate concerns can and should be raised about such regressions, this research identifies a series of robust facts. A second-generation urban econometrics literature uses more sophisticated econometric strategies, ranging from credible instrumental variables to regression discontinuity designs to attempt to identify the effects of human capital stocks and state policies on local growth and wages.[2]

This chapter surveys the key economic research findings on the associations between economic development and urban areas. What types of city have boomed over the last thirty-five years? The fundamental challenge that Appalachia faces is that it does not embody the time-tested formula for achieving ongoing urban growth. This region does not feature any megacities. Its location

I thank the UCLA Ziman Center for Real Estate for research support and James Ziliak and an anonymous reviewer for useful comments.

1. See Glaeser (1998); Duranton and Puga (2005); Glaeser and Mare (2001).

2. See Glaeser and others (1992); Glaeser, Scheinkman, and Shleifer (1995); Durlauf, Kourtellos, and Tan (2008); Moretti (2004a); Holmes (1998).

is far from the coast, and many of its counties feature cold winters. Relative to the rest of the nation its educational attainment is low and its local economies have not specialized in the information technology sector. Instead, large sections of the region have focused on environmentally harmful natural resource extraction. Half of the states in this region are closed-shop states, meaning that union membership is a precondition of employment for those establishments that are unionized, which discourages entry of manufacturing concerns.[3]

Given the challenges that Appalachia faces in recruiting and retaining skilled workers and the businesses that hire them, are there cost-effective place-based investments that the region could make? This chapter focuses on strategies for encouraging the growth of Appalachia's medium-sized cities that emphasize improving household quality of life. Given the persistent poverty in Central Appalachia, it is crucial to identify strategies that can help these areas to prosper. Valuable lessons can be learned from cities such as Pittsburgh—dirty manufacturing cities that have reinvented themselves as high-skill consumer cities. Geographical proximity to growing metropolitan areas such as Atlanta and Charlotte offers a second pathway to gain from urban growth.

Thriving Cities

Major cities such as San Francisco, Los Angeles, New York City, Chicago, and Boston feature high wages and high home prices and are widely viewed as having high quality of life. None of these cities appear to have an inherent exogenous productivity advantage over other cities such as Houston, Atlanta, Detroit, or St. Louis. Usually, skilled people want to locate near other skilled people and the firms that hire them. These thick local labor markets are an important determinant of industrial agglomeration.[4] But where will these clusters emerge? Initial accidents of history can have cumulative effects, but a first-mover advantage is not sufficient. Philadelphia was the nation's capital, but it is seldom regarded as a superstar city. Detroit boomed as domestic car production increased, but its early industrial edge has not offered long-term advantages.

Skilled People

Cities with a skilled workforce experience greater subsequent population growth, housing price growth, and wage growth.[5] James Rauch (1993) and Enrico

3. Holmes (1998).
4. Dumais, Ellison, and Glaeser (2002).
5. Glaeser and Saiz (2004).

Moretti (2004a) show that, conditional on observable worker characteristics, wages are higher in high human capital cities. A 1 percentage point increase in a local economy's college-educated population increases local population growth over a ten-year period by 1.5 percentage points and increases real wages of non-college-educated local residents by 1.4 percent and real wages of local college graduates by 0.3 percent.[6] Jesse Shapiro (2006) concludes that the presence of college graduates increases a city's employment growth rate and that the rate is almost evenly split between productivity growth and quality-of-life upgrades. From 1940 to 1990 a 10 percent increase in a metropolitan area's concentration of college-educated residents was associated with a 0.8 percent increase in subsequent employment growth.

Quality of Life

In this footloose age, a company such as Google seeks to locate in a high quality-of-life area, where its highly skilled workforce will be happy to live and work. Common sense and hedonic pricing research pinpoints the best cities in America. These tend to be coastal cities in attractive, temperate climates featuring sophisticated cultural opportunities. David Albouy's (2009) top nine amenity cities are San Francisco, Santa Barbara, Monterey, Honolulu, San Diego, New York City, Los Angeles, San Luis Obispo, and Boston. Seattle ranks twelfth, Portland ranks nineteenth, and Houston ranks seventy-fourth. Hedonic researchers identify such cities using revealed preference logic: if a city features relatively high home prices, offers relatively low wages, and experiences low outmigration then it is rated as having a high quality of life.

Today major cities such as Los Angeles and New York City compete to be "green" cities.[7] Such cities seek to enhance their environmental quality so as to improve public health and retain the mobile skilled. Today's megacities do not represent Faustian bargains of economic opportunity but poor quality of life. In fact, these cities offer both opportunity and good quality of life. Indeed, major cities in the developed world have reinvented themselves as consumer cities, where the skilled want to live. A virtuous cycle is created as unfettered employers locate in areas where the skilled want to live. This further attracts more skilled workers and high-end commercial restaurants and retail stores to cater to this niche market.[8]

6. Glaeser and Saiz (2004); Moretti (2004b).

7. For example see New York City's plan (www.nyc.gov/html/planyc2030/html/greenyc/greenyc.shtml), and Los Angeles's plan (www.lacity.org/ead/EADWeb-AQD/GreenLA_CAP_2007.pdf).

8. Waldfogel (2008).

In a nation of 300 million people, not everyone can afford to, or wants to, live in these superstar cities. Limits to housing supply in these cities both due to regulations and due to geography raise the cost of new construction.[9] In Los Angeles, New York City, San Francisco, and Boston, an inelastic supply of housing combines with rising demand (due to the skewing of the nation's income distribution) to lead to very high home prices. Facing this price gradient, millions of people have moved to cities such as Dallas, Houston, Phoenix, and Las Vegas, where the winters are milder and it is easier to build. Labor wages and housing rents adjust across cities to reflect spatially tied compensating differentials.[10]

The Challenge for Small Cities

Appalachia does not have many cities, and those that exist are relatively small and far from the desired coastal areas. Relative to bigger cities, small cities feature a less diversified local economy.[11] They tend to specialize in specific industries. When these industries are booming, these towns boom (think of coal towns), but when the world price of the goods that these towns specialize in declines, the town experiences a sharp recession.[12] In these cities, a large share of the workforce works in manufacturing. As world trade has become more global, such cities face increased international competition from areas with much lower wages. This lack of diversification creates high unemployment risk for workers who do not want to move to another labor market. Small cities lack thick local labor markets and diverse industries. This creates colocation problems for couples when both spouses work.[13]

To provide some facts about how Appalachia's biggest cities compare within the national rankings and relative to each other, table 6-1 lists the twenty-eight largest cities in Appalachia and provides some basic quality-of-life and sociodemographic information. Appalachia's cities are small: the aggregate population living in the region is roughly equal to the total population living in the New York City consolidated metropolitan statistical area. Only three Appalachian counties have more than 500,000 people.

Table 6-1 also reports where these cities rank relative to David Albouy's (2009) overall ranking of 288 U.S. cities with respect to quality of life and productivity index. Intuitively, in a compensating differentials equilibrium, a city

9. See Glaeser and Gyourko (2005); Saiz (2010).
10. Blomquist, Berger, and Hoehn (1988).
11. Henderson (1997).
12. See Black, McKinnish, and Sanders (2005).
13. Costa and Kahn (2000); Goldin (2006).

Table 6-1. *Measures of Quality of Life and Human Capital, Twenty-Eight Appalachian Cities, 2000*
Units as indicated

City	State	Albouy's productivity ranking	Albouy quality of life ranking	Fips county codes	County population	College (%)	Annual household income ($)	Average temperature (Fahrenheit)	
								January	July
Pittsburgh	PA	87	188	42,003	1,286,857	0.29	54,747.61	27.85	72.62
Birmingham	AL	65	173	1,073	685,860	0.24	51,849.98	42.44	80.32
Lawrenceville	GA			13,135	613,526	0.34	72,579.16	40.65	78.00
Greenville	SC	98	135	45,045	396,050	0.26	55,880.31	39.65	77.28
Knoxville	TN	171	91	47,093	389,285	0.29	53,063.55	36.54	76.66
Greensburg	PA			42,129	371,652	0.20	48,504.64	26.78	71.03
Wilkes-Barre	PA	168	160	42,079	320,655	0.16	44,283.75	25.52	71.47
Winston-Salem	NC	88	127	37,067	315,714	0.28	56,044.09	37.49	76.90
Chattanooga	TN	144	140	47,065	313,741	0.24	53,406.50	38.54	78.81
Erie	PA	167	183	42,049	282,078	0.21	46,484.30	24.55	69.84
Huntsville	AL	94	215	1,089	279,559	0.34	58,135.64	39.04	78.83
Youngstown	OH	136	213	39,099	258,321	0.17	46,440.12	25.47	70.98
Spartanburg	SC	98	135	45,083	253,795	0.18	47,706.75	39.84	77.51
Warren	OH	136	213	39,155	226,467	0.14	48,092.43	24.86	70.61
Scranton	PA	168	160	42,069	214,234	0.20	46,368.24	25.03	71.11
Asheville	NC	193	23	37,021	213,272	0.25	48,057.68	36.68	74.37
Washington	PA			42,125	204,206	0.19	50,276.88	27.27	71.68
Binghamton	NY	77	203	36,007	201,606	0.23	47,791.12	22.02	69.07

(continued)

Table 6-1. *Measures of Quality of Life and Human Capital, Twenty-Eight Appalachian Cities, 2000* (continued)
Units as indicated

City	*State*	*Albouy's productivity ranking*	*Albouy quality of life ranking*	*Fips county codes*	*County population*	*College (%)*	*Annual household income ($)*	*Average temperature (Fahrenheit)*	
								January	*July*
Charleston	WV			54,039	199,878	0.21	47,392.71	32.51	74.70
Aliquippa	PA			42,007	181,476	0.16	45,862.00	27.46	72.22
Milford	OH			39,025	177,234	0.21	60,336.09	28.75	75.17
Butler	PA			42,019	174,849	0.24	54,419.41	25.47	70.37
Anderson	SC	98	135	45,007	169,708	0.16	46,269.62	41.52	79.29
Tuscaloosa	AL	146	111	1,125	166,141	0.24	47,264.58	43.13	81.04
Kingsport	TN			47,163	158,670	0.18	45,822.73	35.30	75.17
Morgantown	WV			54,061	81,573	0.35	40,500.25	29.88	72.58
Richmond	KY			21,151	71,768	0.22	42,141.19	32.50	75.83
Boone	NC			37,189	44,217	0.37	42,304.48	32.96	70.32
National mean						0.17	44,976.50	31.82	75.82
National SD						0.08	10,545.56	11.60	5.04

Source: Author's calculations and Albouy (2009).

Table 6-2. *Migration Models, Males Remaining in or Moving to Appalachia, 1995–2000*[a]

	Remaining in Appalachia		*Entering Appalachia*	
	Beta	*Standard error*	*Beta*	*Standard error*
Age	0.094	0.004	0.061	0.001
Age squared	–0.001	0.000	0.000	0.000
College graduate	–6.260	0.116	0.171	0.053
College graduate*age	0.257	0.007	–0.032	0.003
College graduate*age squared	–0.003	0.000	0.000	0.000
Graduate degree	1.340	0.185	1.914	0.096
Graduate degree*age	–0.111	0.010	–0.099	0.005
Graduate degree*age squared	0.002	0.000	0.001	0.000
Constant	–0.085	0.063	–4.451	0.021
Observations	1,877,414		48,823,807	
Pseudo R squared	0.068		0.010	

a. Age, education, and geographical location are based on 1995 and 2000 MIGPUMAs and PUMAs; that is, public-use microdata areas and migration PUMAs. The table reports two logit models.

paying low wages and charging high rents must have a high quality of life. Otherwise, why would anyone live there? A highly productive city features high rents and high wages. Otherwise, why would any firm locate there, when factor input costs are lower in other locations? Based on this logic, Albouy's rankings confirm the fundamental challenge that Appalachia's cities face: Appalachia's cities consistently rank in the bottom half of both the quality of life and the productivity national distribution.

Migration data provide clear evidence that the skilled are "voting with their feet," leaving Appalachia if they originally lived there and choosing not to move there if they live outside of the region. To document this point, I use microdata from the IPUMS census of population and housing sample from the year 2000. I restrict the sample to men ages twenty-five to fifty. I use the Mable Geocorr geography engine to determine whether each man lived in Appalachia in 1995 and 2000.[14] As reported in table 6-2, I estimate two logit models, one being the probability that a man who lived in Appalachia in 1995 also lived there in 2000.

14. See http://mcdc2.missouri.edu/websas/geocorr2k.html.

Figure 6-1. *Predicted Probability of Remaining in Appalachia in 1995 and 2000*

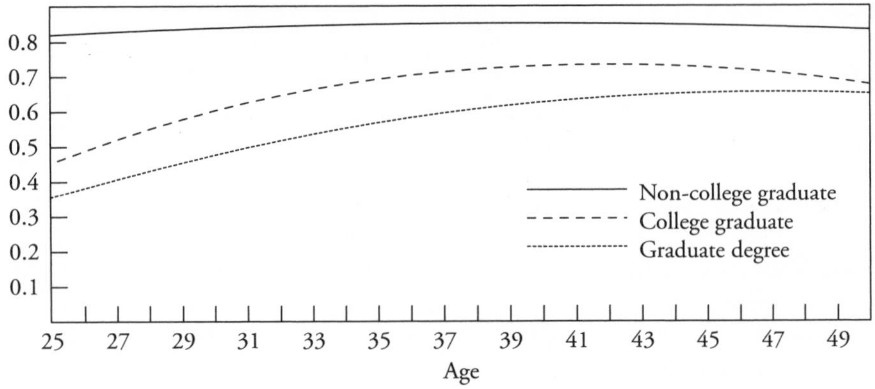

Source: Author's calculations.

I use the estimates from this model to predict the probability that a man remains in Appalachia as a function of his age and education. In figure 6-1, I graph the predicted probabilities as a function of age and education. Relative to less educated men, college graduates are much more likely to leave and men with professional degrees even more likely to leave.

Appalachia is not recruiting enough new skilled individuals to replace those who leave. In a second logit, I estimate the probability of migrating to Appalachia in 2000 for men who lived outside of the region in 1995 (see table 6-2). Figure 6-2 presents the predicted probability of entering the Appalachia region for men who lived outside of the region in 1995. The bottom line is that more educated men are less likely to enter the region. These reduced-form regressions cannot answer why such men are not moving into the region nor can they answer whether men would move in if Appalachia's cities offered higher wages. As a descriptive exercise, they highlight the challenge that Appalachia faces in deciding how it can cost-effectively compete for skilled workers. Figures 6-1 and 6-2 highlight the brain drain the region faces. The skilled are leaving, and too few skilled outsiders are moving in.

These migration results are consistent with findings on the returns to skill in Appalachia relative to the rest of the nation. Christopher Bollinger, James Ziliak, and Kenneth Troske (2011), estimating Mincer-style wage regressions while controlling for Roy-model self-selection, document the low economic returns to working in Appalachia's cities. "Indeed, the wage gap between rural Appalachia and the rest of rural America is virtually nonexistent—the wage gap is driven by

Figure 6-2. *Predicted Probability of Entering Appalachia between 1995 and 2000*

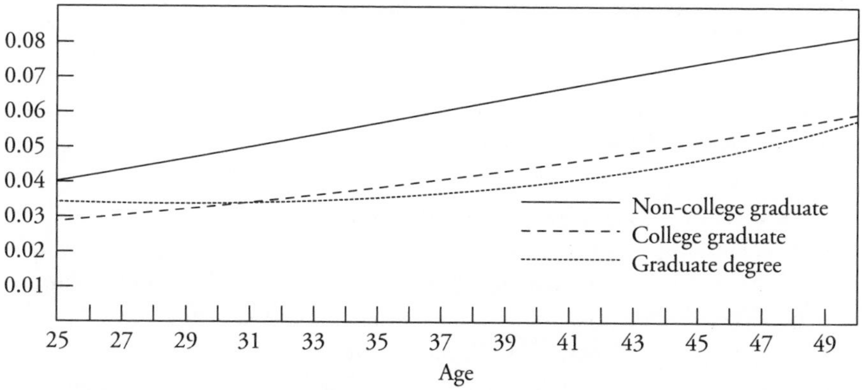

Source: Author's calculations.

weakness in the urban areas."[15] Appalachia's cities could be more competitive if investments in place-based programs increased the region's cities' quality of life or if they boosted productivity.

Place-Based Investment

One strategy for encouraging economic development and reducing local poverty rates is for the federal and state governments to invest in particular placed-based projects. Given its size and political importance, Appalachia represents an important case study for examining the consequences of past place-based investments. Starting in 1965 the U.S. government has invested billions of dollars in Appalachia through the Appalachian Regional Development Act (ARDA). Between 1965 and 2009 roughly $23.5 billion was spent on ARDA programs, around $12.7 billion coming from federal funds and $10.8 billion from state and local funds. Of the total, roughly half was spent on highways and the other half on human services (see James Ziliak, chapter 2, this volume). The Harvard University Kennedy School's 1999 fiscal year report, *The Federal Budget and the States,* documents that West Virginia was in the top six states

15. Bollinger, Ziliak, and Troske (2011).

between 1991 and 1999 with respect to federal spending per capita exceeding federal revenue per capita.[16] The 1999 differential was $2,808 in 1999 dollars.[17] Kentucky was ranked fourteenth in terms of net surplus, receiving $1,595 per capita above what it paid in federal per capita taxes. In contrast, California was ranked thirty-ninth in 1999, paying in $685 per capita more than it received in federal spending.

Place-based investments are costly, irreversible, and risky. Billions of dollars have been spent on place-based infrastructure, not only constructing new rail transit systems, highways, and airports but also bidding to attract industrial facilities. Such investments are irreversible. It is also risky from the public's point of view because it is difficult to predict the effects of the investment.

From the national perspective, are such irreversible investments a good use of funds? As emphasized by Joseph Gyourko and Joseph Tracy (1991), in an open system of cities featuring zero migration costs, if a local government spends a dollar in taxes on services that the public does not desire, then rents will fall by a dollar to compensate the marginal household for facing this tax burden. In this case, local landowners bear the burden of government spending. Conversely, if the federal government funds place-based investments (as is the case with subsidies for rail transit systems, which can be as large as 80 percent of total cost), then local areas will gain access to improved local public goods that will be paid for by all taxpayers. These examples highlight the importance of keeping straight not just what specific place-based investments are being considered but also how they will be financed.

Urban and regional economists, looking at national evidence, are skeptical whether local efforts to stimulate the economy offer benefits to the locals. The work of Timothy Bartik (1991), Olivier Blanchard and Lawrence Katz (1992), and John Bound and Harry Holzer (2000) have convinced many economists that in-migration, in response to increases in local labor demand, is the dominant mechanism for the labor market response to local shocks. In this case, the major beneficiaries of local employment growth are not the local unemployed nor are they incumbent residents who are out of the labor force.

Has past investment in Appalachia been spent effectively? Andrew Isserman and Terance Rephann (1995) conclude that it has raised Appalachia's population and per capita income growth.[18] Edward Glaeser and Joshua Gottlieb (2008),

16. Leonard and Walder (1999).

17. States that were net importers of federal dollars in 1999 include Montana, New Mexico, Virginia, North Dakota, and Mississippi.

using a different methodology in matching Appalachian counties to "twin" control counties, find little evidence that federal investment has helped the Appalachian region to grow. Ziliak (chapter 2, this volume) estimates that ARDA reduced Appalachian poverty over the period 1960–2000 by 4 percentage points relative to border counties, with at least half of the effect realized within the first five years of the act's passage. Leading economists disagree about the impacts of place-based investments in Appalachia. These studies focus on the total effect of special designation status on key outcome indicators such as per capita income and the poverty rate but do not attempt to pinpoint what particular place-based investments are most likely to be effective.

Such reductions in poverty are especially important if the people of Appalachia are unwilling or unable to migrate away from Appalachia. When one is unable to move away from a declining area, place-based programs have direct consequences for household quality of life. When people can easily get up and go, they can protect themselves as news arrives about the economic health of their current location. Such individuals can migrate away from declining areas and move to booming local markets. The young and the educated are the most mobile. In contrast, if poor people do face significant migration costs, then reductions in poverty will enable them to protect themselves from local recessions and decline. In the presence of such costs, poverty reduction efforts that simultaneously target poor people and poor places are more likely to be effective.

Many Appalachian households do not want to leave the region because of nonmarket factors, such as social networks and a specific taste for the amenities their birth region offers. Other Appalachian households may be too poor to finance the moving costs to relocate to an area offering greater employment opportunities. Such households face greater obstacles to escaping from unemployment and poverty. If the experience of being unemployed raises the probability of being unemployed in the future, then declining local labor demand in Appalachia (perhaps caused by a declining world coal price) could have long-run effects on poverty and the next generation's child development.

If people who live outside Appalachia do not want to move in, and if Appalachians would prefer to stay (all else equal), then investments that stimulate

18. Isserman and Rephann (1995) use a technique that resembles a propensity score to identify a nearby twin county for every county in Appalachia. By studying economic outcomes for these twin counties relative to the outcomes for the Appalachian counties, the authors claim to be able to test for the role of the $13 billion that was invested by the Appalachian Regional Commission since 1965.

local labor demand are likely to offer increased wages and opportunities for the region's unemployed and those out of the labor force. Ironically, outsiders' perceptions of Appalachia may actually help it to benefit from place-based investments. Appalachia's boosters have acknowledged that their region faces a fundamental perception issue for outsiders who might be considering moving to the region.[19]

Research exploiting the natural experiment of sharp swings in coal prices documents this asymmetry. Appalachians leave the area when the region is in decline, but people who live outside Appalachia do not enter the region when it is booming: "We do find evidence that the coal boom reduced out-migration of prime-aged men and generated return-migration of prime-aged men that had previously left the region. We also find that the boom increased wages, and reduced both the level and rate of poverty in coal areas, suggesting that the existing residents did benefit from the coal boom."[20]

If this finding generalizes, then Appalachia must focus on a homegrown strategy of educating its own young and then encouraging a large fraction of this group to remain in the region through economic opportunity, social networks, family, and a taste for living in one's region of birth.

If Appalachia could convince more of its young to remain, would this bid up housing prices? Unlike in cities such as New York City and San Francisco, it is relatively easy to build in Appalachia. Such an elastic housing supply means that increased local labor demand will translate into increased home construction and new job creation rather than simply bidding up the prices of existing homes. Joseph Gyourko, Albert Saiz, and Anita Summers (2008) constructed a local housing regulation index for 2,668 places in the United States. I use their overall measure of housing regulatory severity; it has a mean of 0 and a standard deviation of 1 (denoted as *WRLURI*). Positive values for this index indicate more regulated areas. I regress this on an Appalachia dummy that equals 1 if the place is located in one of Appalachia's counties and another dummy variable that equals 1 if the place is located in one of Central Appalachia's counties.[21]

19. A blogger (appalachianview.blogspot.com/2007/04/new-appalachian-stereotype.html) lists the following stereotypes that some outsiders believe: "Appalachian people do not have shoes, indoor plumbing or electricity. Appalachian people cannot read a book and understand what they have read. Appalachian people live in homes with dirt floors." He continues, "These stereotypes apply to a few at best and are downright lies at worst."

20. Black, McKinnish, Sanders (2005).

21. Only eight places in this data set are located in Central Appalachia.

$$WRLURI = -0.035 - 0.500 * \text{Appalachia} - 0.355 * \text{Central Appalachia},$$

where $n = 2{,}668$ and $R^2 = 0.017$.

The Appalachia dummy has a *t* statistic of −6.39, and the Central Appalachia dummy has a *t* statistic equal to −0.99. The omitted category is places that are not located in Appalachia. The *F* statistic for the Appalachia and the Central Appalachia dummies equals 23.18 and is statistically significant at the 1 percent level. This simple regression has important implications. Any increase in local demand to live in Appalachia will be associated with increased regional population growth rather than home price growth.

Place-Based Urban Investment

I divide place-based investments into those that raise urban productivity and reduce poverty and those intended to improve urban quality of life.

Investment in Productivity

Recent empirical research documents the productivity effects associated with investing in luring so-called million-dollar plants.[22] Relative to comparable counties that just missed attracting such new manufacturing facilities, these "treated" counties enjoy improved public finances and spillover gains for other manufacturing industries. Michael Greenstone and Enrico Moretti (2006) identify eighty-two million-dollar plants that opened between 1982 and 1993. Twelve of these plants opened in one of Appalachia's counties.[23] Nine of these twelve plant openings took place in so-called right-to-work states. But seven of the thirteen states that compose Appalachia are closed-shop states, meaning that if the workers join a union all employees must pay dues. These facts are consistent with Thomas Holmes's (1998) finding based on a regression discontinuity framework in which he documents evidence that manufacturing clusters on the right-to-work side of

22. See Greenstone and Moretti (2006); Greenstone, Hornbeck, and Moretti (2010).

23. Future research might investigate whether these twelve treated counties outperformed comparable Appalachian counties over the same time period. Greenstone and Moretti's (2006) control group are counties that just lost out on attracting these new plants. Many of these loser counties are located outside of Appalachia. The twelve winning counties include Allegany, New York; Bartow, Georgia; Berkeley, West Virginia; Chambers, Alabama; Cherokee, Georgia; Clark, Kentucky; Gwinnett, Georgia; Jefferson, Alabama; Spartanburg, South Carolina; Sullivan, Tennessee; Tuscaloosa, Alabama; and Washington, Tennessee.

the border. Given that most of Appalachia's northern states are prounion, attempts to lure new industrial plants to such areas are, all else equal, unlikely to be an effective development strategy.

Investing in broadband Internet access is another strategy for improving Appalachia's productivity and quality of life. Jed Kolko (2010) assesses whether policies to raise broadband availability contribute to local economic development. His empirical strategy relies on the fact that broadband technology has diffused unevenly throughout the United States, thus allowing him to compare economic indicators between areas with high and low broadband availability. He finds a positive relationship between broadband expansion and economic growth. This relationship is stronger in industries that rely on information technology and in areas with low population densities.

Investment in College Towns

Recent research documents the productivity spillover effects of investments in research universities. Roland Andersson, John Quigley, and Mats Wilhelmsson (2009) use a natural experiment provided by the Swedish government's decision to decentralize postsecondary education throughout the country. This policy created new universities in geographical areas that did not previously have universities. Using a double-difference framework, the authors document that the introduction of universities raised local productivity and the number of local patents.

Investing in local universities offers several possible complementary benefits. Improving the quality of research universities will attract and retain high-skilled faculty and students. A base of skilled faculty will attract private consulting firms. Such firms will hire students and faculty for consulting work. This job growth will encourage more students to remain in the area upon graduation and will attract other start-up firms. Small cities such as Ann Arbor, Michigan, have successfully pursued this growth strategy. Enrico Moretti (2004b) documents the external benefits that accrue to an area with high educational attainment.

Investment in Transportation Infrastructure

Recent empirical work has convincingly demonstrated the growth consequences of new roads.[24] Central Appalachian communities have had some success in recruiting branch manufacturing or distribution plants, especially in areas that are metropolitan and adjacent to interstate highways. These venues have been especially attractive because of relatively low wages and land costs. Amitabh Chandra

24. Baum-Snow (2007); Duranton and Turner (2007).

and Eric Thompson (2000) do report evidence supportive of the claim that highways draw economic activity away from adjacent counties. In this case, such a zero-sum game would suggest that infrastructure cannot be at the heart of a regional development strategy. This claim merits future research.

Transportation infrastructure will improve connections between Appalachia and nearby metropolitan areas. Dan Black and Seth Sanders (chapter 3, this volume) document the economic growth in Appalachian counties close to the vibrant southern metropolitan areas of Atlanta and Charlotte. Edward Glaeser and Matthew Kahn (2004) document the growth of employment suburbanization in the United States. This trend offers opportunities to people who live in Southern Appalachia, especially those in the Appalachian counties of exurban Atlanta. There was explosive employment growth in this region between 1969 and 2000 (from 7.6 million to 12.3 million). While many center-city boosters lament the suburbanization of employment, it is important not to forget that there are beneficiaries of this trend. This growth of employment on the fringes of large cities may foreshadow an important trend for Appalachia: its proximity to major booming cities may offer some of its counties an opportunity to thrive.

Investment in Quality of Life

Appalachia's cities could capitalize on the ongoing industrial transition away from mining and focus on the significant public health and aesthetic gains that green cities bring.[25] Pittsburgh's transition from steel to services and high technology offers a salient case study. In 1951, 47 percent of Pittsburgh's workforce was employed in manufacturing. By 2000 only 7.8 percent worked in manufacturing. Between 1969 and 2000 Pittsburgh's manufacturing jobs declined from 188,000 to 68,000, while service jobs grew from 169,000 to 356,000. James Feyrer, Bruce Sacerdote, and Ariel Stern (2007) provide a detailed examination of the Rust Belt's industrial decline. This industrial transition has imposed costs. Research documents that displaced workers can earn $10 less an hour in the service economy relative to their former manufacturing jobs.[26] By the same token, service-based cities are much cleaner and greener than manufacturing cities.[27] Urban air and water pollution problems recede when highly polluting industries such as steel and chemicals contract. Kenneth Chay and

25. For a recent exposé on the hidden environmental costs from water pollution associated with industrial activity, see www.nytimes.com/2009/09/13/us/13water.html?_r=1&ref=us.

26. Neal (1995).

27. Kahn (1999, 2006).

Michael Greenstone (2003 and Janet Currie and Matthew Neidell (2005) document the large infant mortality reduction associated with reducing urban air pollution.

Appalachia's scenic vistas and tourism opportunities offer economic opportunity for the region. Andrew Hackbert and Xiliang Lin (2009) emphasize the possible role of tourism for states such as Kentucky, which feature unique horse riding trails and venues for adventure tourism. In 2008 Kentucky tourism was a $10.1 billion industry, employing 176,840 people.

Developing a reputation for affordable, high quality of life would make Appalachia's small cities more attractive to bargain hunters. This niche could be even more valuable as the baby boomer cohort reaches retirement age. Mark Berger and Glenn Blomquist (1992) document that retired seniors migrate to areas where the amenities are capitalized into wages. Several parts of Appalachia offer plentiful cheap land that is currently not being used for highly productive purposes. New service jobs could be created, offering value added to these senior citizen consumers.

Each of the place-based investments discussed in this section raises two empirical research issues. First, per dollar spent on each of these activities, how much new capital would the people of Appalachia gain from such investments? Intuitively, if universities are expensive to build, then a fixed-dollar investment in new universities will yield only a small increase in the quantity and quality of local universities. Second, we need to know how much heterogeneous households value improvements along the different dimensions presented in this section.

Conclusion

In an open system of cities, skilled footloose workers seek out high-paying jobs in high quality-of-life cities. Firms seek out locations that are business friendly, featuring low input costs, and in areas of the country where their prospective workforce wants to live. Appalachia's cities thus face an uphill fight as they compete for talent and try to lure firms on the national market. They are relatively small, located far from the high-amenity coasts, and endowed with relatively few major universities. Appalachian counties located in closed-shop states will have a difficult time attracting new manufacturing plants. While Appalachia includes many areas of spectacular beauty, the legacy of mining has created a perception and a reality of significant environmental degradation. Parts of the region, especially in Eastern Kentucky and West Virginia, suffer from extremely high rates of poverty.

Facing these realities, what is a promising growth strategy for the Appalachian region? Neither policymakers nor economists are good at picking industrial winners. Cities that offer a high quality of life can be more confident that, regardless of what sector of the economy booms next, their city will adapt to changing market conditions. Urban economists agree that cities that can attract and retain skilled workers will have a bright future. Appalachia's universities must train and retain more graduates, because outsiders, especially those with college degrees, are unlikely to migrate into the region. This chapter advocates place-based investments focused on bolstering Appalachia's university cities and on enhancing the region's productivity and quality of life.

References

Albouy, David. 2009. "What Are Cities Worth? Land Rents, Local Productivity, and the Capitalization of Amenity Values." Working Paper 14981. Cambridge: National Bureau of Economic Research.

Andersson, Roland, John M. Quigley, and Mats Wilhelmsson. 2009. "Urbanization, Productivity, and Innovation: Evidence from Investment in Higher Education." *Journal of Urban Economics* 66, no. 1: 2–15.

Bartik, Timothy. 1991. "Who Benefits from State and Local Economic Development Policies?" Kalamazoo: W. E. Upjohn Institute for Employment Research.

Baum-Snow, Nathaniel. 2007. "Did Highways Cause Suburbanization?" *Quarterly Journal of Economics* 122, no. 2: 775–805.

Berger, Mark, and Glenn Blomquist. 1992. "Mobility and Destination in Migration Decisions: The Roles of Earnings, Quality of Life, and Housing Prices." *Journal of Housing Economics* 2, no. 1: 37–59.

Black, Dan, Terra McKinnish, and Seth Sanders. 2005. "The Economic Impact of the Coal Boom and Bust." *Economic Journal* 115, no. 503: 449–76.

Blanchard, Olivier J., and Lawrence F. Katz. 1992. "Regional Evolutions." *BPEA*, no. 1: 1–61.

Blomquist, Glenn, Mark Berger, and Jon Hoehn. 1988. "New Estimates of Quality of Life in Urban Areas." *American Economic Review* 78: 89–107.

Bollinger, Christopher, James Ziliak, and Kenneth Troske. 2011. "Down from the Mountain: Skill Upgrading and Wages in Appalachia." *Journal of Labor Economics* 29, no. 4: 819–57.

Bound, John, and Harry Holzer. 2000. "Demand Shifts, Population Adjustments, and Labor Market Outcomes during the 1980s." *Journal of Labor Economics* 18, no. 1: 20–54.

Chandra, Amitabh, and Eric Thompson. 2000. "Does Public Infrastructure Affect Economic Activity? Evidence from the Interstate Highway System." *Regional Science and Urban Economics* 30, no. 4: 457–90.

Chay, Kenneth Y., and Michael Greenstone. 2003. "Air Quality, Infant Mortality, and the Clean Air Act of 1970." Working Paper 10053. Cambridge: National Bureau of Economic Research.

Costa, Dora L., and Matthew E. Kahn. 2000. "Power Couples: Changes in the Locational Choice of the College Educated, 1940–1990." *Quarterly Journal of Economics* 115, no. 4: 1287–315.

Currie, Janet, and Matthew Neidell. 2005. "Air Pollution and Infant Health: What Can We Learn from California's Recent Experience?" *Quarterly Journal of Economics* 120, no. 3: 1003–30.

Dumais, Guy, Glenn Ellison, and Edward L. Glaeser. 2002. "Geographic Concentration as a Dynamic Process." *Review of Economics and Statistics* 84, no. 2: 193–204.

Duranton, Gilles, and Diego Puga. 2005. "From Sectoral to Functional Urban Specialization." *Journal of Urban Economics* 57, no. 2: 343–70

Duranton, Gilles, and Matthew Turner. 2007. "Urban Growth and Transportation." Working Paper 305. University of Toronto.

Durlauf, Steven, Andros Kourtellos, and ChihMing Tan. 2008. "Are Any Growth Theories Robust?" *Economic Journal* 118, no. 527: 329–46.

Feyrer, James D., Bruce Sacerdote, and Ariel Dora Stern. 2007. "Did the Rust Belt Become Shiny? A Study of Cities and Counties That Lost Steel and Auto Jobs in the 1980s." Brookings-Wharton Papers on Urban Affairs 2007, pp. 41–89.

Glaeser, Edward L. 1998. "Are Cities Dying?" *Journal of Economic Perspectives* 12, no. 2: 139–60.

———. 2007. "Can Buffalo Ever Come Back?" *City Journal* (Autumn).

Glaeser, Edward L., and Joshua D. Gottlieb. 2008. "The Economics of Place-Making Policies." Working Paper 14373. Cambridge: National Bureau of Economic Research.

Glaeser, Edward L., and Joseph Gyourko. 2005. "Urban Decline and Durable Housing." *Journal of Political Economy* 113, no. 2: 345–75.

Glaeser, Edward, and Matthew E. Kahn. 2004. "Sprawl and Urban Growth." In *Handbook of Urban Economics,* vol. 4, edited by Vernon Henderson and J. Thisse. Amsterdam: North Holland.

Glaeser, Edward L., and David C. Mare. 2001. "Cities and Skills." *Journal of Labor Economics* 19, no. 2: 316–42.

Glaeser, Edward L., and Albert Saiz. 2004. "The Rise of the Skilled City." Brookings-Wharton Papers on Urban Affairs 2004, pp. 47–94.

Glaeser, Edward L., Jose A. Scheinkman, and Andrei Shleifer. 1995. "Growth in a Cross-Section of Cities." *Journal of Monetary Economics* 36, no. 1: 117–43.

Glaeser, Edward L., and others. 1992. "Growth in Cities." *Journal of Political Economy* 100, no. 6: 1126–52.

Goldin, Claudia. 2006. "The Quiet Revolution That Transformed Women's Employment, Education, and Family." *American Economic Review Papers and Proceedings* 96, no. 2: 1–21.

Greenstone, Michael, Richard Hornbeck, and Enrico Moretti. 2010. "Identifying Agglomeration Spillovers: Evidence from Million-Dollar Plants." *Journal of Political Economy* 118, no. 3: 536–98.

Greenstone, Michael, and Enrico Moretti. 2006. "Bidding for Industrial Plants: Does Winning a 'Million-Dollar Plant' Increase Welfare?" Working Paper 9844. Cambridge: National Bureau of Economic Research.

Gyourko, Joseph, Albert Saiz, and Anita A. Summers 2008. "A New Measure of the Local Regulatory Environment for Housing Markets." *Urban Studies* 45, no. 3: 693–729.

Gyourko, Joseph, and Joseph Tracy. 1991. "The Structure of Local Public Finance and the Quality of Life." *Journal of Political Economy* 91, no. 4: 774–806.

Hackbert, Andrew, and Xiliang Lin. 2009. "Equestrian Trail Riding: An Emerging Economic Contributor to the Local Rural Appalachian Economy." *Journal of Business Case Studies* 5, no. 6: 47–58.

Henderson, Vernon. 1997. "Medium-Sized Cities." *Regional Science and Urban Economics* 27: 583–612.

Holmes, Thomas. 1998. "The Effect of State Policies on the Location of Manufacturing: Evidence from State Borders." *Journal of Political Economy* 106, no. 4: 667–705.

Isserman, Andrew, and Terance Rephann. 1995. "The Economic Effects of the Appalachian Regional Commission." *Journal of American Planning Association* 61, no. 3: 345–64.

Kahn, Matthew E. 1999. "The Silver Lining of Rust Belt Manufacturing Decline." *Journal of Urban Economics* 46, no. 3: 360–76.

———. 2006. *Green Cities: Urban Growth and the Environment.* Brookings.

Kolko, Jed. 2010. "Does Broadband Boost Local Economic Development?" Working Paper. San Francisco: Public Policy Institute of California.

Leonard, Herman, and Jay Walder. 1999. *The Federal Budget and the States: 1999 Fiscal Year Report.* Harvard University Kennedy School.

Moretti, Enrico. 2004a. "Human Capital Externalities in Cities." In *Handbook of Urban Economics,* vol. 4, edited by Vernon Henderson and J. Thisse. Amsterdam: North Holland.

———. 2004b. "Estimating the Social Return to Higher Education: Evidence from Longitudinal and Repeated Cross-Sectional Data." *Journal of Econometrics* 121, nos. 1, 2: 175–212.

Neal, Derek. 1995. "Industry-Specific Human Capital: Evidence from Displaced Workers." *Journal of Labor Economics* 13, no. 4: 653–77.

Rauch, James E. 1993. "Does History Matter Only when It Matters Little? The Case of City-Industry Location." *Quarterly Journal of Economics* 108, no. 3: 843–67.

Saiz, Albert. 2010. "On the Local Housing Supply Elasticity." *Quarterly Journal of Economics* 125, no. 3: 1253–96.

Shapiro, Jesse. 2006. "Smart Cities: Quality of Life, Productivity, and the Growth Effects of Human Capital." *Review of Economics and Statistics* 88, no. 2: 324–35.

Waldfogel, Joel. 2008. "The Median Voter and the Median Consumer: Local Private Goods and Residential Sorting." *Journal of Urban Economics* 63, no. 2: 567–82.

STEVEN N. DURLAUF

7

Poverty Traps and Appalachia

In this chapter I provide some general ideas on how to conceptualize poverty traps and speculate on their applicability to understanding Appalachian poverty. My goal is to stimulate thinking on Appalachia that exploits contemporary perspectives in economics on the sources of persistent poverty and inequality. To do this I focus on both the theory of poverty traps as well as issues in the econometric assessment of their empirical salience. Although I describe different definitions of poverty traps below, all of these definitions have the common feature that poverty—be it for a family, a community, or a larger aggregate—is highly persistent. In other words, one cannot expect contemporaneous poverty to simply correct itself except over very long time horizons, if at all.

Why should poverty traps be of particular importance to policymakers? One reason that poverty traps are of particular importance is that they can provide a prima facie justification for government interventions on equality-of-opportunity grounds. John Roemer (1998) argues persuasively that equality of opportunity requires that individual socioeconomic prospects not be affected by factors over which an individual has no control; this perspective provides a way of integrating personal responsibility into the assessment of equality of opportunity. Steven Durlauf (1996b, 2006) uses Roemer's reasoning to provide a justification of government interventions when poverty traps are present. The

I thank Hon Ho Kwok, Hsuan-Li Su, Xiangrong Yu, and Jishu Zong for outstanding research assistance and James Ziliak for comments on a draft of this chapter.

ethical justification for interventions is most obvious if one considers the future socioeconomic prospects of its children. Following Roemer's logic, it is self-evident that children are not responsible for the environments in which they grow up, whether at a family or a community level. While some subtleties exist in translating this lack of responsibility into an ethical case for government intervention (for example, one needs to address the rights of parents to provide differential opportunities for their children), it is fair to say that the presence of a poverty trap provides a prime facie case for government intervention.

By itself, the ethical case for government interventions implied by equality of opportunity or other considerations is inadequate for policy evaluation. A poverty trap generated by deficiencies in early childhood development calls for very different interventions than a poverty trap caused by features of a regional labor market. Hence, a satisfactory theory of poverty traps needs to account for mechanisms as well as the basic facts of poverty persistence.[1]

One natural reason that families in a community may collectively appear to be in a poverty trap is that the individual families suffer from the same initial conditions that produce a poverty trap via family dynamics. In my development of poverty trap definitions I start with family-based models and later incorporate community factors.

My discussion reflects the large body of modern literature on persistent poverty and poverty traps; this modern literature tends to focus on determinants of poverty that are generated at a higher level of aggregation than the family—although, as we shall see, the mechanisms that produce the poverty traps discussed in the modern literature can do so in family-based models. One focus of this modern literature is national economies, so as to understand continuing levels of deprivation in much of the world. Costas Azariadis and John Stachurski (2005) survey poverty traps in development and economic growth. One focus of these studies is on how entire nations can be trapped in poverty. Another focus is the fact that persistent poverty can emerge among a subpopulation in affluent countries such as the United States. Ghettos are a canonical example of a neighborhood-level poverty trap. The neighborhood-effects literature is quite diffuse.[2]

1. I thank James Ziliak for this argument.

2. See Lang (2007) for an overview of the poverty literature; and Durlauf (2004) for a focused review of persistent poverty from the vantage point of neighborhood effects and their attendant effects on inequality. Jencks and Mayer (1990) is a survey of social science research that precedes the modern economics literature. See also Manski (2000) and Durlauf and Ioannides (2010) for surveys of social interactions models that focus on how groups affect individuals.

Regions per se do not represent the usual scale of aggregation at which poverty traps are studied in modern research. In considering a context such as Appalachia, one sees elements of both economywide and local poverty traps. By this I mean the following. Taken as a whole, Appalachia is poorer than the rest of the United States, and so, given its size, one might be tempted to ask whether the mechanisms that produce national poverty traps apply to the region. On the other hand, conditional on the relatively weak economic performance of the region, there is substantial heterogeneity across Appalachia. Central Appalachia in general and Eastern Kentucky in particular appear much closer to being poverty traps than the rest of the region.

While I am not aware of any modern research in economics that explicitly studies Appalachia from the perspective of poverty traps, ideas closely related to poverty traps have long been associated with the region. Over thirty years ago, Dwight Billings (1974, pp. 315–16) described standard thinking on Appalachia:[3]

> The culture of poverty is the most common theory in the literature on poverty and Appalachia alike. . . . Culture of poverty explanations, when applied to Appalachia, take several forms. . . . Emphasis is on the debilitating effects of an atavistic, frontier culture and the socialization of its people into backwardness. The subcultural claim is often buttressed by an assertion that, with the recent introduction of improved roads and mass media, Appalachia is experiencing its first contact with the outside.

Ronald Eller (2008) further argues that culture-of-poverty arguments helped motivate War on Poverty strategies for Appalachia. One use of this chapter, I hope, is to provide a guide to quantitative versions of culture-of-poverty arguments, which can both clarify theoretical thinking and provide insights into how one can assess their empirical salience.

One important feature of modern poverty theories, whether defined at the aggregate or individual levels, is their emphasis on the interplay of a range of causal factors in producing (or eliminating) a poverty trap. This richness comes at a price, as the empirical evidence for any particular factor is consequently difficult to assess. On the other hand, this richness is important in developing poverty-trap perspectives that respect the heterogeneity of individual and subregional outcomes within Appalachia.

3. Billings argues that cultural explanations are overstated, a position maintained in Billings and Blee (2000).

Income Dynamics and Poverty Traps

In this section I outline some baseline models of income dynamics and assess their equilibrium properties from the vantage point of trying to define a poverty trap. The reason for proceeding this way is that there is no accepted formal definition of a poverty trap. Rather, the term encompasses, I believe, three logically distinct, although mutually compatible, qualitative concepts about the nature of poverty:

—Poverty is highly persistent.

—Poverty can be perpetuated indefinitely either across an individual's life or across generations within a family dynasty.

—Poverty is perpetuated by certain features of the socioeconomic environment that are outside an individual's control, so that two individuals (or family dynasties) with identical preferences could end up with different degrees of socioeconomic success.

The absence of a unique and precise qualitative definition of a poverty trap does not, in my view, make the term unhelpful.[4] In contrast, in my view formal definitions of poverty traps are useful to the extent they capture aspects of these qualitative ideas. One important distinction between the first two poverty trap concepts, as opposed to the third, is that the first two refer to properties of the time-series process for income, whereas the third refers to the mechanisms that underlie the income process. What sorts of aggregate or collective mechanisms fall under the third concept? For the Appalachian case, one obvious example is the state of the coal industry. As this industry declines, so do wages; and so Appalachian poverty emerges as a consequence. This explanation may be contrasted with the explanation associating a given region's social norms with the value attached to education; this claim is consistent with (though certainly not proved by) the low educational attainment of Appalachian adults compared to the rest of the U.S. population. These influences are often known as *social interactions* or *neighborhood effects;* I use the term *social interactions* here.

For expositional purposes, I focus on models of intergenerational income dynamics and so do not address issues of intragenerational poverty traps. Focusing on intergenerational income dynamics minimizes the need for formalism to illustrate qualitative ideas. My objective in developing concepts of poverty traps and persistent poverty is to translate qualitative ideas into mathematical equiv-

4. For example, the lack of a precise single definition for poverty traps does not inhibit evaluating whether a given case is a poverty trap. Following an example in Taylor (1998), the absence of a clear definition of money does not diminish the meaningfulness that a dollar bill is an example of money.

alents. These mathematical equivalents are of intrinsic interest but are also important as they provide a segue from qualitative notions of poverty traps and persistent poverty to statistical work on both the measurement and the determination of the mechanisms by which they are generated.

Formally, intergenerational models of poverty traps are constructed by considering the dynamic behavior of a population of family dynasties; these are indexed by *i*. Issues of intermarriage, fecundity, and so on are ignored, so each generation of the family is a single individual who lives for two periods. The pair of indices i,t denotes the adult at time t in dynasty i, so person i,t was born at $t-1$; incorporation of a more elaborate lifetime structure does not matter qualitatively. This structure is known as an overlapping-generations model and is, since the work of Gary Becker and Nigel Tomes (1979), the standard mathematical structure for thinking about intergenerational income dynamics. The framework, despite its many abstractions, allows one to focus on the way in which socioeconomic status at adulthood is determined by childhood (versus adulthood) factors.

Throughout the analysis, adult income is denoted by $y_{i,t}$. While income does not summarize an individual's socioeconomic status, even in this very stylized framework, it is the basis of measuring whether or not the person is in poverty. For simplicity, poverty is defined by an income less than or equal to y^{POV}. The level of $y_{i,t}$ relative to y^{POV} determines whether family i at time t is in poverty and hence—by tracing out the dynamics of the relationship between the poverty level and the income level of different generations—allows one to discuss the persistence of poverty for a given family dynasty and thus to make formal what one means by a poverty trap. Notice that one can engage in comparable exercises for measures of socioeconomic status other than income.

Family-Based Models

One view of intergenerational income dynamics is family specific in that parental income determines offspring income. The formal analysis of this type of model was pioneered by Becker and Tomes and Glen Loury (1981). A deterministic version of this class of model produces the simple law of motion for family income,

$$y_{i,t} = \varphi\left(y_{i,t-1}\right). \tag{7-1}$$

In other words, parental income $y_{i,t-1}$ determines offspring income $y_{i,t}$. The key mechanism in the classical models of this type is that parental income determines human capital investment in children, which in turn determines future adult income. Recent work by James Heckman emphasizes the role of parenting in the production of personality traits, such as conscientiousness, that are distinct from cognitive skills.[5] Further, one can generate persistence of income via persistence in the heritability of intelligence, which has been a long-standing concern. Equation 7-1 elides these distinct sources in order to minimize notation for the basic definitions I wish to develop, but they are essential to account for in empirical work if one is to develop policy responses to poverty traps, for reasons argued above.

This model, and variations (such as equation 7-4) that allow for uncertainty, represents the workhorse for economic models of intergenerational mobility. It is standard (and trivial) to assume that $\varphi(\cdot)$ is nondecreasing in y, which means nothing deeper than that higher income of parents does not reduce the income of offspring. As this model is assumed to apply to all members of the population, the equation is sufficient to describe the evolution of the complete cross-sectional distribution of income over time and, therefore, allows one to characterize the poverty rate, measures of inequality, and other populationwide aggregates. Given a cross-section distribution at time t, the function $\varphi(\cdot)$ determines what the cross-section distribution will be at time $t + 1$.

From the vantage point of an individual family dynasty, an immediate implication of this structure is that, for every initial condition $y_{i,0}$, income will exhibit one of two long-run behaviors. Formally, as t goes to infinity, $y_{i,t}$ will either converge to a limiting value—some finite level of income y such that $y = \varphi(y)$—or it will diverge to infinity. These are the steady states of equation 7-1. Ignoring the latter possibility (which only adds technical complications at this point), the long-run properties of the income dynamics process are fully summarized by the steady states of equation 7-1.

Multiple steady states provide one formalization of the concept of a poverty trap. To see why, consider the behavior of differences in income between two family dynasties i and j, that is, $y_{i,t} - y_{j,t}$. If equation 7-1 is associated with a unique steady state, then it is clear that, regardless of the value of the difference in incomes today, this difference will eventually disappear:

$$\lim_{T\to\infty} y_{i,t+T} - y_{j,t+T} = 0. \tag{7-2}$$

5. See for example Heckman (2008). For a comprehensive survey of what is known about the effects of personality on economic outcomes, see Almund and others (2011).

In words, the uniqueness of a steady state implies that any contemporaneous inequality will disappear over time. While the convergence to the common long-run income level may be slow, it will inevitably occur.

In contrast, suppose that there exist multiple steady states. Further, assume that these steady states are locally stable, which means that, if a family starts sufficiently near either value, it will converge to that value. Finally, designating one of these stable steady states as y^L and another as y^H, suppose that relative to the poverty threshold y^{POV}

$$y^L < y^{POV} < y^H. \tag{7-3}$$

In this case, there exist levels of poverty and nonpoverty that are fully self-perpetuating. Equation 7-3 thus constitutes one formalization of the idea of a poverty trap: moving from specific income values to ranges of incomes, families whose incomes lie in the vicinity of y^L will remain poor forever, while families whose incomes lie far enough away from y^L will not. This situation captures the qualitative poverty trap ideas *i* and *ii.*

Under what conditions can equation 7-3 arise for the dynamics of equation 7-1? Algebraically, the existence of a poverty trap requires that there exist income levels $y_1 < y_2$, such that $\varphi(y_2) - \varphi(y_1) > y_2 - y_1$. If $\varphi(\cdot)$ is everywhere differentiable, this condition requires that $\varphi'(\cdot) > 1$ for some values of $y_{i,t}$; it can also hold if there is jump discontinuity in $\varphi(\cdot)$. When translated into language on the effect of parental income on offspring income, the conditions mean that, in order for this form of a poverty trap to occur, it is necessary that families with higher incomes can, for some income ranges, experience more rapid income growth than families with lower incomes. That is, there must be income ranges in which an additional dollar of parental income leads to more than an additional dollar of offspring income. And what applies across families must also apply within families; that is, it must be the case that, for a given family, income growth is increasing with respect to initial income for some income levels. Notice that there is no requirement that income growth increase at all income levels. Hence over a cross section, one can observe an average tendency for income growth to be negatively correlated with initial incomes, even though a poverty trap is present.

Equation 7-1 is a reduced-form description of equilibrium behavior; so is a black box in that it describes the equilibrium dynamics of income for a family but does not explicitly describe the mechanisms by which income of a parent affects an offspring. In other words, the function $\varphi(\cdot)$ is determined in equilibrium by the underlying decision problems of parents. As noted above, one mechanism that provides an income process consistent with equation 7-1 involves human capital formation.[6] The economic logic underlying these models is straightforward: parents divide income between consumption and human capital investment in children; these human capital investments, in turn, determine income when children become adults.[7] If the level of investment in children is a nondecreasing function of income and the marginal product of human capital investment on adult income is strictly positive, family income will evolve according to equation 7-1, with $\varphi(\cdot)$ nondecreasing in y. Delineating this type of structure is important, as it indicates that one must be careful in talking about causes of poverty traps. As the human capital explanation shows, there is an interplay between the preferences of parents (which determine the relationship between income and human capital investment) and technology (which determines the transformation of human capital into income). These will interact to determine whether or not the conditions for a poverty trap can hold. It is important to be clear that this sort of explanation in no way "blames the poor." When preferences are homogeneous, the investment decisions of the poor are identical to those the more affluent would make in the same position.

While equation 7-1 is consistent with the frameworks of Becker and Tomes and of Loury, poverty traps do not arise in either of their analyses. The reason for this is that each of these analyses places assumptions on the mapping from human capital to income that, in essence, ensure that $\varphi'(\cdot) < 1$ everywhere. Alternative specifications can produce different properties for $\varphi(\cdot)$ and hence generate poverty traps while preserving the behavioral foundations of their models. One way a poverty trap can occur is if the production function exhibits a region of increasing returns to human capital formation. A second way to produce a poverty trap in the family dynasty context is via lumpiness in human capital investment. If transitions across human capital levels require fixed costs to be paid, then $\varphi(\cdot)$ can exhibit a jump, as the poor do not make these investments, whereas the nonpoor do.[8]

The example of fixed human capital investment costs raises an important issue in the economics of poverty traps, namely the question of whether they require some sort of market incompleteness to sustain them. One reason concerns the ability of adults to borrow. Depending on the returns to human capital investment, poor families might wish to borrow in order to invest in their children and

6. See Becker and Tomes (1979); Loury (1981).

7. This formulation is similar to economic growth models in which aggregate economies build up capital stock via savings and consumption decisions.

8. Azariadis and Drazen (1990) is a classic example of a poverty trap driven by jumps.

break a poverty trap. One impediment to borrowing of this type was first recognized by Glen Loury (1981): parents cannot borrow against the future earnings of their children.[9] The human capital explanation implies that there can be efficient redistribution of educational resources in the sense that equalization leads to greater aggregate output.

This first conceptualization of a poverty trap may be fragile in an important sense. Suppose that one allows for randomness in incomes via a variable $\varepsilon_{i,t}$, which summarizes, for example, labor market luck and shocks to ability of offspring compared to parents.[10] It also modifies the income process from equation 7-1 to

$$y_{i,t} = \varphi\left(y_{i,t-1}, \varepsilon_{i,t}\right). \tag{7-4}$$

Questions about poverty dynamics, traps, and so on of course immediately become probabilistic in such a context. For example, long-run differences between families are more naturally described by calculations of objects like the expected gap between two families in the future given the gap in their contemporary incomes. That is,

$$\lim_{T\to\infty} E\left(y_{i,t+T} - y_{j,t+T} \,\middle|\, y_{i,t} - y_{j,t}\right). \tag{7-5}$$

If this expected value is 0, one has a condition that is analogous to equation 7-2, as it says that the expected value of any future gap will shrink to 0 given the current gap between the incomes of two families. Similarly, one can calculate the probability that a poor family will stay poor for the arbitrarily distant future. That is,

$$\lim_{T\to\infty} \Pr\left(y_{i,t+T} < y^{POV}, y_{i,t+T-1} < y^{POV}, \ldots, y_{i,t+1} < y^{POV} \,\middle|\, y_{i,t} < y^{POV}\right). \tag{7-6}$$

If the probability described by equation 7-6 equals 1, then one has the equivalent of equation 7-3 for a random environment; once one is poor, so are one's descendants. On the other hand, it is possible for equation 7-6 to lie between 0 and 1, which provides a richer notion of a poverty trap—that is, a situation in which a family is in danger of being permanently poor, although such an outcome is not

9. Other types of financial market imperfections have been studied; see for example Galor and Zeira (1993).

10. For ease of exposition, I do not introduce separate notation for shocks experienced in youth and in adulthood, as the additional generality provided is not exploited in my discussion.

guaranteed. This intermediate case recognizes the possibility of a Bill Gates being born into a poor family.

Income dynamics as generated by equation 7-4 exhibit very different properties from those implied by equation 7-1. By itself, this is unsurprising; the presence of the random elements $\varepsilon_{i,t}$ breaks the deterministic effect of parental income on offspring income and, hence, the deterministic effect on grandchild income, and so on. Transmission of current income over generations can be disrupted by values of the shocks $\varepsilon_{i,t}$. More surprising, the introduction of even a small amount of randomness can affect the existence of a poverty trap. That is, even if equation 7-3 holds for a world without randomness, equation 7-6 can equal 0. The reason for this fragility again stems from the ability of $\varepsilon_{i,t}$ to overcome the effects of $y_{i,t-1}$ on a given individual. Particular realizations of $\varepsilon_{i,t}$ can mean that, even if a poverty trap exists without shocks, the realizations cause a family to escape the trap. A simple algebraic example can illustrate this possibility. Suppose that income is either high or low—that is, that there are only two possible values, y^L and y^H, and that income dynamics obey the Markov chain

$$\Pr\left(y_{i,t} = y^L \mid y_{i,t-1} = y^L\right) = \Pr\left(y_{i,t} = y^H \mid y_{i,t-1} = y^H\right) = 1. \tag{7-7}$$

Clearly this is an example of a poverty trap in the sense of equation 7-3. On the other hand, suppose that income is stochastic and follows

$$\Pr\left(y_{i,t} = y^L \mid y_{i,t-1} = y^L\right) = \Pr\left(y_{i,t} = y^H \mid y_{i,t-1} = y^H\right) = 1 - \delta. \tag{7-8}$$

No matter how small δ is, one can show that each family dynasty will spend, on average, one half of the time in poverty; further, any rank order in incomes between dynasties at one point in time will reverse itself with probability 1. Hence no family is trapped in poverty; and it is additionally guaranteed that any income differential between two families at one point in time will be reversed in the future. The message of this example is that the introduction of randomness can fundamentally change the predictions of deterministic models, depending on how the randomness interacts with parental income in determining offspring income.

This example—in which an arbitrarily small amount of randomness can eliminate a poverty trap—calls into question the utility of the concept as a literal description of some phenomenon of interest. It does not call into question, in my view, whether models of poverty traps are of intellectual interest. Rather, the import of this example is to call into question whether one should focus empirical analysis on poverty traps as defined by equation 7-6. In my judgment, the upshot of this example is that one should be concerned with developing a notion of a poverty trap that avoids the equating of a poverty trap with permanence of poverty. For the current example, a natural measure of persistence of poverty is the expected number of generations before a poor family transits out of poverty. One can show, for equations 7-7 and 7-8, that the expected number of generations for a poor family to transition to nonpoverty is $1/\delta$. As δ approaches 0, $1/\delta$ diverges to infinity, so that this measure replicates the notion of permanent poverty when there is no stochastic element. Expected passage times, in my view, are the more natural object of interest for empirical studies; put differently, a poverty trap as defined by equation 7-6 is a limiting and in certain ways idealized case of persistent poverty. In contrast, a poverty trap is defined as a condition in which there exist long-expected passage times out of poverty. Doing so better respects heterogeneity in the effects of poverty on individuals, since $\varepsilon_{i,t}$ is nothing more than unobserved individual-specific heterogeneity.

What does this mean operationally? Letting $M^{P,NP}(y_{i,t})$ denote the expected value of the first passage time out of poverty for a family with initial conditions $y_{i,t} < y^{POV}$, one can define families in a poverty trap as those for which

$$M^{P,NP}\left(y_{i,t}\right) \geq K. \tag{7-9}$$

The expected passage of time before escaping poverty is, in my view, a natural statistic of interest if the objective of the analyst is to understand persistence—that is, feature *i* of poverty traps. Of course, K needs to be specified by the analyst, but that is not a defect of the measure but rather acknowledges that it is a judgment as to how much persistence should be designated a trap; the first definition made such a judgment by setting $K = \infty$. The function $M^{P,NP}(y_{i,t})$ itself can be calculated from the data. It is worth noting that calculations of this type are relatively standard in mobility analyses, which focus on Markov transition processes.

A third way to think about poverty traps—one that also permits a smooth transition between nonstochastic and stochastic environments—is to employ the structure of equation 7-4 to uncover how initial conditions affect long-run income levels. Assuming that the shocks $\varepsilon_{i,t}$ are uncorrelated across time (correlation in the shocks is straightforward, although not necessarily trivial to handle, as one simply works with the unpredictable components of $\varepsilon_{i,t}$ instead of $\varepsilon_{i,t}$ itself), one can construct a new time series

$$\tilde{y}_{i,t+T} = \varphi\left(\tilde{y}_{i,t+T-1}, 0\right) \text{ given } \tilde{y}_{i,t} = y_{i,t}. \tag{7-10}$$

The variable $\tilde{y}_{i,t+T}$ represents the family income levels that would occur under the counterfactual that all shocks starting at time t equal 0. It is not a variable that one observes; it is the counterfactual sequence of family incomes that would have been observed if shocks to adult income were to cease. The properties of this time series reveal the extent to which current income inequality is or is not self-correcting as it studies income dynamics after unpredictable future events are purged; as before, this process will, under the assumption that $\varphi(\cdot, 0)$ is nondecreasing in $\tilde{y}_{i,t+T-1}$, either diverge to infinity or possess a well-defined limit

$$\tilde{y}_i^{\lim}\left(y_{i,t}\right) = \lim_{T\to\infty} \tilde{y}_{i,t+T} \text{ given } \tilde{y}_{i,t} = y_{i,t}. \tag{7-11}$$

This limit is expressed as a function of income at time t. The limit may or may not be independent of the value of $y_{i,t}$. Steven Durlauf (1995) first introduced this counterfactual and argues that, if the limit in equation 7-11 depends on $y_{i,t}$ so that long-run behavior depends on initial conditions (in this case income), this property captures what economic historians mean by path dependence. With respect to poverty traps, one can modify equation 7-3 to define a poverty trap as the existence of income levels such that

$$\tilde{y}_i^{\lim}\left(y^L\right) < y^{POV} < \tilde{y}_i^{\lim}\left(y^H\right). \tag{7-12}$$

This concept corresponds to the idea that poverty traps involve the absence of self-correcting mechanisms to overcome current poverty, but it relaxes the requirement that poverty is permanent. The objective in moving to this definition of a poverty trap is to distinguish between cases in which poverty fails to be persistent because of shocks versus cases in which poverty fails to be persistent because of the socioeconomic structure that determines the effect of parental income on their children. This concept of a poverty trap has yet to be investigated.

Turning from concepts of poverty traps to their formulations, equations 7-1 and 7-4 are both limited in that they treat family income as a sufficient statistic for the intergenerational transmission of economic status. For any vector of socioeconomic characteristics $x_{i,t}$, one can consider a more general intergenerational model described by

$$y_{i,t} = \varphi\left(y_{i,t-1}, x_{i,t}, \varepsilon_{i,t}\right) \tag{7-13}$$

and

$$x_{i,t} = \xi\left(x_{i,t-1}, y_{i,t-1}, \xi_{i,t}\right). \tag{7-14}$$

As a mathematical idea, equations 7-13 and 7-14 are a trivial generalization of equation 7-4 in that the system describes the joint evolution of $(y_{i,t}, x_{i,t})$ and so relaxes the assumption that parental income is the only channel by which parents affect offspring.[11] One traditional candidate for an element of $x_{i,t}$ is some genetic factor that is equated with cognitive ability. Without commenting on the importance of this factor, the work of Arthur Goldberger (1977) stands the test of time as a critique of efforts to attribute persistent inequality to genetic differences. My concern is instead with new research pioneered by James Heckman.[12] His research demonstrates the importance of personality traits such as patience and self-control in determining socioeconomic outcomes. A key finding in Heckman's work is that adult personality traits are heavily influenced by early childhood experiences. For the purposes of understanding poverty traps, intergenerational persistence in personality traits, for example, can produce intergenerational persistence in poverty. The transmission of socioeconomically undesirable personality traits from parent to offspring will, I believe, represent an important determinant of the intergenerational transmission of poverty and will increasingly come to be seen as central to the problem of persistent inequality. Heckman (2008) provides an overview of the effects of personality traits on socioeconomic outcomes as well as evidence of the role of families in the creation of these traits.

Location-Based Models

The family- or individual-specific perspective on income dynamics renders the location of the trap irrelevant. In other words, neither the community nor the region matters; if the members of the population were redistributed across different communities or regions, their prospects would be unaffected, assuming that equation 7-1 is a complete description. The only sense in which a region is a poverty trap is that it is composed of families that, because of family influences, are consigned to poverty.

11. The term $\xi_{i,t}$ is introduced in order to allow for unobserved heterogeneity in the determination of $x_{i,t}$. As such, it is simply the analog to $\varepsilon_{i,t}$.

12. See Cunha and Heckman (2007) for a theoretical model of skill development that captures the major stylized facts of human development; and Cunha, Heckman, and Schennach (2010) for empirical implementation of the model. Borghans and others (2008) provide an overview of research from the social and natural sciences on human development. Heckman and others (2010b) demonstrates how intensive interventions in early childhood can generate benefits in adulthood for disadvantaged children; Heckman and others (2010a) show that these benefits involve personality traits as opposed to IQ.

A second class of income dynamics, one in which location matters, may be trivially generated by including vectors of location-specific factors $c_{l,t-1}$ and $c_{l,t}$ in the income dynamics process. Focusing on equation 7-4, such models can be written as

$$y_{i,t} = \varphi\left(y_{i,t-1}, c_{l,t-1}, c_{l,t}, \varepsilon_{i,t}\right). \tag{7-15}$$

The vectors $c_{l,t-1}$ and $c_{l,t}$ capture location influences that occur during childhood versus those that occur during adulthood. So one set of location-specific factors may affect the development of ambition during childhood while a different set of location-specific factors may affect job prospects as an adult.

It is evident that the presence of these location effects can generate persistent poverty. So long as there is sufficient heterogeneity in $c_{l,t-1}$ and $c_{l,t}$ and sufficient sensitivity of φ to these vectors, then it is obvious that family dynasties placed in different locations can exhibit permanent income gaps in the sense of equation 7-5 and that one family can be stuck in poverty in the sense of equation 7-6 while another is not. In this respect, equation 7-15 is able to simultaneously capture all three poverty trap concepts. For this to happen, the location-specific differences will themselves have to exhibit a sufficient level of persistence. Once this is so, then the persistence of the location-specific factors creates a wedge in the incomes of families that inhabit different locations.[13]

Some elements of $c_{l,t}$ may be exogenous; canonical examples include geography and weather. Other locational factors may not literally be exogenous but may evolve sufficiently slowly so that they may be treated as exogenous over the time horizons of poverty dynamics evaluations. Examples include cultural norms and political institutions. For purposes of analyzing income dynamics, the key feature of $c_{l,t}$ is that its behavior may be taken as given without rendering the analysis incomplete. Charles Manski (1993) refers to such factors as contextual effects, borrowing terminology from sociology.

A different way to introduce locational effects involves introducing feedbacks from the behaviors of members of the location to the behaviors of each individ-

13. Notice that family-specific factors could in principle produce poverty traps, a possibility I ignore above. There has not been much interest in permanent family differences given what is known about regression to the mean in IQ. Further, efforts to identify permanent differences in IQ in ethnic groups have been a failure, due to identification problems most effectively demonstrated by Arthur Goldberger. Goldberger (1977) is still the classic study in this regard. I conjecture that the recent work by James Heckman on personality traits can provide a basis for family-specific poverty traps induced by persistent interfamily heterogeneity.

ual. These feedbacks can occur over time or contemporaneously. Focusing first on intertemporal feedbacks, let $y_{-i,l,t-1}$ denote the vector of income levels for families in location l other than i at time $t-1$; introduction of this additional factor generalizes the income process to

$$y_{i,t} = \varphi\left(y_{i,t-1}, y_{-i,l,t-1}, c_{l,t}, c_{l,t-1}, \varepsilon_{i,t}\right). \tag{7-16}$$

It is common to assume that the average income of others, $\bar{y}_{-i,l,t-1}$, is a sufficient statistic for the effects of others on a given adult's income, so that equation 7-16 can be simplified to

$$y_{i,t} = \varphi\left(y_{i,t-1}, \bar{y}_{-i,l,t-1}, c_{l,t}, c_{l,t-1}, \varepsilon_{i,t}\right). \tag{7-17}$$

Equation 7-17 is the basis of an important class of formal models of poverty traps; a study by Glen Loury (1977) is a remarkable early version of this model. In terms of underlying economics, the dependence of adult income on the incomes of the families in the location in which one grows up can occur because of local financing of public schools.[14]

A second source of the intergenerational dependence in equation 7-17 may involve role model effects. If adolescents make schooling choices on the basis of future economic benefits, the assessment of these benefits may depend on the distributions of educational levels and incomes observed in a community. Stratification of communities according to income will correspondingly mean that different locations produce different inferences about the value of education.[15] Research on the economics of identity provides a third explanation for equation 7-17.[16]

Suppose that one effect of educational choices by an individual concerns how he relates his own identity to that of others in his community. If the link between education and identity depends on the characteristics of parents, then it is possible that equation 7-17 is an approximation to the effects of identity on choice. To be concrete, in a community where few parents are well educated, high education can make an individual feel alienated from those with whom he wants to share an identity. This argument has been of long-standing importance in understanding

14. For examples of formal analyses of neighborhoods and the transmission of poverty based on this public finance mechanism, see Bénabou (1996a, 1996b); Durlauf (1996a).

15. See Streufert (2000) for a complete analysis of this type of locational effect.

16. See for example Akerlof and Kranton (2000, 2002).

racial inequality, as a number of authors argue that black educational attainment is hampered by the perception that academic success is a form of "acting white."[17] Suggestive evidence also exists of low aspirations among Appalachian youth.[18] In general, the personality traits emphasized in Heckman's research can plausibly be regarded as determined at a community as well as a family level. One obvious example is the internalization during childhood of shame associated with a failure in self-control. This seems a promising direction for future work on group-determined poverty traps, of which location models of the type I describe are a subset. Note that, while I focus on income as the determining variable, work on personality traits suggests the need to model the social effects for a richer set of socioeconomic variables.

A final modification of the income dynamics equation to include contemporaneous locational influences is no deeper than adding these influences to equation 7-16. Assuming that average income of others is a sufficient statistic, this leads to

$$y_{i,t} = \varphi\left(y_{i,t-1}, \bar{y}_{-i,l,t-1}, \bar{y}_{-i,l,t}, c_{l,t-1}, c_{l,t}, \varepsilon_{i,t}\right). \tag{7-18}$$

When choices are discrete, this model thus corresponds to social interactions models of the type studied by William Brock and Steven Durlauf (2001a, 2006, 2007) and other authors.[19] One source for contemporaneous income interdependences is informational: to the extent that labor market information flows across social networks, economic success by a member of one's network can mean greater information. Empirical evidence of this phenomenon is developed by Giorgio Topa (2001) and by Patrick Bayer, Stephen Ross, and Giorgio Topa (2008). Topa's article also provides a formal theoretical model of information transmission. Other explanations may involve forms of increasing returns to scale of the type pioneered by Robert Lucas (1988) and Paul Romer (1986) for human and physical capital, respectively. If returns to scale occur with respect to human or physical capital, this again suggests the need to move beyond locational income as the mechanism for location-based poverty traps. Charles Manski (1993) denotes the contemporaneous interdependence of socioeconomic outcomes as endogenous social effects, to distinguish them from social effects generated by—from the perspective of time t—predetermined variables. Note that $\bar{y}_{-i,l,t-1}$ is a contextual effect.

17. Fryer and Torelli (2005); Ogbu (2003).

18. See Ali and Saunders (2008).

19. See Durlauf and Ioannides (2010) for a recent survey.

From a theoretical perspective, the introduction of $\bar{y}_{-i,l,t}$ is especially interesting as its presence means that the model has the capacity to produce multiple equilibria for the cross-sectional density of incomes within a given location at a fixed time. In terms of thinking about poverty traps this is of particular importance, as it creates the possibility that two locations with identical distributions of individual and locational characteristics can exhibit different levels of aggregate income. How can this happen? Suppose one considers work effort rather than income as the object of interest. If the productivity of effort is complementary in the effort of others—that is, if the marginal product of increased effort by one worker is increased effort by others—then the effort choices of each individual will affect the effort choices of others.[20] If this complementarity is strong enough, then there will exist multiple effort levels across a population; each of these distributions of effort levels is self-consistent in the sense that they represent Nash equilibria: no one has an incentive to change his effort level given the choices of others. This example illustrates a general principle: when complementarities in individual income levels are strong enough, then multiple equilibria in the total income distribution can result.

When can multiple steady states occur? William Brock and Steven Durlauf (2001a, 2006) show, for discrete choices, that the number of equilibria in a given economic context depends on the interplay of private and group characteristics with the strength of complementarities. Intuitively, if private incentives polarize the population toward one type of behavior, then complementarities cannot create sufficient bunching so that the population on average tips to the other choice. Further, if the distribution of individual-level unobservables generates large draws with sufficient frequency, then the percentage of the population left over to react to other factors will be insufficient to generate multiple distributions of self-consistent bunching. This formalizes the idea that sufficient iconoclasts in a population can break socially enforced conformity among others. As is the case for the individualistic models of poverty traps, the robustness of a poverty trap for a social model of this type depends on the ways shocks impinge on individual decisions. Unlike the family-specific income dynamics model, however, what matters

20. Formally, for a function $f(r, s, \ldots)$, r and s are complementary if $\frac{\partial^2 f(r,s,\ldots)}{\partial r \partial s} > 0$. In words, the marginal effect of increasing one variable is itself an increasing function of the level of the other. One can extend this definition to vectors and generalize to cases where functions are not twice differentiable. See Milgrom and Roberts (1990) and Vives (1990). These works introduce general definitions and launched the study of equilibria of environments with complementarities.

in the locational model is whether enough aggregate heterogeneity is induced by the introduction of shocks to overcome the potential of strong conformity effects tipping the rest of the population toward one behavior or another because of the social interaction effects.

Economic Growth Model

The discussion up to this point focuses on environments in which incomes do not systematically grow. Modern economic growth literature focuses on cases in which interactions can lead to perpetual and endogenous growth. The basic idea, initially proposed in seminal work by Robert Lucas (1988) and Paul Romer (1986), is that the productivity of capital investments, whether human or physical, depends on the investments of others in the economy. Applying these ideas to the Appalachian case, one would say that the effect of human capital on one worker's productivity is increased by greater human capital on the part of others. Lucas and Romer seek to explain long-run divergence between developed and lesser developed economies and so focus on the case in which these spillovers produced "social increasing returns to scale," which means that if the capital levels of others are fixed, a given individual faces decreasing returns to scale mapping of capital into income, while the aggregate economy exhibits increasing returns. For our purposes, their model is a variant of equation 7-18, in which the individual income variables grow without bound.

In terms of the conceptions of poverty traps I describe, perpetual growth requires a modification of the various formalizations. One possibility is to think of traps in terms of relative versus absolute deprivation. This would involve considering the behavior of variables such as $\log(y_{i,t}/y_{j,t})$; the use of logs accounts for the idea that, in growing economies, a fixed difference in income becomes a negligible fraction of the incomes. A relative-deprivation trap could then be conceptualized as one in which contemporaneous inequality can be permanent, with positive probability such as

$$\lim_{T\to\infty} \Pr\left(\log\left(\frac{y_{i,t+T}}{y_{j,t+T}}\right) \geq K, \log\left(\frac{y_{i,t+T-1}}{y_{j,t+T-1}}\right) \geq K, \ldots, \log\left(\frac{y_{i,t+1}}{y_{j,t+1}}\right) \geq K \middle| \log\left(\frac{y_{i,t}}{y_{j,t}}\right) \geq K \right) > 0. \quad (7\text{-}19)$$

To render this notion of a poverty trap operational, the value of the threshold level K needs to be set, just as it had to be set in the definitions of poverty traps in the absence of growth.

One question is whether the sorts of generative mechanism that produce social increasing returns to scale in aggregate economies apply to regional economies. Paul Romer and Robert Lucas put much emphasis on idea generation. Lucas (2009, p. 1) argues, "What is it about modern capitalist economies that allows them, in contrast to all earlier societies, to generate sustained growth in productivity and living standards? . . . What is central, I believe, is the fact that the industrial revolution involved the emergence (or rapid expansion) of a *class* of educated people, thousands, now many millions of people who spend entire careers exchanging ideas, solving work-related problems, generating new knowledge."

One can see analogies to regional development in this statement. Christopher Bollinger, James Ziliak, and Kenneth Troske (2011) find evidence that returns to education are lower in Appalachia than in the rest of the United States, which is consistent with Romer-Lucas type spillovers, although this fact would arise wherever education levels of workers are complementary in production functions.

A Summary Statistical Model

In using any of these dynamic income models to assess data, this discussion indicates the importance of including both individual and location-specific factors. Further, it is necessary to allow for individual and location-specific unobservables. With respect to locations, it seems especially important to distinguish between the unobserved location-specific heterogeneity experienced in youth as opposed to that experienced in adulthood. One reason for this belief is that the social factors germane to development across childhood, such as the formation of norms, seem very distinct from those that matter at adulthood, such as unobserved features of labor market demand. If we define location-specific unobservables as $\eta_{l,t}$, we can combine the various models into a general process for individual income:

$$y_{i,t} = \varphi\left(y_{i,t-1}, x_{i,t-1}, x_{i,t}, \bar{y}_{-i,t-1}, \bar{y}_{-i,t}, c_{l,t}, c_{l,t-1}, \varepsilon_{i,t}, \eta_{l,t-1}, \eta_{l,t}\right). \qquad (7\text{-}20)$$

This specification respects the distinctions between individual and locational influences, observable and unobservable heterogeneity, and contextual and endogenous factors. As such, it naturally corresponds to the type of statistical model one would apply to individual income dynamics.

There is an important dimension, with respect to which this formulation is incomplete: it says nothing about why individuals live in particular locations. In the case of countrywide poverty traps, this is not an important lacuna given international immigration restrictions, but in the case of the United States the determination of residential location needs to be modeled in order to have a complete theory. In the poverty trap literature, the standard explanation as to why poorer families do not move to locations that will maximize human capital in their offspring is that housing prices and rents sustain substantial socioeconomic segregation. When one considers racial inequality, discrimination may act as a separate barrier.[21]

Before turning to econometric issues, it is worth observing that location-specific factors raise the question of interventions to affect the allocation of individuals across localities. In Durlauf (1996b) I term this *associational redistribution.* Many locational factors act as externalities in the sense that they are not directly adjudicated by markets; peer group effects are a standard example. This is so even if prices (that is, house prices or rents) for locations support the allocation of agents.[22] Hence it would seem that there can be efficient interventions in market allocations of individuals across locations. On the other hand, the presence of complementarities between characteristics of agents can render stratification by these characteristics efficient; this is Gary Becker's classic (1973) result on the efficiency of assortative matching, that is, stratification of groupings. One can identify cases in which complementarity does not render assortative matching efficient.[23] A study by Roland Bénabou (1996b) is a standard reference for understanding the efficiency of stratification in the context of school districts when complementarities occur at both local and aggregate levels. Nevertheless, Becker's basic message delimits the probable efficiency gains from government interventions in group formation that are designed to equalize agent characteristics across groups. Location-driven poverty traps may therefore be an example of a trade-off between equality and efficiency.

Identification of Poverty Traps

In this section I discuss the question of identifying poverty traps. The objective of the discussion is to both illustrate the identification problems that arise in producing elements of poverty traps as well as to describe strategies for overcoming these problems. To make the general econometric issues concrete, I consider a specific empirical proposition and its interpretation.

21. See Yinger (1995) for evidence on housing discrimination and Heckman (1998) for a critique of this work.

22. See Becker and Murphy (2000) for a very clear treatment and Bénabou (1996a) for a detailed analysis.

23. See Prat (2002); Durlauf and Seshadri (2003).

Suppose one argues that Appalachia's historically high poverty rates as compared to the rest of the country represent prima facie evidence of a poverty trap. It is straightforward to argue that this empirical regularity, in fact, does not necessarily constitute evidence of a poverty trap with respect to any of the conceptions of a poverty trap mentioned above. The first concept, persistence in individual-level poverty, is not demonstrated by empirical regularity for an obvious reason: persistence in individual poverty does not logically restrict aggregate poverty levels in a location. This follows immediately from the fact that the percentage of a population in poverty does not identify anything about the dynamics of individual poverty processes.[24] Further, one can think of a plethora of reasons why high aggregate poverty rates in a region would be uninteresting from a policy perspective. One reason is migration; persistent poverty in a location can reflect location decisions of agents who would be poor regardless of location; by analogy, the concentration of the poor in low-quality housing does not imply that low-quality housing is a poverty trap but may simply reflect self-selection of the poor into the housing.

The second concept, absence of self-correction of poverty, cannot be deduced from high aggregate poverty for exactly the same reasons. And the third concept, the presence of aggregate reasons for individual poverty, does not follow from persistent poverty either. Here the reason is simple: nothing in the aggregate poverty rate's persistence speaks to its causes. One cannot tell from high aggregate poverty whether it is due to low family-specific investments in human capital because of individual family poverty, a weak tax base for public education, absence of incentives to invest due to the state of the coal industry, particular social norms about education, or other factors. Taking poverty trap ideas seriously requires much more detailed knowledge about individual income dynamics.

Identification through Time-Series Properties

One strategy for generating evidence of poverty traps may be derived from explicit consideration of the time-series properties of individual income dynamics. Calculations of this type directly address the phenomena of persistence and absence of self-correction in poverty. As suggested above, it is important to allow for nonlinearities in the transition function. Despite their commonality in theoretical work, there has been relatively little empirical work on the question of

24. The mathematical point is that poverty in a region is a description of the cross-section density of incomes at a point in time, which does not map one for one back to a particular dynamic process for the incomes.

nonlinearities in the intergenerational transmission mechanism. For the United States, exceptions include Suzanne Cooper, Steven Durlauf, and Paul Johnson (1994), who find little correlation between parental and offspring income outside the tails of the income distribution. A particularly careful analysis for non-U.S. data is that of Francisca Antman and David McKenzie (2007), who estimate nonlinear intergenerational models for fifteen years of individual data on urban Mexican workers and find little evidence of nonlinearity.

In translating the statistical notions of poverty traps into restrictions on the time-series processes for income, it is important to recognize a limitation in using differential income growth rates between the rich and poor to infer the presence of poverty traps: namely, while poverty traps require the possibility that the rich grow faster than the poor, the observation that the poor in fact grow faster than the rich does not imply the absence of a poverty trap. The reason can be seen in the nonstochastic version of the individual-based poverty trap model described by equations 7-1 and 7-3: in the vicinity of each of the steady states described in equation 7-3, one has the property of local convergence; that is, those below the steady state grow toward it while those above it shrink. Andrew Bernard and Steven Durlauf (1996) discuss this problem; one implication of their analysis is that linear models of income dynamics cannot be used to assess poverty persistence; specifically, it is possible to find a cross-sectional correlation between initial income and income growth in an environment with poverty traps because this correlation does not account for any nonlinearities associated with the poverty trap.

A second identification problem concerns nonlinearity versus poverty traps. Following Steven Durlauf, Paul Johnson, and Jonathan Temple (2005), the difficulty arises in the relationship between clustering of behaviors around a discrete number of values and the presence or absence of multiple steady states. Clustering implies that there are few observations that are not associated with the clusters, and hence uncovering transition dynamics toward clusters is difficult. In the context of our model, the problem can occur because of a lack of information about behaviors around the discontinuities in equation 7-1; for the continuous case, the problem would arise if the set of incomes over which $\varphi'(\cdot) > 1$ is small.

A third problem arises with respect to the accuracy of estimates if one treats the definition of a poverty trap as requiring permanent poverty. Such a stark requirement is difficult to assess from data observable over a relatively small epoch, say fifty years. In the time-series literature, this problem arises in the context of the study of unit roots in macroeconomic data. A unit root in a time series requires that some part of the contemporary change in a time series permanently affects the level of a time series, so there is a close relationship to the poverty trap claim that a change can leave someone in or out of a trap. For income y_t, the expected long-run implication of a contemporaneous change in income may be calculated via

$$\lim_{T\to\infty} E\left(y_{t+T}\,|\Delta y_t\right) = \sum_{j=-\infty}^{\infty} \operatorname{cov}\left(\Delta y_t, \Delta y_{t-j}\right). \tag{7-21}$$

Hence calculating permanent effects involves high-order covariances, which are very difficult to estimate accurately without extremely long samples.[25] Thus if one formalized the notion of a poverty trap as requiring that some transformation of aggregate poverty rates exhibit a unit root, evidentiary support will be problematic. The same holds for other conceptions of poverty traps; the semiparametric analyses of Suzanne Cooper, Steven Durlauf, and Paul Johnson (1994) and Francisca Antman and David McKenzie (2007) avoid this problem by focusing on transitions across a single generation, which rules out any higher order temporal dynamics. In my view, this problem reinforces the importance of focusing on probabilities of passage out of poverty for different time horizons.

Identification through Locational Mechanisms

A different strategy for uncovering poverty traps is to focus not on time-series regularities but on the identification of feedbacks from various locational characteristics that correspond to contextual and endogenous social interaction influences on individual outcomes. From this viewpoint, the objects of interest are the derivatives of equation 7-20 with respect to the social interactions variables. If one can uncover these derivatives, one can infer poverty trap outcomes in the sense of the third concept discussed above. This is the strategy employed in the social interactions literature. The most common social interactions models are linear regression variants of equation 7-20; if one were to map this equation into a linear regression it would take the form

$$\begin{aligned} y_{i,t} = {} & \kappa + \alpha_1 x_{i,t-1} + \alpha_2 x_{i,t} + \beta_1 c_{l,t-1} + \beta_2 c_{l,t} + \gamma_1 \bar{y}_{-i,l,t-1} \\ & + \gamma_2 \bar{y}_{-i,l,t} + \eta_{l,t-1} + \eta_{l,t} + \varepsilon_{i,t}. \end{aligned} \tag{7-22}$$

The most important variant of this model is one in which choices are discrete variables. For simplicity, I focus on the binary choice case; denote these outcomes

25. This issue was first assessed in Cochrane (1988).

$y_{i,t} \in \{0, 1\}$. Of course, in this case, $y_{i,t}$ is presumably not income but rather an outcome such as high school completion, use of a regional dialect, and so forth. In this approach, the net utility to choice 1 by agent i at t, $u_{i,t}$, obeys an analog to equation 7-22,

$$u_{i,t} = \kappa + \alpha_1 x_{i,t-1} + \alpha_2 x_{i,t} + \beta_1 c_{l,t-1} + \beta_2 c_{l,t} + \gamma_1 \overline{y}_{-i,l,t-1} + \gamma_2 \overline{y}_{-i,l,t} + \eta_{l,t-1} + \eta_{l,t} + \varepsilon_{i,t}, \quad (7\text{-}23)$$

so that the observed behavior follows

$$y_{i,t} = 1 \text{ if } u_{i,t} > 0;\ y_{i,t} = 0 \text{ otherwise.} \quad (7\text{-}24)$$

My specifications of both the linear regression and the binary choice models are more complicated than the statistical models usually employed to study social interactions—and by implication the models that one would naturally turn to study regional poverty traps. This is because of the attention to distinct determinants of outcomes at different stages of life and because of the explicit attention to unobservables.

Before discussing the identification of these models, it is important to observe that the specifications assume that the elements of x and c are known. This can be problematic since theoretical models of individual and location determinants typically fail to specify how determinants should be measured. For role models, is the correct variable the percentage of white-collar jobs among adults or the percentage of college graduates among adults? This sort of question can be repeatedly applied to the conventionally employed statistical models. Further, my specifications follow the literature in taking locations that define social interactions as known. It is natural to think about agents arrayed in a possibly high-dimensional social space; this may or may not correspond well to counties and neighborhoods, which define the locations as conventionally measured.[26] Finally, my specifications—again following the social interactions literature—assume that each agent places the same weight on the characteristics and behaviors of every other agent. Once one relaxes this assumption, one moves from models of social interactions to models of social networks, and the identification issues facing an analyst become very different.[27] Lawrence Blume and his colleagues (2010, 2011) show how some of the standard identification problems vanish once one moves

26. This is argued in Akerlof (1997).

27. See Jackson (2008) for a clear and exhaustive description of the modern social networks literature.

away from conventional social interactions specifications; they further show that identification can be achieved using particular forms of partial knowledge of social network structure.

Within the contexts of models of the form of equations 7-22 and 7-23, the econometrics literature focuses on three distinct identification problems that arise when one attempts to uncover locational influences when using statistical models of the type described here. Blume and others (2010) provide formalizations of the problems as well as an exhaustive description of the literature; a gentler introduction is Steven Durlauf and Yannis Ioannides (2010). Here, I simply wish to describe the problems a researcher faces.

The first identification problem facing studies of social influences was initially studied in Manski (1993) and is known as the reflection problem. The reflection problem refers to difficulties in disentangling the role of contextual effects $c_{l,t-1}$ and $c_{l,t}$ from the endogenous effects $\bar{y}_{-i,l,t-1}$ and $\bar{y}_{-i,l,t}$. This difficulty arises because the contextual effects help to determine the equilibrium values of the endogenous effects. Manski provides a demonstration that, for cross-section linear models, the reflection problem may render it impossible to identify different locational effect parameters. Brock and Durlauf (2001a) show that the reflection problem does not arise in discrete choice models in the sense that because these models are nonlinear, collinearity between contextual and endogenous effects may be ruled out, so long as there is sufficient variability in the contextual effects across locations. William Brock and Steven Durlauf (2001b) and Blume and others (2010) show that the reflection problem can also be overcome in dynamic contexts because dynamics can affect the degree of linear dependence between the contextual and endogenous effects. Nevertheless, even if identification does not fail per se, the reflection problem indicates that parameter estimates may be highly imprecise.

A second econometric problem derives from self-selection into locations. Following the broader microeconometrics literature, self-selection of locations is typically addressed in two ways. First, instrumental variables may be employed. An early and well-known application of this strategy is by William Evans, Wallace Oates, and Robert Schwab (1992), who study social interactions in schools. To address self-selection in schools, these researchers use school district–level instruments, arguing that self-selection is limited to schools within districts and not to the districts per se. This example reveals some of the difficulties in using instrumental variables. Even if the Evans, Oates, and Schwab argument on self-selection is correct, this is not sufficient to ensure instrument validity. The problem is that $\varepsilon_{i,t}$ contains all factors that are not accounted for by the locational and individual-specific controls. For a district-level instrument to be valid, one must be able to argue that it is not correlated with any of these factors. As a mathematical statement, the presence of $\eta_{l,t}$ is sufficient to make this impossible, except for nongeneric cases. Substantively, the problem is what Brock and Durlauf (2001c) call theory open-endedness: models such as equations 7-22 and 7-23 are not derived from full specifications of individual decision problems and therefore do not rule out determinants outside of those that are included. For the Evans, Oates, and Schwab context, it is not unreasonable to conjecture that an instrument such as district-level dropout rates is correlated with per pupil expenditure or broader social norms that affect decisions.

An alternative strategy is to explicitly model the self-selection process. In turn, there are two ways to proceed. The standard approach is due to James Heckman (1979) and involves introducing a regressor that measures the conditional expectation of the model error modulo a constant of proportionality; this is in fact now known as the control function approach. While implementation of the control function is most often done using parametric assumptions on the probability density of unobserved heterogeneity, there are semiparametric ways to construct selection corrections. An alternative strategy involves coupling the outcome equations with models of the location selection process.[28] This strategy requires complete knowledge of the location selection process.

Either version of the second strategy is, in my view, preferable to the use of instrumental variables. In particular, explicit analysis of self-selection can assist in the identification of social interactions. Brock and Durlauf (2001b) first demonstrated that it was possible for the reflection problem to preclude identification when individuals are randomly assigned to locations; while if locations were chosen, identification was possible. Brock and Durlauf (2006) and Yannis Ioannides and Jeffrey Zabel (2008) extend this approach theoretically, with Ioannides and Zabel applying it successfully to demonstrate the presence of social interactions in housing valuation. Why would self-selection facilitate identification? Selection of locations constitutes an additional choice on the part of individuals and so contains information on the determinants of these choices, determinants that presumably include the social interactions that will be experienced conditional on residing in the location. This information can help to triangulate the presence of social interactions to the extent that the interactions influence locational choices.

A third identification problem derives from the presence of unobserved location-level heterogeneity, that is, the presence of $\eta_{l,t-1}$ and $\eta_{l,t}$ in equations 7-22 and 7-23. In my judgment, the identification of social interactions effects in the pres-

28. Epple and Sieg (1999) is a nice example.

ence of unobserved group effects represents the major existing impediment to developing evidence of the role of social influences. First, it is generally the case that, for those contexts in which social interactions are usually studied, there are many unobserved group characteristics that can be plausibly argued to affect individual outcomes. For Appalachia, factors ranging from the quality of legal and political institutions to geography plausibly matter in explaining poverty, but they are difficult to measure. Second, unlike the case of self-selection, unobserved group factors do not themselves typically derive from a behavioral model the way that location selection does. Hence there is nothing analogous to the control function approach that may be employed to address their presence. Most efforts to address unobserved group effects therefore involve instrumental variables methods or, when the effects are time invariant, differencing of data to exploit temporal variation.

For the reasons I outline, there continues to be considerable disagreement about the empirical importance of social interactions. Recent econometric work focuses on uncovering robust evidence. By robust evidence, I mean evidence of social interactions that explicitly accounts for the presence of various types of unobserved individual and locational heterogeneity.

One approach to developing robust evidence is due to Brock and Durlauf (2007) for binary outcomes and in essence does the following. Suppose that one observes that there exist two locations, l and l', and a vector, z, which is a sufficient statistic for the effects of individual and contextual characteristics on the aggregate locational outcome. What I mean by this is that the only factors that determine the average choice levels outside of z are unobserved group effects and endogenous social interactions. Suppose that one observes

$$\bar{y}_{l,t} > \bar{y}_{l',t} \text{ and } z_{l,t} < z_{l',t}. \tag{7-25}$$

Brock and Durlauf (2007) call this a pattern reversal; the basic idea is that the observable fundamentals suggest one rank ordering of locational outcomes, whereas the observed pattern of outcomes reverses this ordering. Under the behavioral model I describe, a pattern reversal can occur because of the following:

—The group effects, $\eta_{l,t}$, reverse the rank order in outcomes generated by $z_{l,t}$.

—There are multiple equilibria in aggregate outcomes, so that l has coordinated on a high outcome equilibrium, whereas l' has coordinated on a low outcome equilibrium.

When can the first explanation be ruled out? Brock and Durlauf (2007) provide a set of shape restrictions on $\eta_{l,t}$ such that the data would lead one to conclude that social interactions are present. For example, if higher z locations draw from a more favorable η distribution, then an observation consistent with equation 7-25 allows one to conclude that endogenous social interactions are present in the data and that they are strong enough to produce multiple equilibria. As such, this is a form of a partial identification argument. The appeal of the pattern reversal approach is that it focuses on the one feature of endogenous social interactions that other factors simply cannot produce: multiple equilibria.

The Brock and Durlauf (2007) strategy does not apply to linear models for the trivial reason that such models cannot produce multiple equilibria. Some progress has been made on identification in linear models with group level unobservables in Blume and colleagues (2011). The key here is to consider which parameters can be identified under different types of unobserved heterogeneity. While Blume and colleagues focus on cross-section models, their analysis suggests that, for panel data, location-level unobservables may permit identification of some parameters of policy interest, though to be clear this is a conjecture.

A second strategy is due to Bryan Graham's (2008) extension and generalization of work by Edward Glaeser, Bruce Sacerdote, and José Scheinkman (1996) on the impact of endogenous social interactions on the variance of average outcomes across locations. In this approach, one considers the relationship between the variance of $\bar{y}_{l,t}$ and the population size of l. If there are no endogenous social interactions, then this relationship will be different than when endogenous social interactions are present. Intuitively, endogenous social interactions introduce dependencies across individual choices that "slow down" the rate at which the law of large numbers applies. Glaeser, Sacerdote, and Scheinkman's analysis does not allow for group effects; Graham's achievement is to show that if these effects are random rather than fixed, and if the variance is independent of group size, one can uncover evidence of endogenous effects by contrasting variances across group sizes. The random effects assumption implicitly requires that location choices are unaffected by the shocks.

A third strategy is proposed by William Brock and Steven Durlauf (2010) and involves studying transitional dynamics. Their framework considers adoption of a technology; for an educational context one can think of the development of skills to use a new technology, for example computers. Brock and Durlauf (2010) ask what sorts of restrictions are imposed on adoption over time, when the benefits to a technology reflect social interactions. For their model, they show that social interactions can introduce jumps in adoption rates in the economy as well as pattern reversals between adoption rates of those whose private characteristics would suggest they should adopt earlier versus others. To be concrete, suppose that one observed that computer technology diffused more slowly in a high-education location versus another but that there are jumps in the adoption rates of each community considered in isolation. Brock and Durlauf in essence provide sufficient conditions under which one can conclude that social interactions are present.

To be clear, none of these strategies is a panacea. Each requires substantive behavioral assumptions. We began by emphasizing one critical assumption: the uniformity of social interactions between individuals, so that the average characteristics and behaviors of others are a sufficient statistic for characterizing social influence. Other assumptions are implicit in the way that unobserved heterogeneity is modeled. Hence these identification strategies can only be assessed in a specific empirical context.

Identification and Data Collection

Discussion of identification so far focuses on statistical tools as opposed to data collection. One major question concerns the measurement of social groups within a broader social space. The discussion of identification presupposes only that the groups that define social interactions are known a priori. I conjecture that language use may facilitate measurement of social groups. It is well understood that dialects are important sources of identity.[29] Nonstandard dialects in Appalachia have been a major topic in the sociolinguistics literature.[30] Not only could dialect data, in principle, help with the measurement of social networks, they could also help us understand the mechanisms by which networks affect socioeconomic outcomes. Reid Luhman (1990) considers how standard dialect speakers in Kentucky form stereotypes about nonstandard dialect speakers in Kentucky as well as the extent to which these stereotypes are also believed by the nonstandard speakers. I would even speculate that the internalization of stereotypes can, in turn, affect noncognitive traits.

Further, as demonstrated in Blume and others (2010), many identification problems disappear when social networks are known a priori; formally, for known social networks in linear models, the set of linear models under which identification fails can be shown to be nongeneric.[31] Hence data collection that allows the construction of social networks is of first-order value. The current frontier in understanding identification of social effects lies in the study of cases where there is partial knowledge of social networks.

29. See for example Wolfram and Schilling-Estes (2006).

30. Wolfram and Christian (1976) is an especially detailed study.

31. By known social network, I mean not only who affects whom but also the strength of these effects up to a constant of proportionality. In essence, this generalizes the linear in means model by allowing for unequal weights across others in a population.

Footprints of Poverty Traps

In this section I focus on some stylized facts about Appalachia that would seem to hint at poverty traps. While this discussion is admittedly speculative, it reflects impressions I have gleaned from studies of Appalachia as to ways to uncover social interactions that are strong enough to produce poverty traps.

Education

The stylized facts on Appalachian educational attainment are suggestive, in my view, of a poverty trap. Andrew Isserman (1996) documents how Appalachia appears to be an outlier in terms of the high percentage of counties in which less than half of the 1990 adult population graduate from high school. Christopher Bollinger, James Ziliak, and Kenneth Troske (2011) similarly attribute much of the failure of Appalachian wages to converge to those in the rest of the country to lower human capital formation; this study is noteworthy for its careful and sophisticated econometrics. Low human capital investment in Appalachia is a good candidate for a mechanism underlying a poverty trap.

As discussed earlier, one behavioral explanation is that educational investment decisions are interdependent because of both role model and peer influences, so that factors such as parental education and the educational choices of peers affect each individual's decisions. Evidence of social interactions in education has been developed in many studies. A study by Jonathan Crane (1991) is an early example in which interneighborhood variations in high school graduation are associated with the occupational characteristics of parents. Recent examples include Jane Cooley (2008) and Erik Hanushek and others (2003), who focus on peer effects at the school and classroom level. For these reasons, I regard the fact of sustained disparities in education to be a hint of a poverty trap. Nevertheless, by itself, the social interactions/poverty trap interpretation falls prey to the sorts of identification problems I describe.

To proceed, consider two other stylized facts. The first is identified in Andrew Isserman (1996): for socioeconomic indicators other than education, it is much more difficult to identify Appalachia as an outlier relative to the rest of the country. The finding that high school completion behaves differently from other socioeconomic indicators is potentially of great importance in uncovering why it occurs. A second stylized fact is from Thomas Shaw, Alan DeYoung, and Eric Rademacher (2004), who find that the bulk of the Appalachian educational gap is due to Central Appalachia. This is most starkly seen in terms of high school graduation: in 2000, 76.8 percent of Appalachian adults had high school degrees, as opposed to 80.4 percent for the United States as a whole. In contrast, only

64.1 percent of Central Appalachian adults are high school graduates. The high dispersion of education outcomes in Appalachia across subregions provides the sort of variability that helps uncover social interactions.

In what sense might these additional facts help one make an empirical case for an Appalachian poverty trap? With respect to Isserman, the anomalous behavior of education versus other socioeconomic indicators makes an explanation based on unobserved location factors less plausible. The reason is simple: the unobserved factor will need to be one that only affects education, since it evidently does not affect other factors. While this may apply to teacher quality, it does seem plausible from the perspective of social norms. As for Shaw, DeYoung, and Rademacher, if it is the case that, assessing county by county, one finds that the low educational attainment associated with Central Appalachia violates patterns of education as would be predicted by variables described by $z_{l,t}$ above, this would constitute a pattern reversal. Interpretation of these reversals as social interactions would require taking a stance on unobserved group heterogeneity. If the relevant factor is teacher quality, it is plausible to assume that teacher quality is drawn from a distribution that is no better for high-outcome counties than for others. Alternatively, one might wish to assume unimodality of the unobservables and see if one finds conditional multimodality in outcomes. The Graham approach can also be used if one can argue that the unobservables are uncorrelated with z. Daniel Lichter and Linda Campbell (2005) document sufficient heterogeneity in poverty reductions in the 1990s to suggest that this route may be informative.

Migration

Second, I conjecture that substantial information on social interactions can be gleaned from understanding the determinants of migration into and out of Appalachia. Whether or not Appalachia is a poverty trap, socioeconomic conditions would lead one to expect substantial migration away from the region. Actual migration patterns are in fact much more complicated. Phillip Obermiller and Steven Howe (2004) document that in the latter 1990s Appalachia experienced substantial inflows and outflows of population. Underlying these flows are important differences between in- and out-migration. Obermiller and Howe find that central Appalachia experienced nontrivial outflows of more skilled adults, which were largely counterbalanced by inflows of less skilled ones; more generally Robert Baumann and Patricia Reagan (2006) argue that slightly over an eighth of the gap in college graduates between Appalachia and the rest of the United States can be attributed to migration.

There appear to be puzzles in the migration patterns that warrant study in terms of what they say about social interactions. One puzzle, at least to me, is that the out-migration of the highly skilled has not been more rapid, especially in light of the finding that returns to human capital are nontrivially lower in Appalachia than elsewhere.[32] Nor is it clear why low-skilled workers would choose Appalachia as a destination. The retention of high-skilled workers suggests the presence of social interactions effects that make Appalachia more appealing than its observed socioeconomic characteristics would suggest. On the other hand, the in-migration of low-skilled workers suggests that self-selection issues exist with respect to the Appalachian population that mitigate against simple claims of the region being a poverty trap per se; a public housing project is not a poverty trap by virtue of the fact that poor people live there. My point is that analysis of migration decisions can augment social interactions analyses based on various outcomes of Appalachian residents. Comparisons with migration patterns for other disadvantaged regions may also be informative.

Given the sensitivity of Appalachian economic conditions to the price of coal, the time-series properties of these prices may prove a fruitful source for understanding social factors in Appalachia. The utility of coal price shocks in understanding employment and earnings changes was first recognized in Dan Black, Kermit Daniel, and Seth Sanders (2002). My conjecture is that the reactions of migration to persistent changes in the price of coal can be informative about social factors that affect migration just as shocks to coal prices are informative about short-run changes in labor market outcomes.

Conclusion

In this chapter, I try to do three things. First, I describe some formal intergenerational income models that can produce behaviors that capture various facets of the idea of poverty traps. Second, I discuss some of the statistical challenges facing any effort to establish the presence of a poverty trap in a given data set. Third, I use Appalachian educational attainment and migration as examples of where one might wish to begin a systematic search for evidence of poverty traps in light of some established aggregate regularities.

I end with a few comments on policy. First, efforts to ameliorate Appalachian poverty need to respect the level of policymaker ignorance. Theoretical models of poverty traps and formal econometric analyses of the identification of mechanisms that can produce poverty traps are largely divorced from the current body of formal empirical work on poverty. This gap between theory, econometrics,

32. See for example Bollinger, Ziliak, and Troske (2011).

and empirics means that the current literature provides relatively little quantitative guidance on policy construction. This policymaker ignorance should not lead to a Hayekian avoidance of policy interventions. Rather, policymakers should focus on identifying policies that are robust in the sense that their efficacy holds across different specifications of the income determination process for individuals and for communities. Further, given the paucity of formal research on Appalachian poverty, the existing body of qualitative work can play an especially useful role both in policy design and in evaluating the utility of poverty trap ideas.[33]

Second, antipoverty policies should reflect the interplay of locational as well as individual-level explanations of poverty. In terms of direct, targeted interventions, new literature on early childhood development is an obvious source for antipoverty policy recommendations. Social interactions imply that the effects of widespread application of early childhood interventions of the intensity of the Perry Preschool Program (which has been the focus of much of Heckman's research) may, via social multipliers, be even more cost effective than has already been found for specific programs. On the other hand, to the extent that these early childhood interventions need to be intensive in order to be efficacious, budget considerations may require that they are concentrated across a subgroup of locations where poverty is high. This raises complicated equity/efficiency tradeoffs.[34] At the other end of the spectrum, the sorts of place-based policies discussed in Matthew Kahn (chapter 6, this volume) may require that early childhood experiences are such that the potential for a skilled workforce is already latent in the population, in the sense that sufficient levels of noncognitive skills are present in the population to allow these policies to be effective. One example is Kahn's suggestion that improvement of transportation infrastructure is a promising place-based strategy for Appalachia. While I certainly endorse Kahn's recommendation, workers with low noncognitive skills are unlikely to benefit much from connections between Appalachia and other areas. Synergies between individual- and group-level policies give reasons for optimism in reversing persistent poverty even for cases as long-standing as is found in Appalachia, although this optimism, as suggested in my first comment, should be tempered by the limits of our understanding of the specifics of Appalachian policy.

33. See Duncan (1999) for an exemplary study contrasting Appalachia with New England crafts communities and Mississippi Delta sharecropping communities.

34. See Durlauf (2006).

References

Akerlof, George. 1997. "Social Distance and Social Decisions." *Econometrica* 65, no. 5: 1005–27.

Akerlof, George, and Rachel Kranton. 2000. "Economics and Identity." *Quarterly Journal of Economics* 115, no. 3: 715–53.

———. 2002. "Identity and Schooling: Some Lessons for the Economics of Education." *Journal of Economic Literature* 40, no. 4: 1167–201.

Ali, S., and J. Saunders. 2008. "The Career Aspirations of Rural Appalachian High School Students." *Journal of Career Assessment* 17, no. 2: 172–88.

Almund, Mathilde, and others. 2011. "Personality Psychology and Economics." In *Handbook of the Economics of Education,* vol. 4, edited by E. Hanushek. Amsterdam: North Holland.

Antman, Francisca, and David McKenzie. 2007. "Poverty Traps and Nonlinear Income Dynamics with Measurement Error and Individual Heterogeneity." *Journal of Development Studies* 43, no. 6: 1057–83.

Azariadis, Costas, and Allen Drazen. 1990. "Threshold Externalities in Economic Development." *Quarterly Journal of Economics* 105, no. 2: 501–26.

Azariadis, Costas, and John Stachurski. 2005. "Poverty Traps." In *Handbook of Economic Growth,* edited by P. Aghion and S. Durlauf. Amsterdam: North Holland.

Baumann, Robert, and Patricia Reagan. 2006. "The Appalachian Brain Drain." Mimeo.

Bayer, Patrick, Stephen Ross, and Giorgio Topa. 2008. "Place of Work and Place of Residence: Informal Hiring Networks and Labor Market Outcomes." *Journal of Political Economy* 116: 1150–96.

Becker, Gary. 1973. "A Theory of Marriage, Part I." *Journal of Political Economy* 81, no. 4: 813–46.

Becker, Gary, and Kevin Murphy. 2000. *Social Economics.* Harvard University Press.

Becker, Gary, and Nigel Tomes. 1979. "An Equilibrium Theory of the Distribution of Income and Intergenerational Mobility." *Journal of Political Economy* 87, no. 6: 1153–89.

Bénabou, Roland. 1996a. "Equity and Efficiency in Human Capital Investment: The Local Connection." *Review of Economic Studies* 63, no. 2: 237–64.

———. 1996b. "Heterogeneity, Stratification, and Growth: Macroeconomic Implications of Community Structure and School Finance." *American Economic Review* 86, no. 3: 584–609.

Bernard, Andrew, and Steven Durlauf. 1996. "Interpreting Tests of the Convergence Hypothesis." *Journal of Econometrics* 71: 161–73.

Billings, Dwight. 1974. "Culture and Poverty in Appalachia: A Theoretical Discussion and Empirical Analysis." *Social Forces* 53, no. 2: 315–23.

Billings, Dwight, and Kathleen Blee. 2000. *The Road to Poverty.* Cambridge University Press.

Black, Dan, Kermit Daniel, and Seth Sanders. 2002. "The Impact of Economic Conditions on Participation in Disability Programs: Evidence from the Coal Boom and Bust." *American Economic Review* 92, no. 1: 27–50.

Blume, Lawrence, and others. 2010. "Identification of Social Interactions. In *Handbook of Social Economics,* edited by Jess Benhabib, A. Bisin, and M. Jackson. Amsterdam: North Holland.

Blume, Lawrence and others. 2011. "Linear Social Network Models." Mimeo.

Bollinger, Christopher, James Ziliak, and Kenneth Troske. 2011. "Down from the Mountain: Skill Upgrading and Wages in Appalachia." *Journal of Labor Economics* 29, no. 4: 819–57.

Borghans, Lex, and others. 2008. "The Economics and Psychology of Personality Traits." *Journal of Human Resources* 43, no. 4: 972–1059.

Brock, William, and Steven Durlauf. 2001a. "Discrete Choice with Social Interactions." *Review of Economic Studies* 68, no. 2: 235–60.

———. 2001b. "Interactions-Based Models" In *Handbook of Econometrics,* vol. 5, edited by J. Heckman and E. Leamer. Amsterdam: North Holland.

———. 2001c. "Growth Empirics and Reality." *World Bank Economic Review* 15: 229–72.

———. 2006. "Multinomial Choice with Social Interactions." In *The Economy as an Evolving Complex System III,* edited by L. Blume and S. Durlauf. Oxford University Press.

———. 2007. "Identification of Binary Choice Models with Social Interactions." *Journal of Econometrics* 140, no. 1: 52–75.

———. 2010. "Social Interactions and Adoption Curves." *Journal of the European Economic Association* 8: 232–51.

Cochrane, John. 1988. "How Big Is the Random Walk in GNP?" *Journal of Political Economy* 96, no. 5: 893–920.

Cooley, Jane. 2008. "Desegregation and the Achievement Gap: Do Diverse Peers Help?" University of Wisconsin at Madison.

Cooper, Suzanne, Steven Durlauf, and Paul Johnson. 1994. "On the Evolution of Economic Status across Generations." In American Statistical Association, Business and Economic Section, *Papers and Proceedings,* pp. 50–58.

Crane, Jonathan. 1991. "The Epidemic Theory of Ghettos and Neighborhood Effects on Dropping out and Teenage Childbearing." *American Journal of Sociology* 96, no. 5: 1226–59.

Cunha, Flavio, and James Heckman. 2007. "The Technology of Skill Formation." *American Economic Review* 97, no. 2: 31–46.

Cunha, Flavio, James Heckman, and Susanne Schennach. 2010. "Estimating the Technology of Cognitive and Noncognitive Skill Formation." *Econometrica* 78, no. 3: 883–931.

Duncan, Cynthia. 1999. *Worlds Apart: Why Poverty Persists in Rural America.* Yale University Press.

Durlauf, Steven. 1995. "Commentary." In *Macroeconometrics: Developments, Tensions, and Prospects,* edited by K. Hoover. Boston: Kluwer Academic.

———. 1996a. "A Theory of Persistent Income Inequality." *Journal of Economic Growth* 1, no. 1: 75–93.

———. 1996b. "Associational Redistribution: A Defense." *Politics and Society* 24, no. 4: 391–410.

———. 2004. "Neighborhood Effects." In *Handbook of Regional and Urban Economics,* vol. 4, edited by J. V. Henderson and J.-F. Thisse. Amsterdam: North Holland.

———. 2006. "Groups, Social Influences, and Inequality: A Memberships Theory Perspective on Poverty Traps." In *Poverty Traps,* edited by S. Bowles, S. Durlauf, and K. Hoff. Princeton University Press.

Durlauf, Steven, and Yannis Ioannides. 2010. "Social Interactions." *Annual Review of Economics* 2: 451–78.

Durlauf, Steven, Paul Johnson, and Jonathan Temple. 2005. "Growth Econometrics." In *Handbook of Economic Growth,* edited by P. Aghion and S. Durlauf. Amsterdam: North Holland.

Durlauf, Steven, and Ananth Seshadri. 2003. "Is Assortative Matching Efficient?" *Economic Theory* 21, nos. 2, 3: 475–93.

Eller, Ronald. 2008. *Uneven Ground: Appalachia since 1945.* University of Kentucky Press.
Epple, Dennis, and Holger Sieg. 1999. "Estimating Equilibrium Models of Local Jurisdictions." *Journal of Political Economy* 107, no. 4: 645–81.
Evans, William, Wallace Oates, and Robert Schwab. 1992. "Measuring Peer Group Effects: A Study of Teenage Behavior." *Journal of Political Economy* 100, no. 5: 966–91.
Fryer, Roland, and Paul Torelli. 2005. "An Empirical Analysis of Acting White." Working Paper 11334. Cambridge: National Bureau of Economic Research.
Galor, Oded, and Joseph Zeira. 1993. "Income Distribution and Macroeconomics." *Review of Economic Studies* 60, no. 1: 35–53.
Glaeser, Edward, Bruce Sacerdote, and Jose Scheinkman. 1996. "Crime and Social Interactions." *Quarterly Journal of Economics* 111, no. 2: 507–48.
Goldberger, Arthur. 1977. "Heritability." *Economica* 46, no. 184: 327–47.
Graham, Bryan. 2008. "Identifying Social Interactions through Conditional Variance Restrictions." *Econometrica* 76, no. 3: 643–60.
Hanushek, Erik, and others. 2003. "Does Peer Ability Affect Student Achievement?" *Journal of Applied Econometrics* 18, no. 5: 527–44.
Heckman, James. 1979. "Sample Selection Bias as a Specification Error." *Econometric* 47: 153–61.
———. 1998. "Detecting Discrimination." *Journal of Economic Perspectives* 12, no. 2: 101–18.
———. 2008. "Schools, Skills, and Synapses." *Economic Inquiry* 46, no. 3: 289–324.
Heckman, James, and others. 2010a. "Understanding the Mechanisms through Which an Influential Early Childhood Program Boosted Adult Outcomes." University of Chicago.
Heckman, James, and others. 2010b. "Analyzing Social Experiments as Implemented: A Reexamination of the Evidence from the Perry Preschool Program." *Quantitative Economics* 1, no. 1: 1–46.
Ioannides, Yannis, and Jeffrey Zabel. 2008. "Interactions, Neighborhood Selection, and Housing Demand." *Journal of Urban Economics* 63: 229–52.
Isserman, Andrew. 1996. "Appalachia Then and Now: An Update of the 'Realities of Deprivation' Report to the President in 1964." Appalachian Research Center.
Jackson, Matthew. 2008. *Social and Economic Networks.* Princeton University Press.
Jencks, Christopher, and Susan Mayer. 1990. "The Social Consequences of Growing up in a Poor Neighborhood." In *Inner-City Poverty in the United States,* edited by L. Lynn and M. McGreary. Washington: National Academies Press.
Lang, Kevin. 2007. *Poverty and Discrimination.* Princeton University Press.
Lichter, Daniel, and Linda Campbell. 2005. "Changing Patterns of Poverty and Spatial Inequality in Appalachia." Appalachian Research Center.
Loury, Glen. 1977. "A Dynamic Theory of Racial Income Differences." In *Women, Minorities, and Employment Discrimination,* edited by P. Wallace and A. Lamond. Lexington, Mass.: Lexington Books.
———. 1981. "Intergenerational Transfers and the Distribution of Earnings." *Econometrica* 49: 843–67.
Lucas, Robert. 1988. "On the Mechanics of Economic Development." *Journal of Monetary Economics* 22, no. 1: 3–42.
———. 2009. "Ideas and Growth." *Economica* 76, no. 301: 1–19.

Luhman, Reid. 1990. "Appalachian English Stereotypes: Language Attitudes in Kentucky." *Language in Society* 19: 331–48.

Manski, Charles. 1993. "Identification of Endogenous Social Effects: The Reflection Problem." *Review of Economic Studies* 60, no. 3: 531–42.

———. 2000. "Economic Analysis of Social Interactions." *Journal of Economic Perspectives* 14, no. 3: 115–36.

Milgrom, Paul, and John Roberts. 1990. "Rationalizability, Learning, and Equilibrium in Games with Strategic Complementarities." *Econometrica* 58: 1255–77.

Obermiller, Phillip, and Steven Howe. 2004. "Moving Mountains: Appalachian Migration Patterns, 1985–2000." *Journal of Appalachian Studies* 10, no. 3: 359–71.

Ogbu, John. 2003. *Black Students in an Affluent Suburb.* Mahwah N.J.: Lawrence Erlbaum.

Prat, Andrea. 2002. "Should a Team Be Homogeneous?" *European Economic Review* 46: 1187–207.

Roemer, John. 1998. *Equality of Opportunity.* Harvard University Press.

Romer, Paul. 1986. "Increasing Returns and Long-Run Growth." *Journal of Political Economy* 94, no. 5: 1002–37.

Shaw, Thomas, Alan DeYoung, and Eric Rademacher. 2004. "Educational Attainment in Appalachia: Growing with the Nation, but Challenges Remain." *Journal of Appalachian Studies* 10, no. 3: 307–29.

Streufert, Peter. 2000. "The Effect of Underclass Isolation on School Choice." *Journal of Public Economic Theory* 2, no. 4: 461–82.

Taylor, Christopher. 1998. *Socrates.* Oxford University Press.

Topa, Giorgio. 2001. "Social Interactions, Local Spillovers, and Unemployment." *Review of Economic Studies* 68, no. 2: 261–95.

Vives, Xavier. 1990. "Nash Equilibrium with Strategic Complementarities." *Journal of Mathematical Economics* 19: 305–21.

Wolfram, Walt, and Donna Christian. 1976. *Appalachian Speech.* Arlington, Va.: Center for Applied Linguistics.

Wolfram, Walt, and Natalie Schilling-Estes. 2006. *American English.* New York: Basil Blackwell.

Yinger, John. 1995. *Closed Doors, Opportunities Lost,* New York: Russell Sage Foundation Press.

Contributors

Dan A. Black is professor of public policy in the Harris School of Public Policy at the University of Chicago.

Lisa A. Cimbaluk is a graduate student in the Department of Development Sociology at Cornell University.

Janet Currie is Henry Putnam Professor of Economics and Public Affairs and director of the Center for Health and Well-Being at Princeton University.

Steven N. Durlauf is Vilas Professor and Kenneth J. Arrow and Laurits R. Christensen Professor of Economics in the Department of Economics at the University of Wisconsin.

Mariesa Herrmann is a graduate student in the Department of Economics at Columbia University.

Matthew E. Kahn is professor of economics in the Institute of the Environment and Sustainability, Department of Economics, the Department of Public Policy, the Anderson School of Management, and the School of Law at UCLA.

Daniel T. Lichter is Ferris Family Professor of Life Course Studies in the Department of Policy Analysis and Management, professor of sociology, and director of the Cornell Population Center at Cornell University.

Seth G. Sanders is professor of economics and public policy in the Department of Economics at Duke University.

James P. Ziliak is Carol Martin Gatton Endowed Chair in Microeconomics in the Department of Economics and director of the Center for Poverty Research at the University of Kentucky.

Index

MORRIS AUTOMATED INFORMATION NETWORK